For my father
Tapan Kumar Mukherjee

The Racial Order of Things

The Racial Order
of Things

Cultural Imaginaries of the Post-Soul Era

Roopali Mukherjee

University of Minnesota Press
Minneapolis • London

Portions of chapter 4 were originally published as "Regulating Race in the California Civil Rights Initiative: Enemies, Allies, and Alibis," *Journal of Communication* 50, no. 2 (2000): 27–47. Reprinted by permission of Oxford University Press.

Published by the University of Minnesota Press
111 Third Avenue South, Suite 290
Minneapolis, MN 55401-2520
http://www.upress.umn.edu

Library of Congress Cataloging-in-Publication Data

Mukherjee, Roopali.
 The racial order of things : cultural imaginaries of the post-soul era / Roopali Mukherjee.
   p. cm.
Includes bibliographical references and index.
  ISBN-13: 978-0-8166-4705-7 (hc : alk. paper)
  ISBN-10: 0-8166-4705-4 (hc : alk. paper)
  ISBN-13: 978-0-8166-4706-4 (pb : alk. paper)
  ISBN-10: 0-8166-4706-2 (pb : alk. paper)
  1. Civil rights—United States. 2. Affirmative action programs—United States. 3. Equality—United States. 4. Social justice—United States. 5. United States—Race relations. 6. Racism—United States. I. Title.
 JC599.U5M78 2006
 305.800973—dc22

                                            2006014113

Printed in the United States of America on acid-free paper

The University of Minnesota is an equal-opportunity educator and employer.

12 11 10 09 08 07 06   10 9 8 7 6 5 4 3 2 1

Contents

Acknowledgments

Two critical influences mark the development of this book. The first was Patrick Hadley, who spurred me toward a series of introspections about the insistence of race in American life and about our investments in and blindness to the racial order of things in our public and private lives. This book emerged as a way for me to think through our disagreements and to contemplate the vicissitudes of blackness and my stake in them.

I share my joy at having finished this book with a second critical force, a rare bounty of friends and confidants who have for years cheered my ambitions and guided my endeavors. Here I want to mention Priya Jaikumar, my everyday girl, without whom most things are incomprehensible. Madhu Dubey and Michael Curtin read early drafts of the chapters, asking maddeningly difficult questions while offering magical reassurance at the same time. The incomparably fabulous Josefina Saldaña provided gentle care and counsel for every challenge that life in New York presented. I shall be ever grateful to Purnima Bose, Radhika Parameswaran, Dennis Rome, and Cary Boyce, who kept me company and (one must admit) from going all the way insane during my six years in the woods. Anand Dika, Nizan Shaked, Eric Schlaf, and Anuradha Prakash heaped a thousand generosities on me over the years, each of whom I thank deeply. I offer a special note of gratitude to my mother, Kalpana Mukherjee, and Ashok Chokshi for their constant care and guidance. My brother, Sandeep Mukherjee, remains a role model not only because he is brilliant and brave but also because he reminds me often of the importance of being silly. Thank you for sharing your work on the cover. And I would certainly never have finished without Jonah Engle, who turned out to be the most charming cup of coffee they ever served at Tillie's.

I am grateful to the CUNY Research Foundation, the Center for African American Studies at UCLA, and the Dean of Faculties at Indiana University for a series of generous grants and fellowships that supported the writing of the book. I wish to acknowledge Eva Cherniavsky, who invited me into American studies at Indiana University and changed everything as a consequence. Valerie Smith welcomed me to a research fellowship at UCLA, where I began the writing process, and Chon Noriega generously took my ideas to the University of Minnesota Press. At the Press, I am grateful to Jennifer Moore, the initiating editor who responded with immediate confidence to my proposal; Carrie Mullen and later Jason Weidemann, who took over the project and shepherded it through the review process; and my manuscript reviewers (Vijay Prashad, Sanford Schram, and a third who remains anonymous), whose rigorous reports combined to yield a better, more confident book. A number of talented graduate students provided research assistance over the years—Jordan Pascoe, Neecole Johnson, Claire Sisco King, Tonia Edwards, Tim Havens, and the unforgettable Chris Dumas. I thank you for all your work.

Finally, this book is for my father, Tapan Kumar Mukherjee, who, I imagine, never fully understood why I needed to write it but who cheered me on unflaggingly nevertheless. Come back, come back, wherever you are.

Introduction

[T]here is nothing more tentative, nothing more empirical than
the process of establishing an order among things . . . nothing that
more insistently requires that one allow oneself to be carried along
by the proliferation of qualities and forms.

—Michel Foucault, *The Order of Things*

On July 20, 1995, amid widespread student protests, the regents of the University of California adopted a "policy ensuring equal treatment of admissions" that barred the use of race, religion, sex, color, ethnicity, or national origin as criteria for admission to the university. The policy charged the academic senate to develop a series of "supplemental criteria" that would give consideration to "individuals who, despite having suffered disadvantage economically or in terms of their social environment (such as an abusive or otherwise dysfunctional home or neighborhood of unwholesome or antisocial influences), have nonetheless demonstrated sufficient character and determination in overcoming obstacles to warrant confidence that the applicant can pursue a course of study to successful completion" (SP-1: Resolution, section 4).

Like all taxonomies that "tame the wild profusion of existing things," the regents' policy appoints a series of identifiable categories that enable distinctions between the Same and the Other. Race, gender, economic status, home environment, and social influences—each is recognized as a discrete category. Set apart from one another, some categories are pegged as worthy justifications for special consideration for admission to the University of California while others are barred from consideration. All other categories are inconceivable by the terms of this taxonomy. Thus, for instance, applicants' abilities to hail cabs or eat meat, how generous or fashionable they might be, their psychological traumas

1

and psychic abilities are irrelevant. To rank applicants by these standards would be laughable, odd, impossible.

The terms of the regents' policy, moreover, produce "unusual juxtapositions," setting up specific criteria as having no relation to each other and collapsing others by the act of enumeration. Thus, categories like race and sex are comparable to one another but distinguishable from categories like economic standing, home environment, and neighborhood conditions. Economic disadvantage is set apart from race and gender. Social environment is marked as genuinely disruptive while racial and gender circumstances are not. The regents' policy illuminates a remarkable politics of categories, a particular order of things that, as Michel Foucault has suggested, bears "the stamp of our age and our geography" (1970, xv).

Despite its ostensible contempt for identitarian categories, the regents' policy, nevertheless, creates new categories. Like guests on *The Jerry Springer Show*, applicants are asked to parade a range of dysfunctions producing a "competition of victimhood" (Hayden and Rice 1995, 264; Rosen 2003, 55). Consequently, the suburbanite who is a victim of a mugging, the foreign refugee who flees sexual assault in her homeland, the widowed mother of three who is denied admission because existing programs fail to recognize her specific brand of disentitlement each emerge under the policy as new candidates for special consideration. The regents' policy, thus, does not reject categories. It reorganizes them, and, producing unusual juxtapositions, it embraces some groupings and eschews others.

Changes in admissions policies at the University of California, one among several key events marking a turn in the career of the affirmative action concept during the nineties, emerged over the course of the decade from clamoring oppositions over race and privilege, from shifting and coalescing public knowledges about race and gender. As battles over affirmative action rose to the pantheon of divisive, splinter issues like abortion, religion, and gun control, they serve as indexical markers of enduring crises in the cultural imaginary.

Revealing an eerie sameness across efforts to control immigration and immigrant rights, to restrict public support for welfare, and to demonize beneficiaries of affirmative action programs, these debates echo the terms of larger ongoing battles over liberalism and social justice. They are constitutive of the modalities of "new racisms" manifest in claims about the declining significance of race in American public life and in disingenuous erasures of racial oppressions through culturally resonant appeals to individualism and color blindness.

These shifting public policies and the debates from which they emerge offer concrete testimonies to the structures of contemporary knowledges and their claims to truths about racism and the place of race in the contemporary United States. They point simultaneously to the limits of bourgeois Lockean liberalism—held together by abiding celebrations of the sovereignty of the individual, the mythic color-blind meritocracy, and moral imperatives for toil and thrift—as well as a range of ventriloquisms, adaptations, and containments that liberal discourses enabled.

Thus, culturally resonant appeals to individualism and color blindness that had etched programmatic racial reform as the only mechanism that could, ethically and effectively, rectify historical disadvantage and resolve systemic discrimination in the sixties returned in affirmative action debates of the nineties reshaped in the service of other masters. Likewise, combinations of hegemonic collective memories replete with willful cultural amnesias served to conflate white racisms with supremacist hate, locating them in a distant and ignominious national past. These equivalences, in turn, urged the excision of social justice programs on grounds that they mangled the "true intent" of iconic social movements that had pushed them through.

Similarly, reconfigurations of resonant tales of misery and woe stood traditional liberalism on its head, pointing accusatory fingers at the "heady excesses" of the sixties, confident that only neoliberalism could rein in the individual to proper standards of individualism. Thus, from the sixties to the nineties, we find evidence of a remarkable discursive tug-of-war, undulating reconfigurations of claims and counterclaims, shifting from righteous to absurd, plausible to illicit, and back again.

We need only return to the University of California regents' pronouncements to find a case in point. While the regents announced in 1995 that personal hardship and social circumstance would open the doors to special consideration for college admission but race and gender would not, the regents' accommodation for "supplemental criteria" was only the first in a series of iterations that University of California admissions policies took over the course of the nineties.

A few years later, in March 1999, after black and Latino/a enrollments showed precipitous declines at the prestigious Berkeley and Los Angeles campuses of the University of California, the newly elected Democratic governor, Gray Davis, called on the regents to revoke the 1995 policy and, in its place, approve a new standard that would consider all students who graduated in the top 4 percent of their high school classes (Burdman 1999, A1). As had been the case with such experiments in Florida and Texas previously, the "four percent solution" elicited sharp criticism for implicitly favoring racial segregation in school districts. Inviting the top 4 percent of every graduating class to apply, critics argued, would encourage black and Latino/a students to strategically shop around for "low-performing" schools in black and Latino districts to advance their chances of making it to the top of their classes.

As student protests raged, the regents revised admissions criteria once again in November 2001, this time approving a "comprehensive review," which, beginning fall 2002, would judge applicants on not only their academic records but on "special talents or activities" and on their abilities to overcome "personal adversity or hardship" (Schevitz 2001, A1). Reminiscent of "supplemental criteria" conceived in the 1995 regents' policy, the comprehensive review encouraged special consideration for "enrichment programs, volunteer service, leadership, personal challenges, talents and achievements, and educational environment, under which an applicant receives points for attending an academically low-performing school" (Autman 2002, A1). This time, critics on the right argued that such special considerations opened a back door to race- and gender-based affirmative action by carving out exceptions to race- and gender-conscious prohibitions that were required by state law after 1996.

These equivocations, moving back and forth over the imbrications of academic merit and personal circumstances, over how much "special talents" and "life challenges" should count in academic admissions, indicate remarkable disruptions and disunities within dominant knowledge regimes. They point to a series of ambivalences, inherited from the sixties, which simultaneously necessitate acknowledgment of historical racial and gendered disadvantage while demanding repression of race and gender in official decision making. These are public discourses fraught with contradictions, which, on the one hand, celebrate the sovereignty of the individual and, on the other hand, recognize state imperatives for diversity and equal opportunity.

Hence, rather than the facile erasure of certain ways of knowing by others, the discursive assaults of the nineties, escorted by unimaginable forms of categorical complexity, awkward reversals, and the surprising potential of inheritances from the sixties to undo themselves, point to the polyvalent mobility of regimes of truth. Liberal claims to equal opportunity, their appeals to individual rights and responsibilities, that had reigned on the Senate floor during congressional debate over the Civil Rights Act of 1964, did not disappear from the campaigns and pronouncements of rightist assaults of the nineties. To the contrary, they reappeared, with consistency and force, to argue against affirmative action precisely on behalf of the individual and his/her fundamental human potential.

The discursive battles of the nineties, then, do not point to the unstoppable subduction of some knowledges underneath others. Instead, they reveal a continuous clamor of articulation and silence, of dissension and rupture within embattled knowledge regimes. Pointing to complex and contradictory shifts in the "sayable" and the "knowable," policy assaults on social justice and affirmative action, as they played out over the course of the nineties, illuminate the contours of our own system of thought, our ways of knowing.

I pursue a series of overlapping analyses in the chapters that follow, each serving to bring into relief a range of discursive abnegations, reversals, and reinterpretations that mark the turn from the civil rights era of the sixties to the "post-soul epoch" of the nineties (Bonilla-Silva 2001; N. George 1992; Neal 2002). Here, my focus remains on policy discourses, gleaned from public debates and campaigns, and the ideological work of mainstream cinematic portrayals. Tracing cross-pollinations between these discursive domains, this book finds evidence of a profusion of articulations about race in law, public policy, and popular culture. These are articulations imbued with state and cultural authority, voices that carry a special potency to say what counts as "true" (Foucault 1980, 131). Examining the relations between coalescing public knowledges and the workings of power in their claims to truth, this book is, then, first and foremost, a careful study of the epistemic influence of race—as dominant paradigm, as common sense of our time.

Further, the analyses I present here find evidence of a remarkable range of dissension and disruption within our ways of knowing. I trace how categorical distinctions between "majority" and "minority" have imploded in recent years as white victims of "reverse discrimination" trade places opportunistically with "brown-skinned Bill Gates" and "dusky Donald Trumps." Here, the rising tides of postfeminism shore up a vast constituency of white women who, distancing themselves from the subversive impulses of sixties and seventies feminisms, now vote in fierce alliance with white husbands, brothers, and sons. Here, we find evidence of a growing "multicultural conservatism" (Dillard 2001), middle-class blacks, Latinos, and Asians who, eschewing the radical potential of the sixties, now provide a racially correct voice-over for neoliberal claims to individual "responsibilization" (Barry, Osborne, and Rose 1996; Foucault 1978/1991). Thus, the analyses here highlight critical ambivalences within racial claims of the nineties. Revealing its second thematic preoccupation, the book engages the polyvalent discursive mobility of the post-soul moment, its proliferations and contradictions as they distill within the cultural imaginary.

These ambivalences are revealed with critical effect within the ideological contours of mainstream Hollywood genres of the nineties. The analyses included here highlight a willful cinematic silence on formidable dilemmas of race as they linger in the mythic meritocracy, and in contrast, a recurring filmic fascination with tales about women, and particularly white women, as they encounter the apparatus and institutions of the workplace in the post–civil rights era. As later chapters of the book show, female protagonists are variously vilified and valorized in Hollywood texts of the nineties to assuage lingering anxieties about black squatters in the workplace, thus revealing the terms of peculiar cultural ventriloquisms characteristic of the post-soul era.

While others in recent years have focused variously on subversion and equivocation within contemporary black popular culture, taking stock of the politics and poetics of urban vernacular expression (George 2004; hooks 1992; Kelley 1994; Neal 2002; Watkins 1998), this project remains principally invested in hegemonic discourses, their claims to legitimacy, and the epistemic vulnerabilities that invariably lurk within. Far from the "death of civil rights," then (Boyd 2003), my analyses showcase the inescapable endurance of inheritances of the sixties, even when they emerge mangled and distorted by the decade of the nineties.

Bearing the "stamp of our age and our geography," these hegemonic discourses operate as a dominant taxonomy, delineating relations between the Same and the Other and shoring up a reserve of legitimacy and credibility for racisms administered by the contemporary state. As others have pointed out, this is a "governmentalized" state, one that expresses its sovereignty through a decentralized economy of rule and through the economic management of goods and populations (Foucault 1978/1991). Here, transcendent racial discipline withers, adjusting to immanent and diffused technologies of control (Goldberg 2002; Hardt and Negri 2000; Stoler 1995). As state racisms, that is, racisms managed and administered by the state, proliferate through the mechanisms of census protocols, administrative forms, and audit bureaucracies, they work to categorize, subjectify, and control (Barry, Osborne, and Rose 1996; Strathern 2000).

The shifting logics of the racial order in the post-soul moment point to unfolding racial subjectivities that no longer abide pre–civil rights orders of segregation and repression. Rather, they indicate everywhere prolific administrative apparatuses of the governmentalized state. To wit, as the neoliberal state "reforms" welfare, manages immigration to the homeland, and bans affirmative action, its discursive case for doing so, as the analyses here show, rests on the logic of a deracialized, responsibilized self. But as color blindness, the mythic meritocracy, and the striving individual emerge as substantiations of these appeals, we find that race and racial differentiation reappear at each turn. In each chapter, the analyses in this book demonstrate how wholly within the logics of race these neoliberal claims remain—how, for example, admissions and hiring committees must remain ever more watchful of race so they can be sure they are making "truly color-blind" choices, how naturalized ideals of whiteness and masculinity demarcate ethical standards for workers in the meritocracy, and, consequently, how workers, in order to pass as "colorless" and "sexless," contort themselves to fit those elusive ideals.

This is not the state "going color-blind." Rather, these neoliberal imperatives shore up the rationality of governmentalized protocols of state racisms (M. Hill 2003; Omi and Winant 1994; Stoler 1995) and ensure the continuing significance of race in the internalized discipline, or, properly, the control of subjects. It is this sense that—and this is the third and final thematic that weaves though the book—the analyses I offer point to a critical contradiction within the neoliberal state: while it moves to normalize deracialized, responsibilized subjectivities, it simultaneously presumes a vast network of state *savoirs* premised principally upon the logics of race and racial differentiation.

This, then, is not a book about affirmative action per se. Its project is neither the construction of a case for affirmative action nor a critique of these programs. Rather, the analyses presented here are geared toward examinations of a host of linguistic and discursive shifts that, by the decade of the nineties, were witness to a remarkable decline in the legitimacy of racialized social justice programs, programs that had enjoyed widespread public and political favor for thirty years. Together with politico-economic pressures and incentives, these reversals point to shifts and disruptions in knowledge regimes that enabled powerful acknowledgments of race and racism in public discourse during the sixties and Janus-faced repressions of those claims by the nineties.

Offering a careful study of the dynamics of these discursive contradictions and the incessant clamor over truths about race, gender, and
redistributive justice, this book seeks to unearth the contours of dominant knowledge regimes, the workings of power in their claims to truth,
and the vulnerabilities that lurk within. The chapters that follow present
accounts of the rich repertoire of discursive cross-pollinations between
public policy and cinematic forms, between claims made in the sixties
and those proffered in the nineties. Interrogating a range of echoes and
attenuations that mark recent assaults on affirmative action, these accounts
serve to illuminate both the racial order of our time and its discursive
ambivalences.

A Proposition in California

Two events—the passage of Proposition 209 in California during the
general election on November 6, 1996, and the Supreme Court decision
on June 23, 2003, resolving a bitter fight over admissions criteria at the
University of Michigan—serve to bookend a remarkable set of events that
illuminate the linguistic and discursive context within which a series of
intractable disagreements over race- and gender-conscious regimes of
social justice have played out over the past decade.

For some, these events reveal the rise of an envious and racist backlash against gains made by women and people of color over the past thirty
years. For others, three decades of affirmative action had sufficiently
repaid the nation's debt to black Americans whose dependence on "preferences" now exacted an unfair and racist price from white Americans.
Some argued that we had not yet done nearly enough to level the proverbial playing field for Americans within "historically disadvantaged
groups," and still others attested to corrupt and abusive practices that
were now commonplace in a meritocracy that championed "melanin
merit" over other standards.

Marking out a specific time line, these events foreground a diverse
group of actors in the fight over affirmative action—grassroots organizers working out of broom closet–sized offices sponsored in varying ways
by major political factions; incumbent state officials who had access to

the vast ideological apparatuses of the state seeking to parlay public anxieties into electoral gains; white applicants rejected by the colleges of their choice and positioned as a new generation of underdogs ushered to litigation by a host of ideologically aligned, right-wing think tanks and law firms. These contestants, together with their institutional investments, emerge as key players in battles over affirmative action during the nineties, contesting and reworking accepted truths about race and gender.

As it was conceived during the sixties, "affirmative action" is a term that "encompasses any measure, beyond simple termination of discriminatory practice, that permits the consideration of race, national origin, sex or disability, along with other criteria," and that through a variety of mechanisms "provides opportunities to a class of qualified individuals who have either historically or actually been denied those opportunities and/or to prevent the recurrence of discrimination in the future" (U.S. Commission on Civil Rights 1995). By most accounts, the term was first invoked by President Kennedy in Executive Order 10925 issued in March 1961, which asked federal contractors and subcontractors to take "affirmative action" to ensure equality of opportunity.

Nearly ten years after the U.S. Supreme Court had ruled against racial segregation in the nation's public schools (*Brown v. Board of Education* 1954), the Southern Jim Crow system persisted through a combined strategy of violence, intimidation, and appeals to states' rights. The black civil rights movement of the sixties that emerged to challenge entrenched Jim Crow repressions celebrated a critical victory when Congress, under great pressure from the Southern leadership of the civil rights movement, passed the Civil Rights Act of 1964.

A compromise bartered between Northern liberals and Southern Dixiecrats, the Civil Rights Act of 1964 included in its provisions Title VI, which prohibited discrimination on the grounds of race, color, or national origin by all recipients of federal funds, including schools, but which required that affirmative action be taken in admissions only as a remedy for past discrimination. Title VII of the 1964 act made it unlawful for any employer or labor union to discriminate in employment on the basis of race, color, religion, sex, or national origin, and Title

VIII created the Equal Employment Opportunity Commission that was charged with investigating and monitoring cases of racial discrimination in the private sector. Riding the coattails of the landmark 1964 Civil Rights Act, Congress passed the Voting Rights Act in 1965 and the Civil Rights Act of 1968 that prohibited housing discrimination.

Executive Order 11246, issued by President Johnson in 1965, barred discrimination on the basis of race, color, religion, or national origin by federal contractors or subcontractors, and Executive Order 11375, issued two years later, expanded these prohibitions to cover women. Title VII of the Civil Rights Act of 1964 provided the legal basis for affirmative action for female employees in the United States and Title IX of the Educational Amendments of 1972 prohibited sex discrimination in education. Title IX has played a key role in enforcing affirmative action for women, requiring educational institutions receiving federal funds to take "specific steps designed to encourage individuals of the previously excluded sex to apply for admission" and stipulating that such measures be taken not only in response to individual acts of discrimination but also to remedy past exclusions (Johnson 1990, 77–90).

As Manning Marable suggests, these strategies had a profound impact on the political culture of the United States. Crucially, they fueled simmering discontent and racial anxieties among "George Wallace voters," recruiting segregationists like Jesse Helms and Strom Thurmond into the ranks of the Republican Party (1996, 6).

In 1969, President Nixon authorized what became known as the Philadelphia Plan, a program that required federal contractors to set specific "goals and timetables" for hiring African Americans and other nonwhites on government-financed construction contracts. Mandating an outcome-oriented approach to racial equality, these measures visibly increased racial hiring. They set requirements for Federal Reserve funds to be placed in black-owned banks, and minority set-asides to promote black and Latino entrepreneurship. The Nixonian "race and tax agenda" was crucial to the realization of a fundamental goal of the civil rights–era Republican Party—the embourgeoisement of a decisive sector of previously Democratic voters (Edsall and Edsall 1991, 11)—which served to drive a wedge between the prevailing Democratic coalition of blacks, Jews, and labor (Duster 1998, 124).

The creation of a middle-class, anti-government, property-holding conservative identification among white *and* black voters who had previously seen their interests aligned with a "downwardly-redistributive federal government," and who had sympathized "with the importuned rather than with the importuning," now worked to reorient political dispositions and allegiances even though they did not necessarily accompany any genuine movement on the part of such voters into or toward the top half of the income hierarchy (Edsall and Edsall 1991, 11).

Over the course of the seventies, an agglomeration of affirmative action programs was implemented nationally in the public and private sectors under the aegis of the Nixon and Ford administrations. At the same time, the American economy was witness to massive transformations—deindustrialization, foreign competition, and plant closings in many sectors, including the hard-hit automobile and steel industries, which lost a total of 669,000 jobs in one year alone, between July 1979 and July 1980 (Edsall and Edsall 1991, 198). Raising unemployment rates and replacing stable, well-paying positions with part-time, low-wage jobs, these changes impacted workers across color lines, but they took their greatest toll on working-class African Americans, affecting young black males disproportionately and in huge numbers (Moland 1996).

As African Americans bifurcated into upper-class success and working-class poverty and repression over the course of the seventies, social scientists began to describe a process of degeneration in the black community, "a growing army of 'lower class blacks' who had been virtually unaffected by civil rights legislation, affirmative action, and federal government initiatives to diminish unemployment" (Marable 1984, 176–77). Last to be hired and first to be fired, African Americans bore the brunt of the economic changes of the decade.

Nevertheless, racialized resentments among white males interpreted these larger economic changes in terms of a newfound victimhood, a widespread and plaintive "me-too-ism" (Dyer 1988, 45–66), as the emergent figure of the "angry white male" gradually took shape in the cultural imaginary. In 1974, when Alan Bakke sued the University of California at Davis on grounds that black applicants had received unfair advantages under the outcome-oriented admission procedures of Davis's medical school, the case showcased the steady mainstreaming of racial discontent and grievances among whites for whom the meritocracy had devolved into state-sponsored "sets-asides, preferences, and quotas" based on "melanin merit."

Over the next decade, these frustrations would consolidate into a vicious conservative backlash against the legacies of the sixties, marked by a creeping tolerance of nod-and-wink anecdotes about "token hires" and "melanin merit" and a gathering petulance about "sympathy fatigue" and "reverse discrimination." The military debacle in Vietnam and social transformations orchestrated by the civil rights, feminist, antiwar, and gay pride movements disrupted the normalcy of white male dominance and precipitated a cultural crisis of white masculinity by the eighties (Gibson 2000, 496–505; Jeffords 1993). Categories of "hyphenated Americans" proliferated under the auspices of burgeoning discourses of multiculturalism coinciding with massive waves of immigration from Mexico, Central America, Vietnam, Cambodia, Korea, and Taiwan over the eighties. Recasting the masculine as the newly marginalized position within American culture (Wiegman 1995, 123), increasing numbers of white men reported in public polls of the time that there was more discrimination against them than against any other group (American Civil Liberties Union 1996; Gamson and Modigliani 1987, 137–77).

The decade of the eighties, moreover, was witness, on the one hand, to unprecedented numbers of a select cadre of African Americans being invited into high-visibility positions with government and media and, on the other hand, a visceral rage emanating from poor blacks blighted by Reagan's social policies, who communicated their desperation through both the inspired artistry of hip-hop music and style and what some termed a "destructive nihilism" (George 2004, ix–x; West 1993, 18). The eighties also saw the rise of a remarkable range of "crossover cultures" producing new cultural archetypes—wiggers and wannabes, b-boys and buppies (Gubar 1997; Ignatiev and Garvey 1996; Roediger 2002)—and at the same time, the emergence of what Angela Dillard refers to as "multicultural conservatives," African Americans and Latinos who, disillusioned by identity politics, aligned themselves with the New Right and the Republican Party over the course of the eighties and zealously promoted the redemptive possibilities of assimilation, individualism, and neoliberal standards of character and sexual morality (2001, x–xv).

The decade of the nineties took its cues from these shifts and adjustments. Signaling a turn from the civil rights era of the sixties and its specific repertoire of discursive presumptions to a range of abnegations, reversals, and reinterpretations characteristic of the post–civil rights or post-soul era, key distinctions collapsed and new categories emerged (M. Hill 2003; Neal 2002). Neoliberal discourses that had gained acceptance in the context of Ronald Reagan's eight-year presidency reinterpreted the "failures" of liberal Great Society programs, claiming that "measures intended to decrease poverty had actually increased inequality, that attempts to assist the disadvantaged had actually worsened their disadvantage, that controls on minimum wages hurt the worse paid because they destroy jobs" (Rose 1996, 51). Accompanying shifts in cultural discourses celebrated archetypes of entrepreneurial and "enterprised" citizens while dismissing programs for state assistance as burdensome, unnecessary, and illogical. In this context, ideals of individual self-fulfillment and proper standards of work, thrift, and merit assumed the characteristics of a "fundamental and universal paean," that is, as the means to "the complete realization of man" and the "total development of society" (Hunter 1988, 6).

Within this larger discursive context, welfare and social justice emerged as unproductive racial entitlements that created no wealth at the expense of the "productive" private sector in which all national wealth was actually produced (Rose 1996, 51). Emergent ethics of reactionary individualisms placed responsibility for an individual's economic viability entirely on his/her shoulders, creating hated figures of the "welfare queen," the "quota queen," the black/Latina teenage mother as unsavory "baby factory."

As neoliberal discourses renewed Horatio Alger myths about self-empowerment and thrift, individuals themselves were confronting grave economic realities. The extraordinary economic changes that had spun into motion during the seventies lingered into the eighties as the American economy saw staggering trade deficits overseas. Chronic budget deficits transformed the United States from a "creditor to a debtor nation" (Gibson 2000, 503). Policy reforms promulgated during the Reagan presidency "encouraged predatory capital, attacked organized labor, and deepened the impact of inequality by disqualifying economic victims from welfare payments" (Shapiro 1990, 332). Blaming the public educational system for failing to produce an effective and loyal labor force, and charging foreign nations with unfair trade exclusions, these critiques provided justifications for massive cuts to social justice and public welfare budgets.

Focusing the anger of displaced, bewildered, and emasculated white males onto relatively new liberal programs of social justice, the costs of federal policies and programs were articulated "in terms of loss—loss of control over school selection, union apprenticeship programs, hiring, promotions, neighborhoods, public safety, and even sexual morals" and in terms of "what government takes rather than what it gives" (Edsall and Edsall 1991, 11). Increases in the number of new entrants to the American workforce—visible evidence of changes wrought by affirmative action programs—fueled these resentments.

Between 1980 and 1990, the percentage of nonwhite men in professional and managerial occupations almost doubled, from 4.7 percent in 1980 to 7.2 percent in 1990, and the proportion of women of color in these jobs increased from 3.2 percent to 6.9 percent (Hartmann 1996, 78; Holmes Norton 1996, 43). Most notably, white women's share of management jobs increased by about one-third—from 27.1 percent in the eighties to 35.3 percent in the nineties (Hartmann 1996, 78–81).[1]

By contrast, the percentage of white men in the full-time civilian workforce saw a decline of 4.4 percent between 1979 and 1992 (Holmes Norton 1996, 44). Combined with declines in men's wages and the loss of nearly two million male-dominated manufacturing jobs during the eighties, these visible transformations in the workforce confirmed for some that affirmative action programs were racial entitlements that took away jobs previously held by white men and gave them, unfairly and illegally, to women and nonwhites instead. The appointment of large numbers of conservative, right-wing nominees to judgeships nationwide over the eighties, from state courts to federal district and appellate courts to the U.S. Supreme Court, corroborated these circulating laments as the courts eviscerated protections they had previously mandated. Now the Supreme Court, reflecting political shifts enabled by Reagan and Bush appointees to the bench, gave greater weight to claims of "reverse discrimination," outlawed the use of minority set-asides in cases where prior racial discrimination could not be proved, and placed stricter limits on the use of racial preferences at both the state and federal level, stating that affirmative action programs that failed to comply were unconstitutional unless they fulfilled a "compelling governmental interest" and passed "strict scrutiny" tests (*Adarand Constructors v. Peña* 1995; *City of Richmond v. J. A. Croson Co.* 1989; *Shaw v. Reno* 1993).

While this hue and cry about federal contracts and minority set-asides may appear to suggest that by the nineties a majority of federal contracts were being handed over to women- and black-owned firms, of all the federal money awarded between 1990 and 1995, no more than 4.3 percent went to women- and minority-owned business, while 95.7 percent went to white male-owned firms (Harris 1996, 328). Likewise, an examination of discrimination cases filed with the U.S. Commission on Civil Rights shows that 96.7 percent of such cases were filed by women and people of color while only 3.6 percent were filed by white men charging that they were victims of "reverse discrimination" (Harris 1996, 330–31).

Moreover, between 1979 and 1992, while the percentage of white men in the full-time civilian workforce declined by 4.4 percent, jobs were disappearing across the board, so that despite claims that they were the newest victims of racial discrimination, white males were neither alone in their plight nor were they among those who bore the brunt of these losses. Over the same period, black male employment dropped by 5.5 percent and Latino men lost roughly 6.9 percent of their jobs (Holmes Norton 1996, 44). Likewise, from 1964 to 1997, the rate of increase in African American college graduates rose from 4 to 12 percent, but so did the rate of increase among white college graduates—from 10 to 23 percent.

Despite visible changes in the workforce and on college campuses nationwide, affirmative action gains for African Americans did not unseat persistent gaps in earnings and economic mobility between the races. And despite racialized anxieties to the contrary, these gains did not come at the expense of opportunities for whites (American Civil Liberties Union 1997). Comparisons across the races showed with consistency that in every aspect of economic life, white families continued to fare far better than African Americans. More than half of all black children were living in poverty by the mid-nineties, in contrast with less than 15 percent of white children who were growing up in comparable circumstances (American Civil Liberties Union 1996). Likewise, public schools serving inner city black and Latino children received about half the funds per student allocated to public schools in surrounding white suburbs (American Civil Liberties Union 1997). Moreover, empirical studies of the prevalence and continued impact of racial discrimination showed repeatedly that African Americans suffered significant and stubbornly high levels of race-based discrimination in employment, earnings, housing, credit and banking, law enforcement, and other aspects of daily life (Fix and Turner 1998; Glaeser, Vigdor, and Sanford 2001; U.S. Census Bureau 2000; U.S. Office of Professional Management 2002).

The changing circumstances of American workers, irrespective of race, reveals a larger economic context within which the gap between poor and rich has grown exponentially in the last three decades. For instance, the heads of major American corporations receive more than two hundred times the pay and benefits of ordinary workers, a five-fold rise since 1965. Similarly, while wages for college-educated workers dropped 7.5 percent from 1973 to 1993, earnings for the average American CEO increased by 514 percent from 1980 through 1993 (Themba 1999, 15). During this period of ostensible bounty, Fortune 500 companies cut nearly 4.4 million jobs, forcing workers to scramble toward lower-paying, less-secure options. Between 1979 and 1983, more than three-quarters of net new job growth came in the form of low-wage jobs in retail and health care services (Themba 1999, 16).

Despite affirmative action mandates, moreover, white men, who constitute only about 45 percent of the American labor market, nevertheless occupied over 95 percent of top management positions in the largest corporations (American Civil Liberties Union 1996). Indicating the contours of the glass ceiling faced by women and nonwhites, by contrast, women occupy approximately 3 percent, blacks 0.6 percent, Asians 0.3 percent, and Latinos 0.4 percent of these positions (Equal Employment Opportunity Commission 1995; Glass Ceiling Commission 1995). While growing numbers of women have launched their own businesses since the seventies—from around 400,000 in 1972 to almost eight million in 1996—stagnating corporate careers are among the main reasons why women have chosen to start their own shops (Equal Rights Advocates 1999).

Likewise, evidence of sex segregation and income inequity remains significant. In 1994, women were more likely to be schoolteachers, nurses, and social workers while men were more likely to be doctors, architects, and engineers (Hartmann 1996, 81). The wage gap between men and women stands at approximately 85 percent after adjusting for differences in education, experience, and other factors, and this gap is wider still between white men and men and women of color. Latino men, for instance, earn 81 percent and Latinas less than 65 percent of the wages earned by white men at the same educational level (Blau and Ferber 1992; Stith 1996). Thus, while affirmative action programs have enjoyed, at best, a mixed record of effectiveness in opening up American workplaces and college campuses to new entrants, the representation of women and nonwhites in economic life is unlikely to be strengthened by the elimination of policies geared specifically to their inclusion. And yet, attacks on affirmative action, as they took shape over the course of the nineties, did not propose to overhaul existing policies. They sought to end them.

Within this national context of racial impasse and economic transformation, California emerged as the testing ground for a series of neoconservative attacks on social justice during the decade of the nineties. Its population growing more and more racially heterogeneous and multiethnic over the last two decades, California became the first state where nonwhites—Asians, Latinos, and African Americans together—surpassed white Americans as the demographic majority in the year 2000 (California Department of Finance 2000). As conservative critics lamented, by the mid-nineties, taking women into account, nearly 75 percent of all Californians could be included among groups who deserved "special consideration" while white males remained the only category with no claim to such historical disadvantage (Kotkin 1995).

While electronic and aerospace manufacturing, finance capital and agrobusiness had yielded a long boom for the highly diversified Californian economy from 1975 to 1990, "the virtuous circle of investment, employment, and spending" came to a grinding halt with spectacular consequences during the "crisis of 1990–94" (Walker 1998, 284–85). As the state was forced into "collective downsizing in the wake of a decade of over-accumulation of factories, workers, securities, real estate, and executive fat," 1.5 million jobs disappeared (Duster 1998, 123). Southern California was worst hit and accounted for over a quarter of all job losses in the country between 1990 and 1993. The Bay Area was less devastated but it too saw the loss of 120,000 jobs (Walker 1998, 286). Cutbacks in the defense industry accounted for 300,000 of these jobs, and continual hemorrhaging in the manufacturing sector cost an additional 200,000, but the biggest hit of all came in wholesale and retail trades, accounting for 900,000 of all jobs lost in the state (Duster 1998, 123).

As Californians filed 20 percent of the nation's bankruptcies in 1991 and 1992 (Walker 1998, 285) and unemployment reached 9 percent by 1992 (Duster 1998, 123), these changes triggered panic and anxiety about the future of the state. The poor, and in particular the nonwhite poor, were exposed to "the winds of economic destruction and political scapegoating for the debacle" (Walker 1998, 284), and affirmative action and other social justice programs emerged in popular discourse as metonyms for what had gone wrong in California.

Responding to this climate of racialized resentment and economic anxiety, starting in the mid-nineties, state legislators in California made several fruitless attempts to end affirmative action programs statewide (Bancroft 1994, A19; Lucas 1996, A11; Wilson 1995, A1). Then, during the November 1994 general elections in California, voters approved

Proposition 187, a ballot measure that outlawed public benefits for illegal aliens and their families in California. The highly contested "Save Our State" measure made front-page news nationwide and served as the centerpiece of incumbent Republican governor Pete Wilson's reelection campaign. Playing to widespread anti-immigrant fever among Californian voters (Rowan 1994, 42), both Wilson and Proposition 187 won electoral victories in the 1994 elections. By March 1998, a federal judge had ruled Proposition 187 unconstitutional on grounds that federal welfare reform that had passed earlier in 1996 made "states powerless to enact their own legislative schemes to regulate immigration" (Purdum 1998, A12). Nevertheless, the measure's success in the 1994 elections signaled intense public frustration with social justice programs, and the political campaign that had persuaded Californian voters to pass the measure starkly highlighted the racial bases of this frustration (Hasian and Delgado 1998, 245–70; Santa Ana 1999, 191–224).

When Governor Wilson made an abortive run for the Republican ticket in the 1996 presidential primaries, his campaign echoed Proposition 187's appeals to racialized economic anxieties, this time identifying race- and gender-based affirmative action programs as particularly troublesome. Wilson's campaign played to middle-class angst, addressing disaffected and alienated Americans simmering with resentment over being forced to underwrite "costly health and social services for illegal immigrants, provide welfare benefits for unwed teenagers who keep having babies, and watch while job preferences are granted on the basis of race or gender" (Claiborne 1995, A1).

In the midst of these divisive debates, on July 20, 1995, the University of California board of regents adopted its "policy ensuring equal treatment of admissions" that barred the use of race, religion, sex, color, ethnicity, or national origin as criteria for admission to the university. The regents' policy offered Governor Wilson and University of California regent Ward Connerly, appointed to his post by the governor, the first success in what would become a highly effective collaboration in the statewide popular campaign against affirmative action in California (Hayden and Rice 1995, 264). Connerly, an African American businessman from Sacramento, would later emerge as a controversial media figure, serving a strategic role as chairman and spokesperson for the public campaign against affirmative action in California.

During the early nineties, well before the regents' policy came to pass, Thomas Wood, executive director of the conservative California Association of Scholars, and Glynn Custred, a California State University anthropology professor, were outraged by a state bill that required graduating classes at public universities to reflect the ethnic composition of the state's multiethnic population. The proposal was passed by the California legislature twice and was vetoed each time by Governor Wilson (Impoco 1995, 30). Positioning themselves as the voices of white men who had for too long suffered the humiliations of "reverse discrimination," Wood and Custred formed a new group, Californians against Discrimination and Preferences, geared to organizing public opposition to statewide racial preferences.

Wood, a scholar of philosophy, spoke often of an incident where he had "once been told by a member of a search committee at a university, 'You'd walk into this job if you were the right gender'" (Boudreau 1994, A3; Impoco 1995, 30). In an investigative report aired on NBC's *Dateline* in February 1996, Wood's accusations were revealed as uncorroborated by the facts. Nevertheless, his accusations resonated with a ready stock of unsubstantiated but conventional anecdotes about the costs of affirmative action for white males. Custred, never claiming reverse discrimination, explained instead that he objected to affirmative action because these programs "penalized qualified minorities by tainting them as so-called quota hires" and were gradually turning public universities in California into "remedial institutions forced to admit unprepared minority students" (Boudreau 1994, A3).

By 1996, Wood and Custred had authored a carefully worded ballot measure entitled the California Civil Rights Initiative (CCRI) that was included on the ballot for the 1996 general elections as Proposition 209. The measure amended the Californian constitution requiring that "the state shall not discriminate against or grant preferential treatment to any individual or group on the basis of race, sex, color, ethnicity, or national origin in the operation of public employment, public education, or public contracting" (California Constitution, Article 1, § 31[a]).[2] Wood and Custred had sought to have the measure included on the ballot in previous years, and each time they had failed (Impoco 1995, 30). By 1996 however, a number of key events—the economic fallout of the crash of the early nineties, Governor Wilson's electoral campaigns, the controversial success of Proposition 187, and circulating nod-and-wink suspicions about the "real" costs of affirmative action—had converged to produce a discursive environment pregnant with opportunity for a statewide popular campaign to end affirmative action in California.

As chronicled by Lydia Chávez, by mid-1995 the opposition to Proposition 209 coalesced around three loosely organized groups, "civil rights leaders casting about for a strategy to save affirmative action, the Democratic Party looking for a way to win the next election, and women's rights leaders fixed on testing the gender gap's political power" (1998, 85). Divisions quickly emerged among the opposition over campaign strategies, and the split yielded two separate organizations geared to derail Proposition 209.

The Northern Coalition to Save Affirmative Action was led by Eva Jefferson Patterson, executive director of the Lawyers' Committee for Civil Rights; David Oppenheimer, a law professor at Golden Gate University; Jan Adams, an organizer for United Farmworkers; Central American solidarity groups; the African National Congress; gay and lesbian causes; and others. These organizers united behind the belief that Proposition 209 could not be defeated and argued that the only way to save affirmative action was to offer an alternate measure that fixed what voters perceived was wrong with it.

Guided by the strong popular response that President Bill Clinton's "mend it, don't end it" approach had received, the Northern Coalition drafted the Equal Opportunity without Quotas Initiative, which proposed that "the state shall ensure equal opportunity and shall prevent discrimination based on race, sex, age, color, ethnicity, and national origin" (Chávez 1998, 105). The measure proposed changes to the state constitution that would prohibit quotas and the hiring of unqualified applicants, and it imposed fines on anyone who fraudulently benefited from a state affirmative action program. The Northern Coalition argued that it offered what most voters preferred—equal opportunity—while it did away with what voters hated—quotas.

But when legislative analysts in California interpreted the Equal Opportunity without Quotas Initiative as a means to eliminate magnet schools and racially isolated minority school programs, cuts that could save the state "up to 38 million dollars" (Chávez 1998, 108), the Northern Coalition, realizing its proposal might inadvertently harm minority school programs, abandoned the campaign and joined with the Southern Coalition.

This second group brought together the forces of Katherine Spillar, Eleanor Smeal, and Peg Yorkin of the Feminist Majority; Patricia Ireland and others of the National Organization for Women (NOW); Constance Rice and Molly Munger of the NAACP Legal Defense and Educational Fund; Anthony Thigpen, a neighborhood organizer from South Los Angeles; and lawyers from the Asian Legal Defense and the Mexican American Legal Defense and Educational Fund (MALDEF).

In contrast with the Northern proposal, the Southern strategy focused on a No on CCRI campaign that would attack Proposition 209 on its merits without offering an alternative. Their argument was that voters should not have to decide between two evils—outright elimination or severe modifications to affirmative action. Rather, the Southern Coalition argued that if enough minority and white women voters could be cajoled into voting booths on election day, Proposition 209 could be defeated by a slim margin.

Opposition efforts now focused on a $5 million advertising campaign that was later reduced to a budget of $2 million, which was aimed primarily at drumming home Proposition 209's impact on women, a grassroots get-out-the-vote campaign to mobilize minority voters, and a massive education campaign, which was already partly underway under the auspices of nonprofit organizations like MALDEF and Equal Rights Advocates.

Amid continuing internal fractiousness, the opposition split once again in August 1996 into the Stop Prop 209 campaign headed by the

Feminist Majority and NOW, while leaders from the NAACP Legal Defense Fund, Northern organizers from the Lawyers' Committee on Civil Rights, Anthony Thigpen from South Los Angeles, Jan Adams from Oakland, and many others joined forces on the Campaign to Defeat 209 with Patricia Ewing as campaign manager. The Stop Prop 209 campaign spearheaded Freedom Summer '96, a media event that brought hundreds of college students to California in the summer of 1996. Deliberately referencing voter registration drives that had brought thousands of college students to rural Mississippi during the civil rights movement in 1964, Freedom Summer '96 organized voter education drives in the streets of Los Angeles, signature petitions in Santa Monica, and public rallies at the campus of UCLA in Westwood and in Golden Gate Park in San Francisco. Student organizations like the Movimiento Estudiantil Chicano de Aztlan pitched in, and in September 1996 the "Freedom Bus" carrying the Stop Prop 209 message began its journey from Los Angeles to visit churches and schools across the state. It featured the Reverend Jesse Jackson of the Rainbow Coalition, Patricia Ireland of NOW, Eleanor Smeal of the Feminist Majority, and Dolores Huerta of United Farmworkers as traveling speakers.

Part of the Southern Coalition's public education mission focused on the ballot summary for Proposition 209 that was prepared by the state attorney general's office as a means to inform voters about various ballot initiatives they would be asked to decide on election day. Although lengthier voter pamphlets offered fuller details on each ballot initiative, most voters could not be expected to read much beyond the condensed summaries that set the tone and, in the case of Proposition 209, remained silent about the implications of the measure upon state affirmative action programs. Given that public polls found Americans consistently opposed to racial preferences but strongly sympathetic toward affirmative action, opponents of Proposition 209 were keen to have the ballot summary specify the measure's potential impact upon affirmative action programs.

A few months before the general elections in November, opponents approached a superior court in Sacramento asking that the attorney general's voter pamphlets be amended to "specifically state that the measure affects affirmative action programs" (Chiang 1996a, A19). A ballot summary that made reference to preferential treatment but remained silent on affirmative action, they argued, misled voters by making the language of the measure more palatable than it might have otherwise been.

In August 1996, Superior Court judge James Ford ordered the attorney general to revise the ballot summary on grounds that it was "misleading." A week later, a California appeals court and the California Supreme Court both reversed Ford's decision, ruling that "the electorate can hardly be deceived by this essentially verbatim recital of the straightforward text of the measure itself" (Chiang 1996b, A16; Howard 1996, A3).

On election day, Proposition 209 passed by a 54 to 46 majority. Two days later, the American Civil Liberties Union (ACLU), the NAACP Legal Defense Fund, MALDEF, NOW, and several others filed a petition with the District Court of the Northern District of California requesting a temporary restraining order (TRO) on the measure. Opponents primarily argued the legal implications of the new measure stating that it violated the equal protection clause of the Fourteenth Amendment because it specifically targeted race- and gender-based affirmative action programs. They argued, moreover, that Proposition 209 violated the supremacy clause because it created state law that contradicted Title VII of the federal Civil Rights Act of 1964. On November 27, 1996, Chief Judge Henderson of the district court issued the TRO (Ayres 1996, 1) and followed on December 23 with a preliminary injunction on grounds that the measure could cause "irreparable injury" to the plaintiffs' constitutional rights (*Coalition v. Wilson* 1996).

Supporters of Proposition 209 led by Governor Wilson appealed this decision to the U.S. District Court of Appeals of the Ninth Circuit. On April 8, 1997, a three-judge panel of the court of appeals issued an order rejecting Henderson's reasoning and affirmed the constitutionality of the ballot measure. The equal protection clause, the three-judge panel explained, prevents official conduct that discriminates on the basis of race. When the government prefers individuals on account of their race or gender, it correspondingly disadvantages individuals who fortuitously belong to another race or to the other gender. In contrast, "a law that prohibits the state from classifying individuals by race or gender *a fortiori* does not classify individuals by race or gender" (*Coalition v. Wilson* 1997a, 3913). Since it does not classify individuals along race or gender lines at all, the panel explained, Proposition 209 could not be construed as discriminating against individuals based on their race or gender. The three-judge panel concluded that the measure was in compliance with the equal protection clause, and was therefore beyond legal reproach.

Opponents filed an emergency motion for an *en banc* rehearing, which the Ninth Circuit denied on August 21, 1997 (*Coalition v. Wilson* 1997b). A week later, opponents filed a petition for a writ of certiorari to the U.S. Supreme Court together with an application for a stay of the Ninth Circuit's judgment (Biskupic 1997, A10). The Supreme Court denied the petition and on September 4, 1997, allowed Proposition 209 to go into effect (Greenhouse 1997, A16). The measure was the nation's first voter- and court-approved ban on affirmative action.

No sooner had race- and gender-based affirmative action been outlawed in California than news commentators began to describe Proposition 209 as the precedent for eliminating affirmative action nationwide (Conrad 1997, 32; Lesher 1997, A3). California's unique standing as a bellwether state was confirmed and reconfirmed in the aftermath of Proposition 209 as critics of affirmative action programs in Texas, Washington, Florida, Nebraska, and Michigan began to organize efforts to emulate the Californian measure through ballot initiatives, legislative proposals, and legal challenges.

Two years later, voters in the state of Washington approved Initiative 200 during the 1998 general elections, a measure that was modeled so closely after Proposition 209 that it was referred to as the "son of 209" in the popular press ("Initiative 200: Another Blow" 1998, 18A). Meanwhile, Proposition A, a ballot measure specifically outlawing affirmative action in the Houston city charter, failed during elections in November 1997. Observers noted that the Houston measure failed at least in part because it was clearly phrased as an anti–affirmative action measure, thus deviating from the model established by Proposition 209 (Holmes 1998, A25; "Houston Thinks Globally" 1997, A1). By the end of 1998, organizing efforts to get popular initiatives on state ballots modeled closely after the California measure had been reported in as many as twenty-one states nationwide and at the federal level (Freedberg 1997, A1; Honan 1996, 14; Hornbeck 1998, D1; Sample 1998, A10; Verhovek and Ayres 1998, B2).

As the analyses in this book show, these assaults, like the creation of affirmative action programs thirty years ago, confirm that politico-economic practices are not necessarily rational nor always merit-based. They suggest, to the contrary, that hiring and admissions decisions are deeply intertwined with cultural imaginaries about women and non-whites, and their value as workers (Davis 1998/1977, 161–92; Folbre and Hartmann 1989, 90–96; Shultz 1992, 297–338). The implementation of affirmative action programs over the sixties and seventies made explicit questions about opportunities for women and people of color in economic life, and their access to politico-economic power. These programs redefined parameters for entry into politico-economic institutions, limiting an employer's power to shut out female and nonwhite applicants and forcing accountability for sexist and racist impulses in hiring and admissions decisions.

With the elimination of such controls on systemic sexism and racism in California and Washington, these impulses had free rein once again. Thus, for example, prior to the passage of Initiative 200 in Washington, the Plus Three hiring program allowed the state to expand the shortlist of candidates considered for a job by adding the top three affirmative action candidates to the top seven finalists on job tests. In 1998, 226 jobs—roughly 7 percent of all hires—were filled through Plus Three, about 20 percent of who were white men (Brune 1998a, B1). After the passage of Initiative 200, however, only Vietnam veterans and the disabled could legally be among the "targeted groups." Thus, in an ironic turn, the only groups who could legally be granted preferential treatment in state of Washington after 1998 consisted primarily of white men (Brune and Varner 1999, A1).

Similarly, foretelling the impact of "resegregation" upon workplaces and classrooms after the passage of Proposition 209 in California (Katz 1997, 2; Parker 1998), news reports noted that in the months following its passage, California courts ruled that the anti–affirmative action measure could be interpreted as disallowing even "soft affirmative action" such as focused outreach or contract recruitment programs that made specific efforts to hire female and nonwhite subcontractors (Chiang 1999, A22). Accordingly, Proposition 209 limits inclusion mechanisms to the presumption of good faith to hire individuals from historically disadvantaged groups—mechanisms that had remained utterly ineffective until the implementation and enforcement of federal mandates for goals and timetables in the seventies. Mirroring larger concerns over the proletarianization of women of color urged on by the global restructuring of capitalism, such declines would moreover exact the highest price from poor women of color who had reaped the smallest rewards from affirmative action programs while they had been in force.

As state-level anti–affirmative action organizing proliferated nationwide, Jennifer Gratz, a twenty-year-old graduate of Southgate Anderson High School in Southgate, Michigan, applied for admission to the undergraduate program of the University of Michigan. Gratz stood thirteenth in her class of 298 students with a grade point average of 3.765 (Bronner 1997, 24). A student council leader, mathematics tutor, aide to senior citizens in the community, homecoming queen, and cheerleader, Gratz grew up in a blue-collar suburb of Detroit, the daughter of a police officer (Sanchez 1997, A1). When she received a rejection from the University of Michigan, Gratz was convinced that she had been racially discriminated against by the university's admissions policies because she was white.

As Gratz was receiving the letter announcing her rejection, Republican lawmakers in Michigan were issuing public calls to students who believed they had been discriminated against by the university, urging them to file suit (Sanchez 1997, A1). Gratz was among a number of students who responded to the lawmakers' call. Two years later, in October 1997, the Center for Individual Rights (CIR), a right-wing advocacy group, filed a class action lawsuit on behalf of the disgruntled students with the district court in Detroit. Jennifer Gratz and Patrick Hamacher, another of the rejected applicants, were named lead plaintiffs in the case, *Gratz v. Bollinger*. The plaintiffs alleged that the University of Michigan's undergraduate admissions policies used racial preferences, which violated the Fourteenth Amendment's equal protection clause and the Civil Rights Act of 1964.

A few months earlier, in the summer of 1997, Barbara Grutter, a forty-three-year-old mother of two, was denied admission to the University of Michigan's prestigious law school despite a grade point average of 3.8 as an undergraduate, "straight A's" in her graduate courses, and "respectable scores" on the LSAT (Clayton 2001, 14). Grutter had run a consulting business for a few years and had corporate experience, a critical element, she had been told, for admission to law school. When Grutter received her rejection letter, like Gratz, she was convinced it was because she was white.

Prompted by an article in a Detroit newspaper that detailed others' complaints about admission policies, and which showed average test scores and grades of minority applicants to the Michigan law school that were "considerably lower than her own" (Clayton 2001, 14), Grutter decided she would sue. In December 1997, the CIR filed a second lawsuit against the University of Michigan, *Grutter v. Bollinger*, this time challenging the university's use of race as a criterion in law school admissions (Griffith 1997, A12).

The role of the CIR in these proceedings brings into relief the influence of a series of well-funded and well-connected law and advocacy groups that emerged on the national scene over the course of the nineties, and that focused right-wing assaults on affirmative action and social justice. Makani Themba traces the history of these policy analysis and advocacy organizations to the end of World War II, when wealthy patrons like Andrew Carnegie (Carnegie Endowment for International Peace), Margaret Olivia Sage (Russell Sage Foundation), Edward A. Filene (the Twentieth Century Fund), and others began to fund large-scale research and analysis efforts to inform and influence federal policy on a range of complex policy issues (1999, 4–5).

Assembling a formidable network of experts and developing relations with academic institutions and regulatory consortia, business interests came to dominate policy debates both in terms of delineating expert wisdom on policy issues and educating regulators on those issues. The civil rights conflicts of the sixties interrupted the pro-business influence of these organizations, drawing attention to social welfare issues and addressing questions of systemic poverty, unemployment, and racism. The Ford Foundation, the Brookings Institution, the Southern Poverty Law Center, and other organizations emerged during this period, launching ethnic research institutes coast to coast and offering policy research and legal counsel geared to liberal social change.

By the late seventies, however, the influence of these "War on Poverty" social change endeavors dwindled as business-oriented policy organizations took on the War on Poverty as a way to fight for reduced social spending and lower taxes for corporations (Themba 1999, 5). As the cultural backlash of the seventies and the eighties coalesced in response to the gains of the civil unrests of the sixties, these older, more "liberal" policy organizations were targeted by negative media campaigns and were edged out of the limelight by newer, right-wing groups (Themba 1999, 6).

Thus, for example, the Institute for Justice and the Center for Equal Opportunity, a Washington D.C.–based public law firm established by Linda Chavez, who led the federal Commission on Civil Rights during the Reagan presidency, provides Web-based and other forms of legal advice to individuals interested in initiating "reverse discrimination" lawsuits, and the Independent Women's Forum based in Arlington, Virginia, organizes college visits to offer students strategies to confront "political correctness" on campus.

Pursuing a comparable strategy, when legal battles over Proposition 209 drew to a close in California, triumphant University of California regent Ward Connerly announced the creation of the American Civil Rights Institute (ACRI), an organization that would provide Connerly with an advocacy and fundraising platform to assist anti–affirmative action campaigns that were gathering force in a number of other states (Broder 1999, A1; Zachary 1997, A20). When organizers in the state of Washington sought Connerly's assistance with their media campaigns against affirmative action during general elections in 1998, ACRI helped raise funds for the media campaign in support of Initiative 200 (Postman 1998b, A11).

Together with right-wing think tanks like the American Enterprise Institute and the Heritage Foundation, these organizations gradually began to take control of public debate on a range of issues by providing in-house analytical and opinion research. To wit, recent comparisons of "talking head" pundits solicited by network news anchors found that the spectrum of political opinions that finds a voice on the mainstream news has narrowed over the past decade, and that conservative voices have gained attention as experts on the news issues of the day (Dolny 2003). Over the course of the nineties a host of right-wing organizations took up the assault on affirmative action and social justice as their cause célèbre and, with considerable cross-pollination among their executives, constituted a well-organized network of strategic right-wing dissent.[3]

The CIR rose to prominence in this context, its efforts focused on bringing lawsuits against colleges for their race-based admission procedures. The organization had earlier won an important victory when it represented Cheryl Hopwood, the plaintiff in a case against race-based admission policies at the University of Texas (*Hopwood v. Texas* 1996). The CIR had also worked with the Sacramento-based Pacific Legal Foundation to represent California governor Pete Wilson and regent Ward Connerly in suits they brought challenging a number of "offending" state laws that violated Proposition 209 but remained on the books even after the measure had passed in 1996 (Stephens 1998, 12). Now the CIR moved to recruit and represent the plaintiffs Jennifer Gratz, Patrick Hamacher, and Barbara Grutter in landmark lawsuits it would file against the University of Michigan's undergraduate and law school admission procedures.

In May 2002, the Court of Appeals for the Sixth Circuit upheld the admissions policies of the University of Michigan, prompting a long litigation campaign by the CIR to get the U.S. Supreme Court to agree to revisit the issue of affirmative action (Greenhouse 2002, 1). In the meantime, appellate and district courts in California, Georgia, Michigan, Texas, and Washington had issued a host of contradictory decisions on race- and gender-based criteria in university admissions (Firestone 2001, 1; Fletcher 2000, A2; Nissimov 2000, 19; Schemo 2001, 10). The CIR's appeals to the Supreme Court noted these state-level inconsistencies, arguing that the Supreme Court needed to intervene and set a national standard on the question of affirmative action.

The Supreme Court heard oral arguments on April 1, 2003, and on June 23, 2003, the Court issued decisions in both Michigan cases, preserving affirmative action in law school admissions by a one-vote margin and by a 6 to 3 majority invalidating such programs in admissions to the undergraduate program (Greenhouse 2003, 1). The first Supreme Court ruling on affirmative action in higher education since the *Bakke* decision in 1978, the Michigan decisions affirmed the constitutionality of the "diversity" rationale that Justice Lewis F. Powell had staked out in the *Bakke* case, which permitted the use of race as a "plus factor" in admissions decisions (*Regents v. Bakke* 1978).

Writing for the majority in *Grutter v. Bollinger*, Justice Sandra Day O'Connor clarified that remedying past discrimination was not the only permissible justification for race-based governmental action. The Michigan law school, she stated, also has a "compelling interest in attaining a diverse student body."

> Effective participation by members of all racial and ethnic groups in the civil life of our nation is essential if the dream of one nation, indivisible, is to be realized . . . In order to cultivate a set of leaders with legitimacy in the eyes of the citizenry, it is necessary that the path to leadership be visibly open to talented and qualified individuals of every race and ethnicity. ("Excerpts from Justices' Opinions" 2003, 24)

The Court distinguished between the law school's "highly-individualized, holistic review of each applicant's file" in which race counts as one among many factors, and the affirmative action practices of the undergraduate program, which, by using a point system based in part on race, ran afoul of the "strict scrutiny standard" established by Court precedent. As Chief Justice William H. Rehnquist, writing for the majority in *Gratz v. Bollinger*, held, such "mechanical" means that "automatically distribute twenty points, or one-fifth of the points needed to guarantee admission, to every single 'underrepresented minority' applicant solely because of race" fails the "strict scrutiny" test, which requires that these mechanisms be "narrowly tailored" to achieve the "interest in educational diversity that the respondents claim justifies their program" ("Excerpts from Justices' Opinions" 2003, 25).

Ward Connerly, along with representatives from the CIR and other conservative think tanks, disappointed by the Court's rulings, announced the same day that they would begin work on getting a "son of 209" popular initiative on the Michigan ballot in the 2004 general elections. Several others, angered by Justice O'Connor's moderate stance in *Grutter*, announced that when the next vacancy opened on the Supreme Court, they would demand that the president choose a replacement "whose opposition to affirmative action is beyond doubt" (N. Lewis 2003, 1).

In January 2004, the Michigan Civil Rights Initiative (MCRI), bankrolled by Connerly's ACRI, began work on an anti–affirmative action ballot measure, inviting Jennifer Gratz to be spokesperson for the statewide campaign (Pierre 2004, A3; Wiltenberg 2004, 18). By March 2004, however, legal objections and appeals brought by Citizens for a United Michigan and other opposing groups claimed that the MCRI used deceptive and dishonest language in its signature petition forms, which violated state law ("Citizens for a United Michigan" 2004; Fowler 2004). By May 2004, with the signature drive distracted and demoralized by weeks of legal wrangling, Connerly and the MCRI abandoned their efforts, announcing that they would return in two years with a renewed campaign for the 2006 ballot instead ("Anti-Affirmative Action Campaign Will Target '06" 2004; Prichard 2004).

Like the shifting policies of the University of California regents in the wake of Proposition 209 and vacillating court decisions and admissions policies at colleges in Georgia, Texas, and Washington (Ackerman 2004, 20; Brune and Heim 1998, B1; Firestone 2001, A1; Everett-Haynes and Ackerman 2004, 37; Glater 2004, 1), Connerly's strategic failures in Michigan suggest that, at the close of the nineties, the political career of affirmative action remained in flux, thoroughly contested and contradictory.

In particular, they bring into relief the undulating but abiding racial order of the post-soul era. As the chapters in this book highlight, these shifts took form gradually, and in the form of a bricolage of equivocations. Rightist assaults of the nineties, it becomes clear in this context, did not erase race and its concomitant complex of *savoirs* from public discourse any more than did racial reforms of the sixties. The long arm of liberalism, insisting upon objective and neutral standards of excellence in workplaces and college classrooms, did not impede the operation of highly subjective and culturally specific preferences in the sixties any more than contemporary neoliberal proclamations about the "responsibilized" self are color- and gender-blind.

Thus, in the sixties as in the nineties, ideologies of liberalism and neoliberalism alike reveal a vast field of accepted knowledges, which, while they deny their existence, are nevertheless imbued with the logics of race and gender. As the following chapters will show, categories and juxtapositions on the basis of race and gender, while they are viewed as aberrant offshoots of these systems of thought, are nevertheless "inherent to the inclusionary myths and exclusionary practices of democracy and freedom" (Stoler 1995, 24), and the law, public policy, and popular culture are all part of their operation (Crenshaw et al. 1995).

It follows then that the state charged with the efficient management of the population, with inventing techniques and tactics for monitoring race and gender, does not merely intervene in, but is instead intervened by, racial conflict. This "racial state" does not simply mediate racial crises but is itself inherently racial (Omi and Winant 1994, 82). Specifically, as Michel Foucault and others have shown, race and its modern categorizations, its rationale, and functioning rose to prominence among the "normalizing technologies" of government, among "apparatuses of security" of the modern "governmentalized" state (Foucault 1978/1991, 87–104; Goldberg 2002; Stoler 1995).

In this context, racism operates as a "common sense," as unspoken assumptions about morality and character that work to discipline racial subjects, interpellated variously as "model minorities," "token hires," "quota queens," and the like. These categorizations do not arise sporadically in moments of crisis. Rather, they are internal to the "bio-political state," woven into the weft of the social body and internalized within individual subjectivities (Foucault 1978/1990, 135–59; Hardt and Negri 2000, 327–32; Stoler 1995, 69). Racial policies endowed with the authority of the state and its agents, then, work ultimately to secure the centrality of race in the management of the population and to imbue rationality to racisms managed and administered by the state.

In the post-soul moment, the governmentalized state remains a racial state, but one managing a series of searing attacks. Compelled by its critics to peel away layers of its vast bureaucracies and to scale back its profusion of categories, taxonomies, forms, and protocols, the neoliberal state is marked by racial denial and dissonance. Here, in the context of demands for color blindness and erasures of racial privilege, neither binary classifications nor biopolitical repressions are tenable, as categorical distinctions between "black" and "white," "majority" and "minority" have come unmoored.

Likewise, multiracialism and biracialism, reported in growing numbers on managerial mechanisms like the national census, have confounded the state's statistical knowledges in recent years, stymieing its capabilities to order, categorize, and manage the population. Imbricated with circulating imaginaries, its articulations of race-based social justice with "reverse racism" and disarticulations of historical disadvantage from abiding socioeconomic inequities, the neoliberal state navigates a remarkable range of internal contradictions.

We return to California, here in conclusion, to find a notable instance of this range of ambivalences. In March 2002, several years after his Proposition 209 triumph in California, Ward Connerly returned to the airwaves to promote the Racial Privacy Initiative (RPI), a ballot measure that proposed a ban on the collection of all racial data and prohibited state and local governments from "using race, ethnicity, color, or national origin to classify current or prospective students, contractors, or employees in public education, contracting or employment operations" (D. Murphy 2003, 13).

Promoting the vision of a "perfect colorblind polity," the RPI epitomized twin ideals of neoliberalism: it championed responsibilized, self-serving individuals who made no claim to racial or gendered identities in their pursuit of profit and pleasure, while it attacked the state and its capacities for racial categorization on grounds that such mechanisms perpetuated unfair entitlements and an unproductive class of racial dependents. As Connerly had maintained: "This subject is more important to me than all the others [because] there is something fundamentally flawed about a nation that prides itself on equality and wanting to be color-blind, yet [asks] people to identify what their race is" ("Interview with Ward Connerly" 1999).

For Connerly, who served as spokesperson and organizer for the public campaign for the RPI, "the very act of classifying people divides us" (Schevitz 2002, A1). "If you can't ask people about their classification," he explained, "you can't begin to confer benefits on that basis" ("Interview with Ward Connerly" 1999). Moreover, for Connerly, the RPI raised the "fundamental notion that race won't matter." Its challenge was that "the whole concept of race, the legitimacy of race" would disappear (Murphy 2003, 13). Thus, emphasizing his distaste for "odious systems of racial classification," Connerly attacked the "stupidity" of the U.S. census, explaining that, in California,

> One out of nine babies born in 2002 was multi-racial. The Federal Census acknowledges this by allowing individuals to tick as many race boxes as they consider applicable, producing sixty-three possible race categories . . . This system of racial classification, which tracks us from cradle to grave, is arcane and inconsistent. (2003, 26)

Connerly's critique is remarkable for our purposes in that it positions the state's abilities to categorize racial identities at the heart of practices of racism and racial discrimination. As Daniel HoSang observed with incredulity, "the initiative's campaign argues that 'racial classifications' themselves—rather than racist institutions and bigoted beliefs—[are] the foundation rather than the consequence of racist atrocities" (2001). The end of racism, by these logics, is guaranteed by the erasure of racial categories, and, in particular, by disabling the state's management of these categories.

For opposition groups, the ideal of a color-blind society could not be reached by simply removing racial data from public records. Focusing precisely on the administrative apparatuses of the state, the NAACP and MALDEF argued that not collecting racial data would make it impossible to demonstrate racial discrimination or to evaluate the effectiveness of policies intended to eliminate discrimination. Likewise, social science and public policy researchers argued that the prohibition would vitiate efforts to track critical facts like Latino birthrates and African American academic achievement. Medical researchers and health insurance providers claimed the proposal limited their abilities to study correlations between racial identity and health propensities and to provide adequate public health services. And law enforcement agencies argued ironically that not having racial data would stymie efforts within police departments to monitor patterns of racial profiling (Burdman 2002, 18–20; Burdman 2003, 40; Nieves 2003, A4; Schevitz 2002, A1). Even Glynn Custred, author of Proposition 209, disagreed with Connerly, arguing that, "suppressing racial data, rather than rendering affirmative action unworkable, will render the ban on it impossible to enforce" (as quoted in Caldwell 2003).

Together, Connerly's case for the RPI and the broadly articulated opposition that succeeded in defeating the measure[4] typify contestations and ambivalences within the racial order of the post-soul era. Here, multicultural impulses inherited from the sixties and seventies and neoliberal imperatives of color blindness and individualism meet and mutate. Thus, we find, among the justifications for the RPI, the proliferation of unanticipated and open-ended racial self-identifications that subvert static, unchanging formulations of racial categories in census forms and other administrative protocols of the state. And we find, in Connerly's claims themselves, evidence of the neoliberal state scurrying to proliferate its statistical categories apace, evidence, as David Theo Goldberg argues, of how state mechanisms of counting, categorization, and control always lag behind, always attempting to catch up to the "irreducible heterogeneity" of lived identity (1997, 32).

Moreover, beyond opposition concerns that the RPI would impede the capacities of state agencies from managing a whole field of racial claims and counterclaims, even conservative critics of race-based programs acknowledged that "to erase the objectionable use of race in public governance, [one] must first ferret it out with unceasing relentlessness" (Nakao 2003, E14). As the journalist Annie Nakao remarked wryly, "For a guy who's the standard bearer for 'colorblindness,' University of California regent Ward Connerly can't see anything but race" (2003, E14). Thus, the contours of public debate over the RPI, witness to a proliferation of arguments for the erasure of racial classifications as well as claims that such classifications served crucial public ends, highlight the abiding logics of race and racial differentiation within the administrative apparatuses of the neoliberal state, and within recurring contests over their legitimacy.

Revealing the relentless centrality of racial claims in both neoliberal imperatives and race-conscious critiques, the RPI serves to highlight key ambivalences within the racial order of the post-soul moment. Insisting simultaneously upon the proliferation of racial taxonomies as a guarantee of race blindness and the necessity of racial protocols as a defense against racism, these public debates offer us critical insights into the abiding racial order of this moment and the rich repertoire of its discursive ambivalences.

As contemporary public discourse in the United States is yoked to the logics of neoliberalism and those logics in turn shape-shift their way toward hegemonic control, the analyses that follow here serve to mark and specify, through careful study of the affective domains of public policy and cinematic representation, the epistemic order of this post-soul epoch, its proliferation of categories and juxtapositions, its particular regime of taxonomies and truths.

I offer these analyses in four chapters as follows. The first chapter, "Race, Gender, and the Constitution of Subjects: Enemies, Allies, Alibis," explores questions of voice, delegation, and silence in the constitution of cultural identities in the policy arena. Here I focus my attention on representational claims on behalf of racialized and gendered subjects to make visible the ways in which categories such as "blackness" and "women" have performed subtle yet significant discursive work in recent public debates over affirmative action. Combining elements of documentary, discourse, and textual analysis, this chapter draws attention to the operation of the public policy process as a key site where cultural identities are formed, recognized, legitimated, and delegitimated.

The second chapter, "The Affirmative Action Film of the Nineties: Hollywood Cinema as Racial Regime," pursues critical resonances across cinematic texts and policy debates. Presenting textual and figural analyses of recent Hollywood texts—*Disclosure* (1994), *Courage under Fire* (1996), *G.I. Jane* (1997), and *The Contender* (2000)—the chapter focuses on cinematic dramas about the burdens of workplace integration with depictions of a range of difficulties arising from the introduction of women and blacks into the workforce. Marked by their difference from the norm and their uneasy assimilation into the American workplace, these racial and gendered others offer narrative evidence of the follies of race- and gender-conscious social justice programs. Pursuing a range of cross-pollinations between the cinematic and public policy, this chapter highlights the representational context provided by narrative cinema within which policy pronouncements about race, merit, and fairness variously shift and cohere.

The third chapter, "Civil Rights, Affirmative Action, and the American South: Eyewitnesses to the Racial Past," focuses on the politics of public memory, highlighting how social power privileges dominant versions of historical pasts, how one version edges out another in successive retellings, and how some versions are mangled or lost over time. Seeking to understand the ways in which contemporary assaults on affirmative action engage a wistful nostalgia about the sixties and a willful amnesia about aspects of the racial past, the analysis pursues overlaps and divergences between dominant and less familiar versions of the racial past— canonized versions of events and icons of the sixties as well as those that have been relegated to obscurity.

Illuminating aspects of "roads not taken" in public memory, the chapter offers a single comparative analysis that reads Joel Schumacher's *A Time to Kill* (1996), a mainstream Hollywood film that dramatizes racial conflict in a small town in present-day Mississippi, against an independently produced documentary, *Waking in Mississippi* (Christine Herring and Andre Alexis Robinson, 1998), that chronicles the making of Schumacher's film on location in the small Southern town of Canton, Mississippi. Together with network news programs such as *Lights, Camera, Canton* (1995), which aired on CBS's hour-long news magazine *48 Hours*, the analysis interrogates the shaping of a tidy civil rights past that now infuses national debates over affirmative action and the implications of these dominant collective memories.

In the fourth and final chapter, "Of Heroism and Healing, Racism and Redemption: Tall Tales and Short Lists," I focus on the operation of narrative and counternarrative within knowledge regimes. Relying upon newspaper coverage in the mainstream press and returning to legislative records of the mid-sixties, I present a comparative reading of authorized narratives of the anti–affirmative action campaigns of the nineties in the context of analogous and overlapping tales from congressional debate over the Civil Rights Act of 1964. Escorted by a profusion of articulations about race, equality, and discrimination, these events were each witness to intense contests over intersecting and overlapping narratives of heroism and resistance, of bigotry and redemption. Attention to these moments in time illuminates the workings of power in narratives, as well as the ways in which narrative practices are implicated in the production of dominant knowledges about race and racism in the public policy process.

CHAPTER 1

Race, Gender, and the Constitution of Subjects: Enemies, Allies, Alibis

> We live in fragments like speech. Like fits of wind, shivering against
> the window. Pieces of meaning, pierced and strung together.
>
> —Amiri Baraka, *Tight Rope*

Benjamin Kepple, editor of the *Michigan Review*, the conservative student newspaper at the University of Michigan, may be among a new band of American heroes. "Among those of us who oppose affirmative action," he laments, "very few speak out because of the criticism we receive . . . I can't go a day without being called a racist or a bigot" (George 1998, 1A). Like him, John Alberti, a resident of the state of Washington, complains that "if you take the pro-equality side, you tend to be smeared as a racist" (Beason and Brune 1998, A1). Giving voice to a "churning discontent," Kepple and Alberti take their place at the vanguard of popular resistance against "the poisonous atmosphere of political correctness" where "people are tiptoeing around trying not to rock the boat" (Carlson 1998, B5).

For Ward Connerly, chairman of the campaign for California's Proposition 209, it is no surprise that these "warriors of democracy" are angry (1997). As he explains, "if anyone is discriminated against because of his or her color, they have a right to be angry. And, we should all share in that anger" (1996a). Giving voice to "long-simmer[ing] discontent over racial preferences," these voices incur the wrath of "bigots [who] come in all shapes and colors" (Connerly 1996a). For John Carlson, chief spokesperson for the 1998 anti–affirmative action campaign in the state of Washington, this new generation of American heroes seeks only to "move Americans beyond race" (1998, B5).

Beyond the ways in which Kepple, Alberti, and others like them bear witness to a rising tide of frustration over the ferment that programs like affirmative action appear to have silently bred, these voices mark and particularize the "angry white male" archetype in contemporary culture. Their opposition to race- and gender-conscious regimes locates the irrational racial regime that reigns in America as a cumbersome inheritance from a distant racial past. Kepple and his generation can be mistaken for neither pathological white supremacists of the moment nor white racists of previous generations. Their attack on the lingering racial order, as they argue, is pragmatic and principled. Once marginal and extreme, these voices have moved to center court, their outrage to the mainstream of contemporary public discourses.

The authenticity of circulating accounts of how token blacks are included because of their blackness hinges on the presumption that white applicants for college admissions and jobs are excluded because of their whiteness. Thus, concurrent with the "Negroization" of affirmative action beneficiaries (Takaki 1980, 217–18), victimized whites are whitened in the context of affirmative action. Contemporary contests over such programs then are sites where a particular modality of whiteness is articulated and confirmed with keen and eloquent reassurances of the ways in which it is not black.

Contrasting with Richard Dyer's argument that whiteness retains much of its power by remaining on our visual periphery (1988, 44–65), recent assaults on affirmative actions are witness to paradoxical unveilings of the category of whiteness. Within the fraught politico-economic context of the early nineties, with visible markers of demographic shifts in the American population fueling fears of decline and displacement among whites, outrage over affirmative action programs specifies a whiteness that is no longer invisible or hard to see. Its claim to normalcy—the silent hegemony of its centrality—disrupted by epistemic shifts since the civil unrests of the sixties, the category of whiteness, and white masculinity with it, appears to have tumbled toward crisis. Unable to make seamless claims to legitimacy, a racially self-conscious whiteness emerged by the nineties, speaking for a constituency of racialized victims, "minoritized and injured" (Wiegman 1999, 117).

Kepple's whiteness no longer masks itself, for the dangers of silence at this moment outweigh the liabilities of visibility. Instead, we find white males engaging in various strategies of self-naming, "outing whiteness" to specific political ends (Shome 2000, 366–74). Such self-naming reasserts a white, masculinist claim to the American meritocracy within which people of color and women are rendered hypervisible, exceptional, and abnormal. Kepple's laments, by these logics, work to strategically recenter whiteness (Projansky and Ono 1999, 151). Equating perversions that have sullied the American meritocracy with the decline in white male authority over that meritocracy, these voices of outrage focus mainstream attention on the ways in which nonwhite and nonmale assimilation into the American workforce has enabled a loosening of white male normativity as the workplace standard. Thus, recentering and resecuring the power and privilege of whiteness, Kepple and his cohort conflate white masculinity with an authentic American nationhood where white males who dare to call out the real racists in America are modern patriots, a new breed of warriors for democracy.

Scholars within the developing field of whiteness studies have argued that the history of whiteness has entailed a "history of modifications to renegotiate the centrality of white power and authority" (Projansky and Ono 1999, 152).[1] Temporary and strategic unveilings of whiteness, what Robyn Wiegman refers to as "strategies of particularization" (1999, 118), that came to force over the course of the nineties offer late editions of this history of whiteness and are comparable to the crisis of Southern white masculinity descriptive of the fifties and sixties, for instance. Revealing the terms of renegotiations that work to renew a white, masculine claim on economic and political control, racialized assaults of the nineties are analogous to unveilings of whiteness epitomized, for example, by the formation of segregationist white citizen's councils in the South of the fifties. As later chapters of this book will show, these historical unveilings were disciplined into invisibility by the hegemonic Northern agenda for civil rights reform. Eschewing vulgar displays of anxious masculinity that had emerged to champion Southern segregation, the Northern agenda for reform in the sixties recuperated and salvaged white nationalized masculinity to its rightful place with liberal scripts of color blindness and racial fairness.

Common across these episodes of crisis, whiteness emerges recuperated not as a cultural and historical category but normalized as "not . . . anything in particular" (Dyer 1988, 44; Hanke 1992, 186). In the sixties as in the nineties, these episodes serve to reduce the experience of racism to "discrete acts of racial discrimination" and to reestablish race as an "irrational attribute" that is irrelevant within the terms of the American meritocracy (Crenshaw et al. 1995, xiv–xv). They serve critically to facilitate a discursive return from the racialized and gendered to the neutral and objective. Much like the hegemonic work of the Northern agenda for reform in the sixties, here again we are witness to reinvestments in hegemonic truths that normalize a "meritorious self," keenly distinguished from a "racialized self." Registering echoes of their genealogical past, these strategies are reformulated within contemporary debates on affirmative action and leave their mark on our view of normalcy.

Within the terms of larger discursive shifts from traditional to "advanced liberalism," deracialized meritorious subjects perpetuate standards of neoliberal "responsibilization" (Burchell 1996, 29–30). Simultaneously making room for white claims of "reverse discrimination," these strategies erase their reference to race even as they re-inscribe it (Fergerson 1997, 126). Returning whiteness to its position of hegemonic invisibility, they enlist categories like merit, equality, and anti-discrimination toward a racial discipline articulated in color-blind and universalized terms.

While these racialized critiques assume an obviousness, a taken-for-granted transparency, they obscure other explanations, including the possibility that the economic realities that white males confronted in the nineties were not a consequence of racial favoritisms that excluded them, but rather that dramatic transformations in the American economy forced workers of all races into less secure, lower-paying jobs over the past few decades. The possibility that domestic labor, both white and black, has lost to free market incentives of predatory capital, profit shelters, and cheap labor overseas is eclipsed by authorized racial anxieties. Thus, white male outrage over race- and gender-conscious remedies, viewed so sympathetically by Connerly, absolves and, moreover, valorizes an economic system that has emerged as a significant factor in the changing circumstances of American labor in the nineties. What survives instead are rearticulations and reiterations of racialized and gendered scripts that affirm particular knowledges of equality, merit, and affirmative action that are ontologically connected to authorized truths about black, white, woman, and so on.

I begin this chapter with the foregoing discussion to draw attention to the operation of the public policy process as a key site where cultural identities are formed, recognized, legitimated, and delegitimated (Butler 1996, 75). Shaped by economic, political, and discursive pressures, public policies and the debates from which they emerge tacitly structure functioning truths about cultural identity and difference. Accepted public policy legitimizes a limited but powerful knowledge of cultural identities, and as Sanford Schram explains, "policy discourses and public policies themselves are implicated in the construction and maintenance of identities in ways that have profound implications for the allocation of scarce resources" (1993, 249). Thus, circulating imaginaries about identities and differences give shape to and are shaped by knowledges authorized in the public policy process, and in turn, the politics of identity formation are pervasive in public policy choices. Not unlike the mass media, then, the public policy process operates as a powerful site for the production of race and gender.

This chapter attends to representational claims on behalf of racialized and gendered subjects in recent public debates over affirmative action to make visible the ways in which the categories such as "blackness" and "women" have performed subtle yet significant discursive work. Here, the analysis seeks to understand how sanctioned truths about these cultural categories work, as Barbara Christian has argued, as "hidden, though powerful, construct[s] in the anti–affirmative action arsenal" (1996, 120). Within the wider arena of cultural representation and politics, this analysis interrogates a range of cultural meanings that were drawn on and constructed within public policy debates over affirmative action. It seeks to offer a rough genealogy of enemies, allies, and alibis constituted within these debates and asks where such cultural meanings come from, and how they are worked over and recirculated as "true."

Model Minorities, Model Majorities

Visibly en-raced and gendered spokespersons crowded the frontlines of recent assaults on affirmative action programs. In California, Ward Connerly, a wealthy black entrepreneur and University of California regent, and Pamela Lewis, a white attorney and Clinton Democrat, joined Pete Wilson, then governor of California, as co-chairs for the Proposition 209 campaign. Similarly in Washington, the black Republican Mary Radcliffe, together with the former state senate majority leader Jeanette Hayner and the conservative activist Pat Herbold, joined John Carlson, talk radio host and chairman of the conservative Washington Institute for Policy Studies, to "diversify leadership" of the statewide public campaign against race- and gender-based programs.

A strategic and deliberate representational politics is visible here. As Connerly, a black man, and Lewis, a white woman, are positioned at the forefront of race- and gender-blind attacks on affirmative action in California, their opposition is effective, erasing its reference to race and gender even as it secures much of its discursive force from visible displays of their en-raced and gendered identities. Echoing familiar, all-American mythologies of individuals who pull themselves up by their bootstraps, Connerly often told the story of his life as a black man growing up in a racially segregated South and rising out of poverty on his own merits. Lewis similarly extolled the virtues of color and gender blindness, narrating her experiences as an attorney who represented white males in reverse discrimination lawsuits.

By their very presence, these individuals offered proof not only that racial discrimination against blacks and sexual discrimination against women were surmountable in America but that, by the nineties, such forms of discrimination were a thing of the past. Embodying the distance that blacks and women had traveled since the sixties, they lent credence to idealized visions of a color- and gender-blind meritocracy. Embodying the mythic American Dream, Connerly and Lewis appeared in television advertisements for the Proposition 209 campaign, expressing their frustration and fatigue over race- and gender-based programs with the chorus "We're tired of people dividing us by race and gender" (Skelton 1996, A3).

Lewis's presence among the spokespersons for Proposition 209 is almost a cliché in the context of stories of breakthroughs in gender equity that dot the landscape of contemporary public knowledge. Major news stories of women ascending to powerful cabinet offices, high executive ranks in business, and positions of command in the nation's space program make for a comforting view of the distance women have covered since the inception of equal opportunity programs. Statistical evidence lends credence to these claims as white women more than tripled their rate of college completion between 1960 and 1993 and increased their share of management jobs by about one-third—from 27.1 percent in the eighties to 35.3 percent in the nineties (Hartmann 1996, 78–87).

With the overwhelming majority of affirmative action beneficiaries reported as being middle-class white women (American Civil Liberties Union 1996; Marable 1996, 9), Lewis's presence served as a reminder of the ways in which social justice programs of the sixties had enabled members of historically disadvantaged groups to make precisely the kinds of material advances that the social movements of the sixties had sought. Her career as a successful attorney, her access to law schools and law offices, and her presence in circles of influence and prestige underscored the ways in which race- and gender-based mechanisms had opened up the American workplace and classroom. The success story of her life gestured to how well affirmative action programs had fared. And yet, Lewis emerged within the Proposition 209 effort not as a poster woman for the triumphs of the sixties but instead to mark affirmative action as unfair, discriminatory, and un-American.

Like other homegrown G.I. Janes, fiercely individualistic and scornful of such policies, Lewis appeared in campaign spots to authorize knowledge of declining gender bias in the workplace and to argue that it was an egregious miscalculation of liberal intentions of the sixties to preserve affirmative action programs into the nineties. Archetypal, hegemonized subjects, these women constitute a "model majority," performing significant work by their very presence, representatives of a broad category of model women who play by the rules, for whom gender is irrelevant, and who deny their debts to social justice programs (Mukherjee 2002, 100–111).

The constitution of such a model majority operates as a site of discipline for women in much the same way that the myth of the model minority works to discipline Asians and other groups of color, as Ronald Takaki has shown (1993, 414–17). Anti–affirmative action campaigns in the nineties served up familiar formulations of "the daughter of a third generation Chinese-American family" who is passed up by preferences for "applicants who are in this country illegally," or "the Vietnamese student who is turned away from Berkeley or Irvine, despite his high grades, in favor of a wealthy underrepresented minority . . . with the explanation that we are getting 'too many Asians' at those campuses" (Connerly 1996a). With formulaic representations of model minorities that serve as alibis for systemic color privilege—it can't be racism if Asians are succeeding—Connerly contrasted Asian American "success" with black "failure":

> Vietnamese people, one of the more recent immigrant groups, come to our country and open up doughnut shops and other low-capital enterprises and insist that their kids go to school and get a good education. They sacrifice themselves so that their children may someday enjoy the American Dream . . . They often come here with nothing more than a belief in themselves, a can-do-it-attitude. Blacks on the other hand, perpetuate the self-defeating and corrosive myth that we cannot do it without help from someone else . . . It is this "I can't do it" attitude that largely accounts for the fact that Asians are receiving significantly higher grade point averages than blacks. (Connerly and Brown 1995, 156)

Playing a critical role within the machinery of racial and gendered discipline, the mythic model minority reiterates the promise of the meritocracy and the American Dream, standards held up as fundamental and universal. The myth of the model *majority* works in much the same way, disciplining successful women as effectively as it does those who "fail." Denying the internal complexities and indeterminacies of the category of women, the myth of the model majority normalizes the experiences of white women to women as a whole. Such deployments minimize the circumstances of class and color among women with critical effect, constructing exceptions to gender bias as the rule and fictionalizing the experiences of poor, nonwhite women. As economically successful white women like Pam Lewis are held up as model women, representatives of an imagined majority that no longer needs state assistance, the experiences of working-class women of color are delegitimated. Transparent in its whiteness, this model majority exerts racial discipline even as it is inscribed in race-blind terms.

Like Katie Roiphe, Christina Hoff Sommers, and others who appear on news programs as "resident sages" who are invited to articulate the "feminist perspective" although they have spent the bulk of their careers attacking women's rights, leaders, and goals, Lewis and her ilk are carefully crafted as allies in the "new civil rights movement." A mythic majority of middle-class women is thus constructed as naturally equipped with knowledge of the dangers of affirmative action. As the conservative commentators Sally Pipes and Michael Lynch tell it, "Women are mothers, wives, daughters and sisters. No one is better placed than a woman to see the double-edged nature of racial and gender preferences. It is clear to a mother that an institutional preference for her daughter is institutional discrimination against her son" (1996).

Armed as they are with an essentialist, particularly womanist knowledge of the paradoxes of affirmative action, women are justified in looking around and seeing that "by employing a woman we are taking a job away from her husband" (Marks 1996, S5). Invoking old-fashioned scripts, white women are located standing dutifully by their men, narrating cautionary tales about how programs like affirmative action victimize their husbands and sons. Thus, in commercials used by congressional and assembly candidates in northern California during the 1996 elections, a young white husband walks dejectedly into the kitchen to tell his wife that he did not get the job because of quotas. Her face lined with sympathy and frustration, the wife turns to face the camera and declares, "It's just not right."

Constituted within traditional heterosexist and gendered roles—wives, mothers, daughters—women, and particularly white women, are strategically positioned on the same side of the debate as white males. Such solidarities have served strategic and reactionary ends at other moments in time as well, suggesting that white women have historically served a critical role in the history of whiteness, recruited as allies during episodic turns from crisis to recuperation. Thus, for example, at the height of debates on the civil rights bill in 1964, Southern congressmen proposed a series of amendments as a ploy to bog down debate on the measure. One of these amendments, offered by Representative Howard W. Smith (D-Va.), a vocal opponent of the civil rights bill, proposed that discrimination by "sex" be included among the bill's prohibitions along with race, color, religion, and national origin. For Smith, the amendment served more as obfuscation than any serious effort toward gender equality. As he put it, "This bill is so imperfect, what harm will this little amendment do?" (Kenworthy 1964b, 1).

Representative Martha W. Griffiths (D-Mich.) quickly added her voice in support, stating, "Without the protection of this amendment, white women would be at the bottom of the list in hiring after white men and Negro men and women." She continued, "It would be incredible to me that white men would be willing to place white women at such a disadvantage" (Kenworthy 1964b, 1). Representative Catherine May (R-Wash.) joined in, pleading, "I hope we won't overlook the white native-born American woman of Christian origin." Thus, even though the case for gender equity emerged during congressional debates of the sixties as a tongue-in-cheek suggestion, offered disingenuously to deride the idea of civil rights for black Americans, the proposal nevertheless stirred white women to particularly racialized responses.

As Northern women were riled up during debates of the sixties as political pawns in Southern ploys to muddle and overwhelm the objectives of the civil rights bill, contemporary moves to deploy white women's stories in an effort to discredit affirmative action sound a familiar tone.

But whereas such arguments remained trivial and impractical decades ago, ultimately failing to confound the civil rights agenda of the sixties, they emerged in the nineties refashioned as urgent and reasonable. By the nineties, the experiences of model white women served to highlight the ways in which affirmative action programs had deteriorated into systemic *racial* favoritisms that discriminated against white women in much the same way as they excluded white males. The Initiative 200 campaign in Washington in 1998 described the experiences of Katuria Smith along these lines:

> Ms. Smith, who is white, earned good grades as an undergraduate, did well on her Law School Admission Test, and had to work her way through school as the child of a single mother heading a low-income family. Yet she was refused admission to the University of Washington School of Law, which takes into account "diversity factors," including race and ethnic background, in choosing students. According to university records, just over half the minority applicants admitted had grades and test scores lower than Smith. (Knickerbocker 1998, 3)

Smith's experience tells a story of "reverse discrimination" that is left out in stories of such practices as they frustrate white men. Smith's example is an important one within the anti–affirmative action campaigns of the nineties in that it reveals the racialized politics of division that characterize authorized discourses of the moment. As it draws anxious white men and model women together as allies, Smith's experience serves effectively to divide the category of women across color. These strategic alliances were highly effective in terms of electoral results over the course of the nineties as 51 percent of white women in Washington voted in support of Initiative 200 to end affirmative action statewide. Similarly, in California, exit polls showed that 48 percent of women voted to end affirmation action in the 1996 referendum ("Women Helped Push" 1996, A3). Since all nonwhites, men and women both, made up only 26 percent of the Californian electorate, a sizable proportion of the pro-vote from women in California reflects the opinions of white women (*Los Angeles Times* Exit Poll 1996). As Cathy Allen, vice president of the National

Women's Political Caucus, explained: "I think two things are happening. One is that almost every white woman has had a husband, boyfriend, brother, or son gripe about losing a job or a promotion to a black person. It gets to the point where women themselves talk this anecdote to death and to the point where it becomes institutional memory" Jackson 1998, A27).

By the nineties, then, authorized discourses of neoliberalism had edged out traditional liberal cultural scripts to privilege a specific brand of individualism and self-fulfillment. These evolving truths universalized the naturalness of entrepreneurial subjects within an "enterprise culture" (Rose 1996, 57–58). Celebrating individuals who exhibit a "can-do-it-attitude," as Connerly puts it, evolving discourses of neoliberalism champion individuals who "enterprise" themselves to the demands of free markets and who take responsibility for their successes as well as their failures. Conforming to these standards, model white women emerged over the course of the nineties in empathetic accord with white men to celebrate neoliberal standards of enterprise and self-help.

Of Strippers and Sisterhood
By the fall of 1996, a small coalition of organizers in California headed by the Feminist Majority and the National Organization for Women had split away from other organizations to form the Stop Prop 209 campaign. A Louis Harris and Associates public opinion poll commissioned by the Feminist Majority in the spring of 1995 had shown that affirmative action for women and minorities continued to enjoy broad support with a majority of Californians, but that the impact of Proposition 209 upon affirmative action programs remained unclear in the minds of most respondents (Harris 1995). Harris recommended that the effort to oppose Proposition 209 must concentrate on the gender gap.

In response to these findings, a few weeks before the November 1996 elections, the Stop Prop 209 campaign aired a series of radio commercials that worked thematically to emphasize gender and called for an explicit defense of affirmative action programs. The commercials used the voices of Hollywood celebrities speaking in chatty, conversational tones to persuade women voters that "high on the priority list of the extreme right are plans to cut back on and even wipe out choice on abortion and measures to weaken and ultimately wipe out affirmative action programs" (Chávez 1998, 153). Thus, the film and television actress Candice Bergen urged listeners in one advertisement to pay attention to the hidden and confusing consequences of Proposition 209. "Anyone who depends on a working woman's wage should listen carefully," Bergen cautioned. "If 209 passes, we could lose maternity benefits . . . 209 will cut funding for rape crisis centers . . . Don't make a permanent change to the constitution that will hurt young girls, women, and minorities. Vote no on 209!" The comedienne Ellen DeGeneres appeared in another commercial, asking: "Don't you think it's odd that the people most against a woman's right to choose are usually men? Turns out the same anti-choice boys are trying to wipe out affirmative action for women and people of color. That's right: Pat Buchanan, Newt Gingrich, David Duke— all anti-abortion—all supporting Proposition 209."

The implications of Candice Bergen and Ellen DeGeneres testifying against Proposition 209 deserve careful examination here. Both women are etched in public memory at the epicenters of recent gender wars— Bergen for her "irresponsible celebration of single motherhood" in the CBS situation comedy *Murphy Brown*, as former vice president Dan Quayle put it, and DeGeneres for "normalizing the homosexual lifestyle on primetime television" in the ABC comedy *Ellen*, as leaders of the religious right accused.

Each commercial implicitly trades on the notoriety of the speaker. Cultural archetypes of the single working mother and the lesbian, laden with subversive potential and consequently demonized in mainstream culture, are thus drawn to the center of the Stop Prop 209 campaign. These appeals justify affirmative action as a means to protect groups of women who, as it turns out, are typically reviled in dominant culture. Thus, the opposition's radio commercials sought to make a case for affirmative action by offering up scandalous, troublesome women, publicly denounced in recent years as epitomizing the "excesses of the sixties."

The linguistic emphasis of the campaign explicitly identified the category of "women" as its political constituency and thus addressed a niche audience presumed sympathetic to historical solidarities formed in the social movements of the sixties. Deploying the liberal, humanist cliché that "we are all sisters under the skin," the campaign urged the renewal of "sisterhood is powerful" myths that were championed by second-wave feminists during the sixties and seventies. Miscalculating the persuasive appeals of single mothers and women marginalized by race, sex, and class, the radio commercials of the Stop Prop 209 campaign overestimated the strength of interracial and interclass sisterhoods that had remained an utopian ideal even at the height of the civil rights era (hooks 1984, 43–65; D. King 1995, 294–318; Lorde 1984, 66–71; Shah 1997, xii–xxi). The chances that such nostalgic appeals would propel a majority of middle-class heterosexual women into solidarity with diverse constituencies of nonwhite, single, poor, and homosexual women during the nineties may have been more than optimistic.

Critical discursive shifts by the nineties had effectively vilified feminists and ridiculed the idea of solidarity among women (Douglas 1994, 269–94). Decades of economic changes and evolving discourses of neoliberalism set up keen distinctions between "armies of entitlements" on the one hand and responsible, entrepreneurial subjects on the other. Thus, by the time affirmative action emerged as "toxic for the American polity," appeals to "sisterhood" across race and class served mainly to close ranks, preaching primarily to the proverbial choir. Emphasizing women's political realities and their imperiled economic fates, the Stop Prop 209 commercials may have found a sympathetic audience among feminists and marginalized women, but they simultaneously distanced state programs like affirmative action from the broad center of middle-class, heterosexual women who, as the Harris polls had predicted, were crucial for the opposition.

None of the Stop Prop 209 commercials managed to link the career successes of professional women to affirmative action, and none divested the audience of circulating fears that affirmative action programs diminished job prospects for husbands and sons. Rather, the radio advertisements confirmed allegations from the right that the progressive agenda of the sixties had produced tedious balkanization among Americans. Constructing an "us versus them" ethos that contrasted sharply with the "bring us together" mantra of the Proposition 209 campaign, the Stop Prop 209 campaign identified ultra-right-wing male voices as foes of women's rights, warning women to watch out for such enemies as the "anti-choice boys."

The African American screen actress Alfre Woodard appeared in one of the Stop Prop 209 advertisements enumerating "five reasons to vote no on Proposition 209—Newt Gingrich, Pete Wilson, Pat Buchanan, Jesse Helms, and David Duke—they're all for 209." Woodard continued, "Here are some people I trust a little more when it comes to defending equal opportunity. Jesse Jackson asks that you to vote No on 209 to keep the dream alive . . . The League of Women Voters, the NAACP, the National Organization for Women, and the Rainbow Coalition are all against 209." Bergen set up a similar opposition when she pointed to how confusing political advertising can be. "Take Proposition 209. They say it prohibits discrimination, but 209 will eliminate affirmative action for women and people of color. That's like the Ku Klux Klan calling itself 'the Martin Luther King Society.'" Naming specific civil rights organizations, these commercials drew up key battle lines, separating enemies from allies, but on the basis of unsubstantiated presumptions of gender solidarities and waning feminist sympathies.

During the last weekend before the November elections, the Stop Prop 209 campaign aired its only television commercial.[2] As Chávez explains, the commercial was conceived and produced in twenty hours by a group of volunteer screenwriters, producers, and editors and was designed to be provocative (1998, 232). Referred to as the "stripper ad," the commercial sought to emphasize a specific set of consequences of Proposition 209 for women:

(Shots of white woman in black lingerie, a black jacket dangling from her right shoulder. She strikes strip show poses to music.)
MALE CHORUS: Take it off. Take it all off.
FEMALE ANNOUNCER: Want to be a doctor? Police officer? Hard hat? Forget it.

MALE CHORUS: Take it off. Take it all off.

FEMALE ANNOUNCER: How about women business owners? Forget it! Want your daughter going to math, science, or sports? Counting on a pension? Or just a job? Well, there's always . . . *(a man's hand reaches in and yanks the woman's chin sideways toward him)*

FEMALE ANNOUNCER: Don't strip away our future. Vote No on Proposition 209. Save affirmative action for women.

The advertisement was immediately controversial. Without mandates for affirmative action and protections against sexual harassment, it suggested, workplaces would revert to draconian fraternities of sexist men for whom women workers would serve primarily as sexualized objects of desire. Campy and exaggerated, the advertisement was a hard sell for a number of reasons. For one, budgetary constraints of the Stop Prop 209 campaign restricted its time on the air to one brief weekend prior to the November 1996 elections. As Chávez argues, the campaign may thus have suffered from both doing too little too late and unrealistically expecting a single commercial to make a lasting impression at a time when the audience would have been bombarded with political messages of every stripe.

Positioning female workers at the bottom of the economic totem pole, always and imminently only a few precarious steps away from destitution, the commercial dramatized the impact of Proposition 209 as a nightmare of disempowerment, de-skilling, and despair. Without the protective mandates of affirmative action programs, it warned, Proposition 209 would pimp women and girls into sex work and economic dependence. In doing so, the campaign, once again, miscalculated its target audience. The women most likely to face the debilitating consequences dramatized in the commercial are not the broad center of middle-class, white women that the Stop Prop 209 campaign sought to woo. Rather, the stripper advertisement described a fate more likely reserved for working-class and unspecialized women workers for whom the costs of Proposition 209 would be the greatest. Overestimating the salience of "sisterhood is powerful" mythologies that consistently faltered in their efforts to build lasting solidarities among women across race and class, the commercial remained unpersuasive to the campaign's target audience—white middle-class women.

The stylistic exaggerations of the commercial, moreover, narrated the systemic sexisms of the workplace as unabashed and lustful patrons at a peep show. The commercial ultimately held sexist men, rather than sexism, responsible for declining economic opportunities for women. It became possible to deride chauvinistic men who patronize strip clubs and whorehouses for their personal tastes while systemic and structural constraints remained invisible. As strip show patrons were indicted for their role in women's economic subordination, these malefactors could not be mistaken for the vast majority of husbands and sons whose laments over reverse discrimination and outrage against affirmative action remained free of culpability by these standards. Establishing key ethical boundaries thus, the Stop Prop 209 campaign misdirected its ire and, inadvertently perhaps, effaced the complicity of the vast majority of men who remain beneficiaries of systemic race and gender privileges.

Beyond these concerns, the stripper advertisement, like the radio spots that preceded it, remained unpersuasive for the ways in which it departed from circulating imaginaries of individual rights and authorized ethics of color and gender blindness. Arguing explicitly for benefits that accrued to women as a group, the advertisement specifically enumerated affirmative action programs like math and sports programs for girls, public contracts for women-owned businesses in nontraditional fields like highway construction and masonry, and outreach programs used by police academies and medical schools to recruit women, hailing them as mechanisms that ensured equality for women as a historically disadvantaged group. Offering examples of programmatic benefits that affirmative action programs had made available for women, the advertisement plainly acknowledged that women as a group had enjoyed particular and targeted dividends as a consequence of such programs.

Moreover, the focus on struggling single women and their lived proximity to destitution presented them as precisely the kind of troublesome, immoral, and unproductive individuals that neoliberal discourses lamented. The stripper advertisement echoed rightist critiques that identified an unproductive welfare and racial entitlements sector that created no wealth at the expense of the "productive" private sector in which all national wealth was actually produced (Rose 1996, 51). The proletarianization of women that the stripper advertisement sought to highlight served contrarily as a reminder of the difference between responsible, entrepreneurial subjects on the one hand, and state-run "measures intended to decrease poverty [that] had actually increased inequality" and "attempts to assist the disadvantaged [that] had actually worsened their disadvantage" on the other (Rose 1996, 51).

Within the context of such evolving dominant discourses and decades of economic shifts, the radio and television commercials of the Stop Prop 209 campaign registered as isolated rants from outmoded feminists and parasitic dependents. Hyperbolic excesses offered in public statements like the stripper advertisement undercut the power of stories about women workers and their lived struggles, thus evacuating their potency as political messages. Moreover, the Stop Prop 209 campaign failed to highlight how and why the discursive strategies of identitarian movements of the sixties should remain politically efficacious, particularly for middle-class, white women in the nineties. Instead, "bad girls" of popular culture combined with far-fetched narratives of sex workers to produce a freak show while the critical white female support base for the opposition slipped through, untapped.

Learning from these mistakes, the No!200 campaign organized in opposition to Initiative 200 in Washington enlisted representatives of the model majority who would link the career successes of professional women to affirmative action. Testimonials were gathered from women like Anne C. Symonds, president of Symonds Consulting Engineers, one of about four thousand companies in Washington that were registered as "women- or minority-owned" and were thus covered under state programs intended to ensure that such companies were represented in government contracting. Almost $3 million of the $3.8 million in contracts that Symonds's company earned in 1997 came through affirmative action programs (Jackson 1998, A27).

In the testimonial, Symonds recalled how difficult it was "to get

[her] foot in the door with certain clients" before affirmative action, how government agencies dealt with an "old-boy network" of firms and had no obligation to look elsewhere.

> If every woman saw power like I do, they might see it differently. When I bid on contracts and have to negotiate, I see who is on corporate boards . . . who the CEOs are . . . who makes the final decisions. It's still almost all men . . . Within the past year, I had a top man at a state agency tell me that my company didn't get a job because women engineers were seen as too feminine or . . . too aggressive. I was told, "You're never going to get jobs like this, because we always deal with that other company."

Everyday instances of favoritism that exclude women workers and entrepreneurs that are given voice in the Symonds advertisement bring to light the persistence and prevalence not of reverse discrimination against white men but its obverse as it affects women in the workplace. The advertisement highlighted systemic gender and race privileges that have faded from public view but nevertheless exact a heavy price from individuals who are by overwhelming margins women and/or nonwhite. Thus, forcing attention to the quotidian presence of race and gender in the everyday of the workplace, Symonds's testimony gives voice to experiences of systemic racisms and sexisms. Her voice hints at dockets full of grievances and complaints pending before courts and commissions, filed in overwhelming numbers by African Americans and women, counterevidence to authorized truths about merit and color and gender blindness.

Symonds offers a glimpse into "hidden transcripts" that indicate gaps and flaws in official versions of the truth, alternate accounts that circulate "offstage" beyond direct observation by power holders (Scott 1990, 3–4). Attempting to wean the audience away from authorized versions of the achievements of the sixties and dominant knowledges of sexism and racism, the testimonial asks mainstream viewers to suspend disbelief. In the face of the mythic edifice of the American meritocracy, of Horatio Alger scripts and paeans to rugged individualism, and of "experiences" that locate America's race problem in the historical past, Symonds's testimony jars. The hidden, and consequently unfamiliar, transcript of her experiences is thus less than effective in interrupting the credibility of model women like Pam Lewis. Within the context of authorized discourses of neoliberalism, where women like Lewis echo a familiar refrain, Symonds, in contract, urges attention to points of view that remain laughable, odd, impossible.

Single Moms and Quota Queens

Within dominant discourses of entrepreneurial subjects, anti–affirmative action campaigns of the nineties enlisted a range of "failing" women who would demarcate key differences between neoliberal standards of enterprise and indolence. A peculiar racial politics is visible within these maneuvers as white female "failures" were etched as unfortunate victims who, much like their male counterparts, served to foreground the costs of affirmative action in terms of reverse discrimination. By contrast, damning portraits of dark and delinquent quota queens appeared systematically in anti–affirmative action campaigns of the nineties, reconstituting figures of hated females, lurking within the cultural imaginary, in the service of strategic ends.

The Proposition 209 campaign in California created a poster woman of Janice Camarena, a white single mother whose experiences provided powerful evidence to render affirmative action unfair and unethical. Campaign advertisements recounted her story as follows:

> MALE ANNOUNCER: The following actually happened January 19th, 1994.
>
> CAMARENA: The teacher said to me, "You have to leave."
>
> MALE ANNOUNCER: Because you're white.
>
> CAMARENA: Yes. Then I left. (door slams shut—sound undercurrent)
>
> MALE ANNOUNCER: As she went out the door, students laughed. (laughter fades) But for this young, widowed mother trying to enroll in a class at a public college, racial quotas were no laughing matter.
>
> CAMARENA: I thought that discrimination was illegal.
>
> MALE ANNOUNCER: But the law allows preferential treatment.
>
> CAMARENA: Another class was for Mexican American students only.

MALE ANNOUNCER: These programs are based not on merit, or even on need, but on race. Janice Camarena Ingraham is white. Her deceased husband was Mexican American.

CAMARENA: Recently our public school asked the race of my children. I said the human race.

MALE ANNOUNCER: Janice is now one of many men and women leading the campaign for Proposition 209. Proposition 209 prohibits discrimination and preferential quotas. It protects men and women of all races.

Resonating within a discursive context that reiterates the nightmare of race and gender preferences using a variety of narratives of reverse discrimination, token hires, and diversity candidates, racial entitlements emerge as being at cause for quotidian and structural inequalities that single mothers endure.[3] Condensing a vast repertoire of hearsay and rumors, received second- and third-hand, Camarena's story confirms racist suspicions that existing affirmative action programs fail to provide assistance to the most deserving individuals at least in part because they enable unfair preferences for unfit, nonwhite others.

Camarena's story is as instructive in its articulations as it is in its silences. Well within the parameters of hegemonic reproductive moralities and conventional standards of the "truly needy," Camarena is precisely the type of woman who deserves assistance. She is a widow. She seeks responsible ways to provide for her children. She tries to complete her education to get a better job. She makes several attempts to enroll in local training programs. But she is laughed out of programs that were supposed to assist her. If Pam Lewis epitomized model women who no longer needed affirmative action, Camarena confirms that the beneficiaries of these programs are no longer those who truly need help—working-class and, perhaps, white women—but rather, other, less deserving and, perhaps, nonwhite women.

Within a larger discursive context rich with narratives of irresponsible and unfit black and Latina single mothers, the tragic but conscientious Camarena emerges in stark contrast. Dark and delinquent quota queens who have access to racially exclusive outreach programs are recalled in the silences in Camarena's example. Her story is authenticated in the context of circulating images of "the circle of poverty" where, as Adolph Reed Jr. clarifies, out-of-wedlock births and female-headed households are pathologized, and female economic dependence on men is naturalized as a necessary condition for restoring traditional family values (1999, 191). Echoing the gendered character of underclass imagery that has lingered in the political imaginary since the publication of the Moynihan Report in 1965, Camarena's story bears pernicious policy fruit. An effective alibi for the state's failure to embark on basic institutional changes to end black and white poverty (Moynihan 1965; Rainwater and Yancey 1967, x), her example equates the poorest households in the United States with black cultural pathologies and erases the complicity of inadequate and ineffective state programs in the life chances of poor families, irrespective of race.

Indictments delivered in the Camarena advertisement reveal the potency of hated figures like the "quota queen" and the "welfare queen" who silently occupy what Jackie Jones has referred to as the "space of the accused" (1992, 96), women who serve as exemplary scapegoats within the divisive and racialized semiotics of contemporary class warfare. The figure of the quota queen offers one example of the ways in which gendered and racialized scripts serve to demonize poor and typically black women in public policy debates. The media spectacle surrounding the nomination of the African American law professor Lani Guinier in the spring of 1993 to President Bill Clinton's cabinet provides discursive context for these assaults on affirmative action, revealing how working-class women of color are indicted as a matter of course for the nation's economic and ethical dilemmas. Guinier's public denouncement and ultimate removal from consideration for the post of attorney general in charge of civil rights is a visible moment in the constitution of black female identity in the public sphere, and a vocal moment of articulation that served to conflate poor black women with the hated figure of the quota queen.

Public responses to Guinier's nomination reveal her progression from legal scholar to quota queen and "extreme, left-wing activist" (Leff 1993, 36). Referring to Guinier and Norma Cantu, Clinton's nominee for assistant secretary for civil rights in the Department of Education, as

"Clinton's Quota Queens," Clint Bolick offered strident objections to Guinier's appointment. In a column that appeared in the *Wall Street Journal*, Bolick chided Guinier for her calls for "racial quotas" and, as he put it, her "in-your-face civil rights agenda" (1993, A12). *Newsweek* followed a few weeks later, publishing its first report on the Guinier controversy in an article entitled "Crowning a 'Quota Queen'?" (Cohn 1993, 67). Bob Cohn, author of the *Newsweek* article, justified his use of the term "quota queen" in his title by suggesting that "the term was around town. It was the way most people identified her" (as quoted in Leff 1993, 36).

The emphasis on quotas in these reports and the insistent tagging of Guinier as "quota queen" worked to fit Guinier and her writings within a preconceived and familiar view of what counts in debates about race (Savage 1993, A1). Marking equivalences across Guinier's black femaleness and her alleged calls for racial quotas, these reports shed light on the ways in which common presumptions about Guinier's black femaleness functioned within the public outcry over her nomination. As Erwin Chemerinsky asked, "if she wasn't a black woman would it have come out that way?" (Leff 1993, 36). The choleric response to Guinier's nomination compels attention to the ways in which the quota queen, whether or not Lani Guinier deserved such a label, serves as powerful shorthand for black females who deserve to be treated with hostility and suspicion.

Complicating authorized knowledges of the parasitic and freeloading figure of the quota queen, the attack on Guinier is explained not simply by her writings, which reveal her as a vocal proponent of black civil rights, but also by her position as a potential voice for that corps of silent but reviled black girls and women who exist in the space of the accused. Thus, black single mothers, constructed as embodiments of excess, indolence, and waste, never achieve the position of sympathetic victimhood reserved for white women like Janice Camarena. The quota queen is designated black as forcefully as the white single mother is discursively immunized from these characterizations. Janice Camarena deserves nothing but our compassion. Lani Guinier and her constituency of quota queens, in contrast, warrant nothing but our repugnance.

Such deployments of contradictory and racialized figures of the single mom and the quota queen, in turn, enabled appeals for race-blind but class-conscious solutions for "the problem" with affirmative action in paradoxical ways. For Connerly and other advocates of Proposition 209, if inclusion mechanisms should properly help those who really needed help, they were to focus on factors that "truly disadvantage individuals." Thus, mechanisms for preferences were permissible, but only if they were geared to the "truly needy," in other words, as long as they were specifically race and gender blind (Connerly and Rhodes 1997, A20; Custred 1997, 15).

Censorious of racial thinking, authoritative vernaculars of color blindness are seen working to vilify race consciousness either as a "stupid race mentality" ("Interview with Ward Connerly" 1999) or as a "new racism masquerading as self-awareness" (Carlson 1998, B5). Such celebrations of race blindness disingenuously exclude race while they purport to target poverty as a site for state assistance. With deliberate disregard of race as a systemic factor in economic life, the operation of racism as an invisible system of economic hierarchies and oppressions is muted. Systemic privileges associated with whiteness and structural burdens faced by the black poor remain veiled.

Resonating in the context of popular mythologies of "average folk," for whom, as Proposition 209 organizers argued, "there is no special interest lobby" ("Longing for the Days" 1995, 40), the class-but-not-race emphasis in the Proposition 209 campaign worked divisively. Provoking paranoid discourses of scarcity, narratives of economic disadvantage positioned women like Camarena as emissaries of the marginalized white working class. While her experiences do indeed bear witness to the frightening realities of systemic economic inequities, deployed within anti–affirmative action campaigns, they place blame for Camarena's circumstances on poor, nonwhite women.

As subtle imbrications of class and race give meaning to authorized tales of affirmative action, assurances of color-blind affirmative action elicit overwhelmingly racialized reactions. Silencing the ways that white, working-class women highlight systemic gender inequities, Camarena instead emphasizes the ways in which the division of the working classes remains a structural characteristic of contemporary capitalist economies

(Balibar and Wallerstein 1991, 2). Its radical potential eviscerated, Camarena's example appoints nonwhite others who must bear the blame for her circumstances while it affirms the meritocratic free market, which, it is presumed, will accommodate any "qualified" applicant irrespective of race or gender.

Superblacks and Sellouts

Comparable with white female allies who have served a historical role in recuperating white masculinity out of its episodic crises, campaigns to eliminate affirmative action appointed an indispensable corps of entrepreneurial and highly successful African American voices to serve as the public face of neoliberal critiques of the nineties. Providing "a racially correct voice-over to narrate the story of black pathology and dependence" (Crenshaw 1997, 281), these black voices appeared perforce in anti–affirmative action campaigns of the nineties.

Mary Radcliffe, an outspoken critic of race-based affirmative action programs, often wrote letters to the editor of the *Seattle Times* stressing self-reliance and color blindness. Radcliffe, a black woman, worked a variety of jobs over the years from live-in maid to sales representative, raising her daughter as a single mother. During June 1998, Radcliffe was invited to serve as co-chair of the Initiative 200 campaign to end race- and gender-based affirmative action in the state of Washington. Accepting the invitation, she stated preemptively that she was not "Washington state's Ward Connerly" (Brune 1998a, B1), thus precisely implicating herself within the rhetorical strategies and public persona of the outspoken UC regent.

Not unlike the Proposition 209 effort in California, which admitted to recruiting Connerly as campaign chair to "use affirmative action to defeat affirmative action" (Brune 1998a, B1), Radcliffe served the Initiative 200 effort as no white spokesperson could. Marking themselves as authentically black and thus authorized to speak on questions of race, both Radcliffe and Connerly spoke publicly over the course of the campaigns about their experiences of racism and discrimination. "I know there is discrimination," Radcliffe avowed. "I live with it everyday. But we can't say discrimination against other people is okay because it happened to us in the past" (Varner 1998, B1). She explained: "I don't think of myself as a particular color, but others remind me that I am, and the reminders always come in a negative fashion . . . I'm a black woman, and I know what the real world is about. I'm not looking at the world through rose-colored glasses. I'm not allowed to."

Similarly, Proposition 209 organizers scripted reminders that the man leading the fight against affirmative action in California was black. In one campaign advertisement, Connerly speaks pleasantly to the camera, stating: "Proposition 209 would prohibit discrimination and preferential treatment in public employment, education, and contracting. For men and women of every race, Proposition 209 keeps all existing protections against discrimination. If it didn't, *I* wouldn't be its campaign chairman" (emphasis in original).

Connerly also appeared in highly visible public debates with other blacks including the mayor of San Francisco Willie Brown, retired Army general Colin Powell, and the reverend Jesse Jackson. These appearances positioned Connerly at "the head of a political movement" (Connerly 1996c, 14A) and as the leader of the "civil rights movement of the 1990s" (Connerly 1996b, A22). He explained:

A black San Francisco contractor who regularly benefits from minority set-asides has been quoted as saying of me: "For someone to stand within the ranks and say, 'I'm not black,' but use it to destroy his own people—that's the kind we brand as a traitor" . . . My opponents think that the color of our skin should dictate what we think: If I'm black, I either go along with the politics of Willie Brown, Marion Barry and Jesse Jackson or I'm a traitor. (1996b, A22)

These statements worked simultaneously to authenticate and exceptionalize Connerly's blackness. As Derrick Bell writes:

When a black person makes a statement or takes an action that the white community . . . deem "outrageous," the latter [i.e., whites] will actively recruit blacks willing to refute the statement or condemn the action. Blacks who respond to the call for condemnation will receive superstanding status. Those blacks who refuse to be recruited will be interpreted as endorsing the statements and may suffer political or economic reprisals. (1992, 118)

Within a larger context of intraracial exchanges over the authenticity of blacks like Supreme Court justice Clarence Thomas, right-leaning academics like Thomas Sowell and Shelby Steele, and others who have gained precisely the kind of superstanding that Bell describes, the appointment of Connerly and Radcliffe to recent anti–affirmative action campaigns reveals the ways in which a particularly entrepreneurial and assimilationist blackness is valorized to provide the salve to soothe lingering doubts about racism in America. Radcliffe and Connerly emerged as mavericks among blacks, their disavowal of race-based programs striking an individualist, all-American chord.

Moreover, such "superblack" representatives of black Americans work forcefully to shepherd black political resistance and to mainstream black political opinion (Marable 1992, 61–85). In Connerly's America, blacks live in a society where not only can racism be overcome but blacks, particularly those who rely on gifts from the government, are responsible for much of the racism they encounter. Similarly, Radcliffe is mortified by the very idea of racial preferences. As she puts it, her "grandmother would roll over in her grave if she thought I was taking something that I did not earn" (Brune 1998a, B1). Thus, by their very presence, Radcliffe and Connerly reinforce the perception that black Americans who support affirmative action simultaneously condone discrimination and thus are the real racists in contemporary America. As Connerly lamented:

It pains me to say that within the past year, I have experienced more hate from my fellow black Americans than I have seen in the previous fifty-five and a half years of my life. For example, a black state senator, Diane Watson, recently said that I want to be white, that I consider myself colorless, that I have no racial pride—all because my wife is white and because I oppose racial discrimination and racial preferences. The one thing

I have learned from this experience is that bigots come in all shapes and colors. (1996a)

Radcliffe occupied an equally embattled position over the course of the Initiative 200 campaign, superblack by some counts and sellout by others. She described how she was forced to resign from a committee formed by the Episcopal Diocese of Olympia in Washington—a group seeking to address racism and diversity within the church and the community, and to which she had been elected co-chair in early 1998—when members of the committee learned Radcliffe had agreed to serve as a spokesperson for Initiative 200 (McBride 1998, B4). Radcliffe revealed emotionally that "a part of [her] soul died" when blacks called her a "white man's slave" and a traitor to her race at committee forums (B4). She stated: "Here I am living in America, and because I have a different point of view, I am being attacked . . . I have never had black people treat me like that. I never had white people treat me like that. I never had anyone treat me like that" (McBride 1998, B4).

Connerly and Radcliffe both offer emotional testimonials of how they were derided and scorned by their "fellow black Americans." From their superblack vantage point, Connerly and Radcliffe detect a new brand of bigots who are outspoken, belligerent, and, most egregiously, black. Thus, it becomes possible to shift the onus of racism and bigotry away from the structures of white privilege and toward blacks, who, as Connerly suggests, "peddle a form of racism and bigotry that is just as destructive of democratic principles as the bigots of yesteryear" (Connerly 1996a). Reprimanding their "own people" for being the new racists, Connerly and Radcliffe perform critical racially correct work for the Proposition 209 and Initiative 200 campaigns, nudging widespread consent to policies that African Americans overwhelmingly opposed.

Racialized Enemies Within

Patricia Songstreng, a resident of Tacoma, Washington, who voted in support of Initiative 200 based on "personal experience," explained her decision at the polling booth as follows: "My husband's a longshoreman.

He's a union member. But before he belonged to the union, he was a middle-aged white male. And it's very hard to get a job as a white American male" (Brune 1998b, A1). Similarly, Christine Griffiths, a mother of two from Bothell, Washington, argued, "My son was nearly a 4.0 student. He had a 3.989, and you can't get much closer than that. But all the scholarships offered by the state went to minorities . . . everybody seems to be a minority except white males" (Brune 1998b, A1).

In Washington, a state that was 88.9 percent white (U.S. Census Bureau 1998), and where Asian Americans constituted the largest ethnic minority—a group to whom affirmative action programs do not apply—racialized anxieties about how "all the scholarships offered by the state [go] to minorities" remained authorized during the 1998 elections.

Likewise, Proposition 209 proponents in California typically characterized affirmative action policies as unfair because they routinely gave special breaks to individuals of the "preferred race." Ballot pamphlets in California read:

> Two wrongs don't make a right! Today, students are being rejected from public universities because of their *race*. Job applicants are turned away because their *race* does not meet some "goal" or "timetable." Contracts are awarded to high bidders because they are of the preferred *race*. That's just plain wrong and unjust. (Wilson, Connerly, and Lewis 1996, emphasis in original)[4]

Promising a return to color blindness, these appeals target their attacks primarily on race-based programs while they remain noticeably silent on questions of gender. The Initiative 200 campaign echoed these strategies, airing television advertisements that deliberately amplified racial scenarios. In one such advertisement, children reciting the Pledge of Allegiance serve as background for a little girl who looks innocently into the camera, asking, "Does it matter what color someone is? Should it matter?" A male actor then explains that under current state policies someone could get a job or a contract or a spot in school "based on the color of that person's skin" (Postman 1998a, A7). Constructing affirmative action as either unnecessary or racist or both, anti–affirmative action campaigns of the nineties thus reveal a strategic and overwhelming emphasis on the *racial* implications of such programs.

From public speeches and television interviews by campaign spokespersons to brochures and bulletins available at Proposition 209 and Initiative 200 Web sites, there is little evidence of any serious discussion of the benefits that women have reaped from affirmative action programs nor of the impact that eliminating such programs may have on them. Even when these campaigns addressed women voters, questions of gender were frequently silenced and on the sidelines of campaign strategy. If the majority of beneficiaries of affirmative action over the past few decades have been white women, recent assaults on affirmative action programs could have been expected to raise gender issues more centrally and more frequently. White women may have been identified as at least partly responsible for reverse discrimination against white men and at minimum may have been implicated in the affirmative action equation. Instead, as this analysis has shown, women and particularly white women were located either among a mythic model majority that no longer required state protections against discrimination or as victims of racial discrimination, suffering the brunt of unfair affirmative action programs much like their husbands, brothers, and sons.

Campaign strategies to diffuse gender issues may reveal "the delicate but pragmatic recognition that the politics of gender are less volatile than the politics of race" (Boxall 1996, A1). Placing a prominently racial face upon affirmative action issues, the eclipse of gender may have facilitated what Barbara Christian refers to as the "trigger effect" of racial appeals. Velma Eastwood, a Washington resident who voted against Initiative 200 and in support of affirmative action, articulates this effect:

> We know of a black person who was given a promotion over a white person, and it appeared to me that the white person was better qualified. For that reason, we were tempted to vote in favor of the initiative. Then we got thinking about the women. They are not getting paid or receiving credit for what they do. So that's why we decided to vote against it. (Brune 1998b, A1)

Framing it as a racial issue, the Eastwoods measured their opposition to affirmative action by fundamental principles of equality and merit, their sympathies turning on the observation that "the white person was better qualified." But when they considered the implications of the ballot measure for women, the general logics of individualism and merit were drowned out by circulating knowledges of women who "are not getting paid or receiving credit for what they do." Thus, even where No!200 strategies managed to convince voters to reject the ballot measure, suspicions about racial entitlements remained influential within dominant knowledges of affirmative action.

Beyond their preoccupations with race, anti–affirmative action organizers in California and Washington directed their loudest and most vociferous attacks specifically at *black* inclusion. This emphasis on black villains defies explanation given that, in 1996, African Americans constituted a small 8 percent of the population in California in contrast with Hispanics and Latinos who made up a hefty 30 percent (California Department of Finance 2000). Organizers of Proposition 187, the state ballot initiative that won the public vote in 1994 to end public benefits for illegal aliens and their families in California, had served up a campaign that directed its racist ire at Mexican immigrants without much self-restraint (Hasian and Delgado 1998, 245–70; Santa Ana 1999, 191–224). But the anti–affirmative action campaign in 1996 was remarkably silent on the specter of burdensome Latinos and their claims to public employment, education, and contracting. Instead, Proposition 209 campaign materials consistently identified black inclusion as particularly problematic, and black Americans as most commonly the "real villains" in affirmative action situations.

In both California and Washington, anti–affirmative action campaigns located black Americans in a variety of stereotypical images, each in its own way geared to the elimination of affirmative action. Every mention of black Americans over the course of the campaigns described them as "unqualified," "less-qualified," "lagging behind," and "lower-achieving," their inclusion "unmeritorious" as a matter of course. These portrayals reveal strategic deployments of "blackness" that served the anti–affirmative action campaigns in critical ways. Locating blame for contemporary racial troubles exclusively on black Americans and within black culture, such deployments reiterated a variety of social pathologies historically associated with blackness. As Connerly pronounced:

> We have to convince black Americans, a group which has become addicted to the drug of a powerful central government, that their rights can be no more secure than anyone else's when we empower government to make decisions about people's lives on the basis of a government melanometer which measures melanin levels. None of our rights are secure in a game of racial self-interest. (1996a)

Middle-class and wealthy black beneficiaries of affirmative action programs, by these logics, frustrate opportunities for others who may be "truly needy." These undeserving black beneficiaries were portrayed as "addicted" to state allotments of rights. Elimination of affirmative action would rehabilitate these "quota addicts" out of their toxic reliance on race-based inclusion mechanisms. Blacks so rehabilitated would play by the rules. They would deny their debts to race-based mechanisms and authorize knowledge of declining racial bias in the workforce. Successful career blacks would engage in self-conduct, and, typical of such subjects, they would ultimately facilitate dominant economic and state interests (Burchell 1996, 23–29).

Entanglements of race and class made visible in Janice Camarena's example are revealed here again, as Proposition 209 advocates singled out "wealthy sons and daughters of 'underrepresented minorities' who receive extra points on their admissions applications to the university, while higher-achieving Asians and whites from lower income families are turned away from the university" (Connerly 1996a). Such efforts to narrate the follies of affirmative action with narratives of nonwhites who may be getting ahead by unfair means provoke age-old and particularly racialized anxieties that blacks may be climbing out of the bottom of the well while leaving poor whites behind.

Racially inscribed appeals that blame "wealthy minorities" for the economic circumstances of poorer whites work within the racialized semiotics of contemporary class divisions where racial anxieties spur apprehensions about class status in much the same way as class-based anxieties provide the impetus for racial resentments. In a fundraising letter in support of Proposition 209, then House Speaker Newt Gingrich wrote: "I urge you to give your financial support to the effort to put the CCRI [the California Civil Rights Initiative] on the California ballot. You will be helping your children and grandchildren and indeed our entire nation. We must work to eliminate what I call legalized discrimination" ("Longing for the Days" 1995, 40).

Promising the end of "legalized discrimination," Gingrich's words etched images of white children and grandchildren who are left out by existing programs. Such appeals lent force to circulating suspicions about "dusky Donald Trumps and brown-skinned Bill Gateses who have grown rich from affirmative action programs" (Varner 1998, B1). Together, these images build on the shorthand that "when the bottom of white society loses, the top of black society gains" (Roediger 1997, 52). Moreover, they reveal that recent assaults on affirmative action, while inscribed in race-neutral terms, remained motivated by and consequently contained within race.

Along similar lines, working-class and poorer persons of color were portrayed as preoccupied with the pursuit of "racial pride," such attitudes breeding, on the one hand, belligerent and paranoid suspicions about whites and, on the other, a "slavish reliance" upon dependency and domination myths (Connerly and Brown 1995, 156–57). Expressing his disapproval of blacks who saw themselves as an oppressed minority victimized by a dominant majority—categories that, according to Connerly, no longer existed—the UC regent suggested that poorer blacks who "fail" do so simply because they have not pushed themselves to the standards of the meritocracy. He argued: "We [blacks] all too often don't even try. Instead of developing a successful attitude, telling our kids that they can do anything they set out to accomplish, we plant and fertilize seeds of failure, which take form in policies and practices such as affirmative action" (Connerly and Brown 1995, 156–57).

Locating the failure of black students in attitudes internalized by working-class black people—their unhealthy reliance upon racial quotas, their willful connivance with a perverse system of racial spoils—these indictments recalled images of poor blacks that informed anti–civil rights appeals forty years ago. As Senator Barry Goldwater put it during his presidential campaign in early 1964: "The idea that poverty and unemployment were caused by lack of education was like saying that people have big feet because they wear big shoes. The fact is that most people who have no skill have no education for the same reason—low intelligence or low ambition" (Mohr 1964, 1).[5]

Such arguments, whether in the mid-sixties or within more recent debates over affirmative action programs, add weight to circulating suspicions about the difficulties, even impossibility, of educating hundreds and thousands of "deprived children." Faced with "the disinterest and apathy of slum parents" who "have not taught their children to be interested in education" (Currivan 1964, 61), these arguments shift the problem away from underfunded and deteriorating schools to "unteachable children" of unfit parents. Such images made their mark on the civil rights agenda of the sixties, as later chapters of this book will show, and re-emerged within recent assaults on social justice. They point forcefully to the futility of efforts to teach the unteachable. Lost causes in the heroic effort toward racial equality, these children and their parents are marked by color, their blackness amounting to a tragic failing.

Thus, the Proposition 209 campaign urged blacks who "fail" to dissociate themselves from programs like affirmative action and simply try harder. Black abdication of race-conscious programs is offered here as a "serum for 'denegrification,'" making it possible, as Frantz Fanon has suggested, for "the miserable Negro to whiten himself and thus to throw off the burden of that corporeal malediction" (1967, 111). Pathological conditions of black life in America are made a stable reference point for defining the path to progress, as the elimination of race-based programs is validated on grounds that "if you behave like a black, you will be . . . treated as one" (Goldberg 1993, 88).

As Ronald Reagan substantiated the black welfare queen and George

H. W. Bush the Willie Horton menace, anti–affirmative action organizers of the nineties substantiated preferences for black quota addicts as a significant site of racial discrimination. In neat packages, these formulaic distillations bear on public consciousness. As "welfare" and "the urban underclass" became encoded racialized terms that erased their reference to race even as they reinscribed it (Fergerson 1997, 126), anti–affirmative action appeals served to camouflage racial discrimination as "rational discrimination," that is, as the conservative critic Dinesh D'Souza explains, "discrimination against those who ought to be discriminated against" (as quoted in Cose 1997, xv). Race provided the "silent justification" for renewed police and disciplinary power in the context of criminality that has typically been inscribed as black (Davis 1997, 264–79) in much the same way as race provided the silent justification for the discipline of "quota addicts" who were assumed without much hesitation to be black.

Mirroring coverage in the mainstream media, anti–affirmative action campaigns of the nineties posited a simple zero-sum game between black beneficiaries and white victims of race-based programs (Entman 1997, 32–52). A significant omission here was a sizable roster of previously "white" people who made official acknowledgment of their Native American and other nonwhite heritage while affirmative action policies were being enforced during the sixties and seventies. The bureaucratic push toward recording the racial and ethnic heritage of public employees during this period witnessed acknowledgments, hitherto unseen, by white males who now willingly revealed precise measures of their native and other nonwhite ancestry. Faced with federal goals and timetables mandating opportunities for members of "historically disadvantaged groups," employers scurried to report these newly calculated multiethnic workers toward proof of the diversity of their existing workforces. And employees who were considered "white" prior to the enforcement of affirmative action mandates during the sixties and seventies were now able to stand in as alibis for other potential beneficiaries of affirmative action.

The pervasive emphasis on black-white antagonisms in the affirmative action context also erases a sizable constituency of "affirmative action alibis," neither black nor white, who do not share the same history of oppression as American blacks (Chakravorty-Spivak 1990, 62). As Vijay Prashad argues, the entry of thousands of South Asians from India and Pakistan, for instance, into techno-professional jobs over the decades of the seventies and eighties facilitated the inclusion of *desis* into the model minority category (2000, 166–70). Complicit with structural racisms directed at black Americans, these newcomers contributed, with characteristic compliance, to the diversification of American workplaces by being hired into positions instead of or vacated by blacks. Like Southeast Asians before them, these affirmative action alibis—while they did not count toward federal goals and timetables for equal opportunity— nevertheless served as visible evidence of efforts by employers to meet diversity objectives in the workplace. Championing model minority discourses of responsible newcomers inching their way toward the American Dream, these strangers from foreign lands served to soothe ethical dilemmas associated with racist corporate cultures.

Ignoring the presence and impact of these alibis within the affirmative action equation, current assaults, like media coverage of these debates, remained strategically preoccupied with black-white racial binaries, appointing black beneficiaries of state favoritisms as familiar and visible "enemies within." Such enemies were defined in various ways by their "irregularities, anomalies, and departures from the norm" (Foucault 1979, 298–99; Stoler 1995, 19–54). These undeserving and unqualified beneficiaries of state assistance were seen willfully perpetrating a fraud on the American meritocracy. Their nonchalant acceptance of preferences that excluded others who may be more deserving, their role in perpetuating the fiction that blacks continued to be oppressed by a racist white majority, and their collusion with a system rife with racial favoritism combined to construct beneficiaries of racial preferences as "dangerous individuals" (Foucault 1978, 1–18), individuals who did not play by the rules and who deserved, therefore, to be disciplined into conformance.

The demonization of black beneficiaries within these assaults, moreover, implicated the state-sponsored programs that harbored them. It reflected the growing authority of images of a state plagued by crises in its abilities to manage the meritocracy. Neoliberal critiques of the state as an Orwellian monster rapaciously perpetuating abuses of public funds and threatening the fundamental freedoms of its citizens through unfair anti-white quotas and preferences specified the "arrogance of government overreach, of the dangers of imminent government overload." Echoing shades of traditional liberalism's deep distrust of government, such critiques reproduced liberal imperatives for "a retreat from the state," for "a lessening of political concern with the conduct of conduct" (Barry, Osborne, and Rose 1996, 9). By the nineties, these critiques invoked unworthy, black beneficiaries of government-imposed quota systems to explain the collapse of the welfare state.

As programs of social justice emerged as key sites for neoliberal reform, abandoning affirmative action promised to restore public confidence in state authorities as gatekeepers of the meritocracy. Renewing constructions of black Americans as either clowns or crooks, ruefully ill-equipped to fully participate in economic life, these anti-government discourses paradoxically defined positive tasks for government. Claiming to foil the "special interests that have hijacked the state," and to heal a people "terrorized by quotas, set-asides, and preferences" (Wilson, Connerly, and Lewis 1996), proponents proffered the elimination of racial and gendered criteria as the means to invigorate the effective management of the population.

In doing so, however, they attenuated ever more subtle and implicit tactics of racism and racial governance. For within post–affirmative action workplaces and college campuses, strict surveillance over race and its classifications is necessitated to ensure *against* race-based hiring or admission. College officials must probe into race ever more closely to ensure race-neutral admissions, and the recruitment process must be ever more watchful of race to ensure that institutions are in fact applying a "truly race-neutral standard" (Bowen and Bok 1998, 289). Thus, even in its elimination, or perhaps as a consequence of its elimination, race-based affirmative action remains a normalizing technology of state power, essential for the management of the population.

Allies from the Past

Ineffective though they ultimately remained in both California and Washington, supporters of affirmative action programs organized themselves in a variety of ways in response to the Proposition 209 and Initiative 200 campaigns. Working in their own way to appoint superblacks and angry white men alike as the real racists in the contemporary United States, these voices took aim at anti–affirmative action proposals, referring to them as the "Jim Crow, Jr. Initiative" and the "Civil Rights for Whites Initiative" (Asadullah 1996, A7; Guillermo 1995, 11). As the mantle of "real racist" was passed around in public debates of the nineties, these battles over taxonomies—what racism is and who the real racists are—foregrounded the ways in which specific labels and categories coalesced under the auspices of authorized discourses.

Working at a tangent from the Stop Prop 209 campaign organized by the Feminist Majority in California, the breakaway No on 209 campaign focused on indicting white male support for Proposition 209 as a renewed and virulent brand of white racism. In October 1996, with financial support from the Democratic National Committee, the No on 209 campaign aired what it described as a "nuclear bomb" of a television commercial. Working with a street poster campaign that used slogans like "The Klan supports 209. Should you?," the television spot began with images of the ex-Klansman David Duke dressed in a business suit smiling and waving at an audience. The image then morphed into an older image of Duke wearing a white robe digitally dropped in front of a burning cross while a male voice announced:

> He's not just another guy in a business suit. He's David Duke, former head of the Ku Klux Klan. And he's come to California to support Proposition 209 . . . Don't be fooled. David Duke didn't come to California to end discrimination. Vote no on 209.

Student organizers in California had earlier invited Duke to a campus forum on affirmative action at the California State University at Northridge, hoping to indict the anti–affirmative action effort in California as the work of "racists of the worst order" (Chávez 1998, 200).

As Lydia Chávez reports, Duke had been vocal on California radio, obligingly damning affirmative action and minorities and accusing blacks and Latinos of raping white women, as he put it, "by the thousands" (1998, 201). Producing a rare moment of media interest in campaigns seeking to preserve affirmative action in California, Duke's presence invigorated the languishing and fractious student campaign against Proposition 209 and guaranteed the No on 209 campaign local news coverage of the controversial advertisement.

However, spectacular displays of overt racial violence commissioned by the Klan and its various descendants in contemporary times are newsworthy *because* they are exceptional. The spectacle of these acts attests to their utter marginalization within contemporary culture. Thus, despite the brief media attention, the No on 209 campaign, like the student organizers at Northridge, remained ineffectual in their efforts to dislodge ethical distinctions, authorized in the cultural imaginary, between white supremacy and white male ferment over race-based public programs. As Connerly, who refused the invitation to appear with Duke at the Northridge debate, put it: "I am not worried about the skinheads, the Ku Klux Klan, and the Aryan Nation. In our time, we have discredited them and their brand of racism" (1996a).

By the decade of the nineties, the anxious vulnerabilities of reasonable white men could not be mistaken for virulent hatreds espoused by white supremacists. The positioning of an ex-Klansman as representative voice for the mainstream of white men in contemporary America jarred. The campaign's effort to locate the voices of white college students and middle-class entrepreneurs on par with "racists of the worst order" served contrarily to authenticate frustrations associated with reverse discrimination. The Northridge debate and the No on 209 campaign thus emerged as strategic failures in the campaign against Proposition 209 in California, having misidentified the victim of racial programs as the morally repugnant supremacist rather than the middle-class white college and job applicant.

Whereas in the mid-sixties such narratives had effectively constructed the Southern segregationist as irrational and un-American, resurrected in

1996 California, the Southern bigot was a straw man, and the advertisement a resounding flop. Benjamin Kepple and others of his ilk could not be mistaken for white racists of previous generations. Neither were they, as Vijay Prashad argues, "like those egregious racists who dragged James Byrd down a dirt road in Jasper, Texas" (2000, 164). These new patriots exculpated themselves from "a vulgar, lower-class kind of racism" (164) and were thus insulated from being read as white supremacist by any standards.

Indeed, the exceptionality of white supremacist racial dogma and the irrationality of Klan appeals amplified the normalcy and credibility of everyday accounts of reverse discrimination. The contrast offered by the rabid white supremacist added legitimacy to the mainstream dictum of reverse discrimination offered by "average white guys." Now it became possible to wield the accusatory device of reverse discrimination as a trump card, operating without much need for evidence or substantiation. The very mention of reverse discrimination authenticated its accusatory impact, solidifying circulating knowledge that the white supremacist deserves rehabilitation in much the same way that the victim of reverse discrimination warrants compensation.

Organizers of the Proposition 209 campaign protested Duke's presence at the campus forum fiercely ("Prop. 209 Chair Condemns" 1996; "Sacramento Bee Editorial" 1996) and argued instead that they could not be constructed as bigots because even Martin Luther King Jr. himself would have supported an end to affirmative action. Identifying Proposition 209 with "the civil rights movement of the 1990s" (Connerly 1996b, A22), organizers appropriated King's words to argue that "individuals should be judged by the content of their character, not the color of their skin" (Gingrich and Connerly 1997, 15).

A series of television advertisements attacking affirmative action used footage of King's "I have a dream" speech to argue that his dream of a color-blind America remained unfulfilled as a result of liberal programs like affirmative action, which attempted to right one wrong with another. Although broadcast of the advertisements was preempted by the King estate ("State GOP Pulls TV Ads" 1996, A3), they are telling of proponents' efforts to have black voices speak authentically about the true character of affirmative action and its inconsistency with civil rights. Affirmative action, now synonymous with preferences, was characterized as "a 'corruption' of the civil rights laws of the '60s" while Proposition 209, officially and strategically entitled the California Civil Rights Initiative, was described as "the true heir to the American civil rights movement" (Pashler 1996).

The opposition to Proposition 209 sought to claim these heroes as allies as well. Thus, the radio commercials of the Stop Prop 209 campaign asserted their genealogical claim to heroes of the sixties. In one radio advertisement, Dolores Huerta, co-founder of the United Farmworkers Union, proclaimed: "Proposition 209 is a lie. It aims to take away our civil rights. It aims to close the doors of opportunity that have opened for us . . . Many people gave their lives so that we could better ourselves—César Chávez, Rubén Salazar. Together we can defeat this Proposition 209." In another, the African American screen actress Alfre Woodard spoke of the Reverend Jesse Jackson of the Rainbow Coalition and his plea to "keep the dream alive." The Reverend Jackson himself appeared in a commercial, arguing: "We've fought too hard, bled too much, and died too young, to see the precious gains of the civil rights movement snatched away. Vote no on Proposition 209. It's misleading. It's not civil rights. It's civil wrongs. They tried to manipulate Dr. King's words and make him stand against us with David Duke, Pat Buchanan, and Pete Wilson. How vulgar."

César Chávez, Rubén Salazar, and Martin Luther King Jr. are invoked by name as a means to draw upon the ethical reserves of beloved and charismatic heroes of the past. Dolores Huerta and the Reverend Jesse Jackson themselves are heroic figures from the sixties. Claiming a faultless bloodline for affirmative action, like its supporters, organizers against Proposition 209 sought to position themselves as true heirs to the social revolutions of the sixties. But by invoking images of legions of black and Chicano protestors marching and striking for the rights of entire ethnic groups, the campaign's strategic return to the historical past of the social movements of the sixties echoed logics of restitutions for historically disadvantaged groups that now emerged as outmoded within authorized discourses of neoliberalism.[6]

The advertisements of the Stop Prop 209 campaign thus reproduced a cultural nostalgia for specific historical pasts without explanations for why modes of opposition that were successful decades ago would stand a chance or need popular support at the present time. As deployed within the radio commercials, such appeals were ineffective in opening up authorized tales of the present to incredulity and contestation. Neither Huerta nor Jackson denaturalized the authority of pro-209 claims that while state-sponsored mechanisms may have been necessary during the sixties, they had outlived their purpose by the nineties. Nor did these commercials adequately unearth vulnerabilities in the official knowledges of the present—that racial and gender discrimination remained pervasive in specific and quotidian terms and that thousands of women and nonwhites would be imperiled in specific ways if state protections for equal opportunity were eliminated. Untranslatable into the grammar of individualism, appeals by Huerta and Jackson located themselves in the past and, paradoxically, served as reminders of ethical contrasts between the battles of the sixties and those of the present.

Within the campaign for Proposition 209, the voices of civil rights leaders served to evoke memories for whites and blacks who had been allies in the social movements of the sixties. Dipping into the ethical reserves of black leaders of the civil rights movement of the sixties, the campaign for Proposition 209 offered Californian voters a "second chance." Thus, ballot pamphlets stated: "A generation ago, we did it right. We passed civil rights laws to prohibit discrimination. But special interests hijacked the civil rights movement. Instead of equality, governments imposed quotas, preferences, and set-asides" (Wilson, Connerly, and Lewis 1996). Now Proposition 209 granted these voters the opportunity to reclaim their "hijacked" efforts and redeem the civil rights movement by voting to end affirmative action. Appropriations of civil rights discourses enabled reversals of objectives pursued by the civil rights movement, so that civil rights appeals based on liberal imperatives of individualism and color blindness now served to discipline subjects against race-based affirmative action and to make opportunistic claims to civil rights allies from the past.

CHAPTER 2

The Affirmative Action Film of the Nineties: Hollywood Cinema as Racial Regime

> They [women] are stronger, they're smarter, and they don't fight fair.
> It's the next step in human evolution. It's like the Amazons—
> keep a few of us around for sperm and kill off the rest.
>
> —Barry Levinson, *Disclosure*

> If I were a man, nobody would care how many sexual partners I had
> when I was in college. And if it's not relevant for a man, it's not
> relevant for a woman.
>
> —Rod Lurie, *The Contender*

John McTiernan's *Die Hard with a Vengeance* opened in theaters in the summer of 1995 to cheering audiences and high returns at the box office. Third in a series of action-adventures featuring John McClane (Bruce Willis), the perpetually hung-over but heroic police detective, *Vengeance* presents the biracial buddy formula, introducing the character of Zeus Carver (Samuel L. Jackson), black owner of a corner electronics repair shop in Harlem, who is the reluctant but reliable sidekick to McClane. True to formula, McClane and Carver are "trapped in circumstances where they must form an uneasy alliance to resolve [a] disruptive criminal situation for the benefit of the dominant social order" (Guerrero 1993, 242). The narrative follows the main characters as they are forced to play a deadly game of "Simon Says" with a stereotypical German baddie who orchestrates a reign of terror in the streets of New York, detonating bombs in department stores and drilling through the basement depositories of the Federal Reserve Bank to make away with $140 billion in gold bullion.

Over the course of the eighties, Ed Guerrero suggests, the black presence on screen was presented "in the protective custody, so to speak, of the white lead or co-star, and therefore in conformity with dominant white sensibilities and expectations of what blacks should be like" (1993, 239). By the nineties, however, this tactic of representationally condensing blackness with the feminine shifts and, as Robyn Wiegman has argued, the interracial buddy formula works instead to inculcate the black buddy into the "province of the masculine," marking such masculinization as the "precise measurement of America's democratic achievement" (1995, 118). For Wiegman, rescuing the black male from the feminine is a necessary cultural assertion by the nineties as a mean of negotiating the threat of militant black masculinity and phallicized discourses of Black Power. Transforming long-standing tensions between black and white men into a "democratic fraternity," thus, the biracial buddy film of the nineties celebrates "America" as an exclusively masculine realm (118).

Zeus Carver, the black male sidekick in *Die Hard with a Vengeance*, starts out as mulish and paranoid. Recalling characters from the heyday of the Black Power movement, he espouses separatist dogma and harbors a belligerent suspicion of whites. Rehearsing an at-home lesson about the realities of life in contemporary America with a pair of neighborhood children at his store early in the film, Carver asks them, "Who are the bad guys?" "Guys who sell drugs, guys who have guns," the children reply. Carver continues, "And who are the good guys?" "We're the good guys" they respond. "And who's going to help you?" "Nobody." "So who's going to help you?" "We're going to help ourselves," the children reply. "And who do we not want to help us?" "White people," they reply. "That's right!" Carver responds, breaking into a satisfied smile and waving the boys off to school.

A key moment in the film's treatment of Carver's racial consciousness occurs when he accompanies McClane to Tompkins Square Park in the East Village of Manhattan to defuse a bomb that Simon, the villain, has waiting for them. At the park, a panicked and heated exchange builds between the two, reaching a climax when Carver accuses McClane, screaming, "You were going to call me a nigger, weren't you?" Balking at the charge, McClane yells in response, "You got some fuckin' problem because I'm white, Zeus? Is that it? Have I oppressed you? Have I oppressed your people somehow? I'll tell you what your problem is. You don't like me because you're racist. You don't like me 'coz I'm white." Stunned into silence, Carver breaks eye contact and changes the topic, turning his attention back to the ticking bomb at hand.

As the scene at the park suggests, *Vengeance* serves in compelling ways to mark black racial consciousness as dysfunctional, to position it as "the thing against which normality, whiteness, and functionality [are] defined" (Kelley 1997, 3). The white hero is resolutely color-blind and thus epitomizes hegemonic racial ideology. "Have I oppressed your people?" McClane demands in a move that rhetorically extricates him from the role of oppressor. White men like McClane, the scene suggests, do not and have never oppressed black people and are not accountable for the nation's racial past or present. Moreover, they now make claims for their own cultural exclusion, thus, as Susan Jeffords points out, recasting the masculine as the newly marginalized position within American culture (1993, 207).

In all the ways that the scene portrays white males as having moved beyond race, Carver serves contrarily as a representative of contemporary blacks who remain captive to their racial dogmas. Carver, the scene suggests, is more likely than not to think racially, to make things about race when they are not, and to anticipate racisms where none exist. The exchange at the park, moreover, does not allow Carver any response. He turns away from McClane's accusation, relinquishing what have been for him until then guiding principles about racism in black life to concentrate on matters more urgent. Thus, at the end of the scene at the park, black racial dogma is portrayed as typical, and Carver, the working-class black man from Harlem, is pegged as the racist with the proverbial chip on his shoulder.

The parameters of everyday race relations legitimized in *Vengeance*, including the film's unambiguous allegiance to dominant white expectations of what blacks should be like, serve critical hegemonic ends. As Carver is disciplined out of his anachronistic mind-set, he is forced to acknowledge that McClane is just another honest police detective who, like other ordinary white Americans, may not be racist at all. Such is the ethical force of McClane's reprimand at the park that the question of race never resurfaces as a problem between the protagonists for the remainder of film and Carver appears transformed by the episode.[1] The hardboiled and battered white action hero thus gives voice to mainstream white indignation at black racial consciousness and, shifting blame, speaks for legions of whites in the audience for whom race would disappear from the American landscape were it not for the tedious racial fixations of black Americans.

I begin with scenes from *Die Hard with a Vengeance*, a film with no particular and certainly no stated claim to racial themes, to call attention to the ways in which dominant truths about race and discrimination are woven into the narratives of Hollywood formula films. Their didacticisms masked, films like *Vengeance* serve in notable ways to reinforce racial and gender hegemonies. Typical of popular cinema, that "theatre of popular desires . . . of popular fantasies," as Stuart Hall refers to it, "where we find who we really are, the truth of our experience" (1992, 32), *Vengeance* works its discipline in subtle but effective ways. Constructing racial and gendered subjectivities in narrowly hegemonic terms and addressing racialized and gendered threats to social order, the film exemplifies the work of Hollywood cinema as racial regime.

In this chapter, I consider the complex repertoire of cultural imaginaries of workers and workplaces, of merit and indolence as they circulated in mainstream cinematic texts of the nineties. I trace the porous boundaries between Hollywood narratives and public policy campaigns toward a genealogical analysis of contemporary knowledges about race and gender, and to understand the workings of power in their claims to truth. Thus, I analyze film portrayals of outrage over race- and gender-conscious programs, and conceptions of effort, acumen, and merit to reveal how these scripts take hold in the cultural imaginary as contemporary truths. I consider how cinematic heroes and villains of the mythic American workplace bear on cultural consciousness, working over and recirculating images of rogues and victims in policy debates over affirmative action. Such analysis reveals a range of discursive cross-pollinations between mainstream cinema and policy campaigns that have served in recent years to reinforce the persuasive appeal of neoliberal assaults on social justice policies and programs.

The Affirmative Action Film of the Nineties

Key within the filmic repertoire of the nineties, a series of texts appeared for the first time that offered dramatic critiques of bureaucratic improprieties and structural injustices occasioned by what were perceived as stagnating and burdensome inheritances from the civil rights era. Shaping contemporary portrayals of race, gender, and cultural equality in crucial ways, these "affirmative action films" assert a wry disillusionment with liberal intentions of the sixties and take contemporary anxieties over racial and gender integration as their central problematic. Drawing on themes from four such affirmative action films—Barry Levinson's *Disclosure* (1994), Edward Zwick's *Courage under Fire* (1996), Ridley Scott's *G.I. Jane* (1997), and Rod Lurie's *The Contender* (2000)—this chapter examines a range of cultural imaginaries of work and workplace dramatized in mainstream cinematic texts of the nineties.

Linked thematically in their attention to crises occasioned by the introduction of nontraditional workers into workplaces, these texts cover a variety of scenarios from the frustrations of qualified white men who get passed over on the corporate ladder by conniving career women to racial fantasies that play out as exceptional white females batter through workplace glass ceilings. All are major Hollywood studio productions featuring actors and directors with established marquee values. All were released over the decade of the nineties.

Exemplifying discursive engagements over race, gender, and social justice occurring in a host of Hollywood productions at this time, affirmative action films are in some senses *unexceptional* cultural productions of the nineties. There were certainly scores of mainstream texts, like *Die Hard with a Vengeance*, that addressed race in oblique gestures of hegemonic conformance. Roger Donaldson's *White Sands* (1992), Tony Scott's *True Romance* (1993), Harold Ramis's *Multiplicity* (1996), Andrew Niccol's

Gattaca (1997), and Brett Ratner's *The Family Man* (2000) are other examples that toe the official line on "the problem of race and gender" while asserting no particular claim to racial themes. In so doing, these films set the limits of a representational baseline for the affirmative action genre of the nineties. They construct the ideological and allegorical backdrop, the mise-en-scène, if you will, for social critiques wrought centrally into the narratives of affirmative action films.

These texts may be located within the social problem genre that has been a staple of Hollywood since the thirties and forties. Combining didactic social analysis and interpersonal conflict, the classical social problem film dramatized the relationship between individual and society, taking a highly cynical attitude toward social institutions. The earliest social problem films, epitomized by such releases as Archie Mayo's 1935 classic *Bordertown*, lingered on images of a hostile urban environment where, as Peter Roffman and Jim Purdy explain, the hero had to be "tough and amoral in order to endure in a society crumbling under the weight of its own corruption and ineffectuality" (1981, 16).

Key to the genre was the "assimilation narrative" that focused on immigrants to America and their quest for assimilation and the American Dream (Ramirez Berg 1992, 29–46). The plot typically pursued a range of barriers facing the new entrant, who is ultimately forced to realize the vacuity of mainstream success, the hopelessness of his/her efforts, and the depth of incompatibilities between American success, on the one hand, and values espoused by the immigrant's root culture, on the other. Thus, a crucial moment in the social problem narrative is the protagonist's realization that American success is inherently dangerous when practiced by ethnic others, often inducing moral decay, madness, even death. Forced to return to the barrio or ghetto where s/he began, the new entrant is ultimately left to cope with the negligible opportunities available to him/her there. Playing out endless variations on moral lessons about the station of immigrants in American society, the classical social problem film raised critiques of cherished mythologies of the melting pot in American culture.

Problem films from the postwar years included such films as Elia

Kazan's *Gentleman's Agreement* (1947) and Joseph Mankiewicz's *No Way Out* (1950) and focused on ethical dilemmas raised by abuses of state power, postwar race riots, and nonwhite characters who urged racial tolerance and integration (Bogle 1997, 178). Capitalizing on and contributing to the cross-racial popularity of the Hollywood star Sidney Poitier, social problem films of the sixties included such hits as Stanley Kramer's *Guess Who's Coming to Dinner* and Norman Jewison's *In the Heat of the Night*, both released in 1967, and showcased desexualized and exceptional black male protagonists who would be successfully integrated into white enclaves because of their infallible assimilability.

Critical to these narratives were dramatizations of dilemmas confronting beleaguered whites who would ultimately be persuaded to racial integration by the strength of ethical claims. Balancing the sheer humanity of its black characters with white protagonists of conscience and heroic adaptability, the problem film of the sixties remained resolutely celebratory of civil rights–era white liberal ideologies and worked therapeutically to reassure the audience of "brotherly-love everything's-going-to-be-dandy escapisms" (Bogle 1997, 219). By the seventies, in the face of growing audience fatigue with such "Negro-struggle films," cinematic texts invented a new brand of black protagonist who "shouted back to whitey" and "bucked a corroded system" even as decency, duty, and moral intelligence dictated his or her actions (Bogle 1997, 176, 179–80).

Turning away from these preoccupations, the social problem that deserves moral condemnation in affirmative action films of the nineties is neither the hypocrisy nor the irony of contemporary racial ideologies but rather the frustrations of white male Americans who are no longer in control of their environment. Drawing on themes from media representations of the eighties that produced, as Herman Gray suggests, "an aggressive and largely effective attempt on the part of the new right to reconfigure and establish a conservative hegemony . . . which set its sights on such issues as affirmative action, multiculturalism, the welfare state, immigration, big government, and patriotism" (1995, 16), the affirmative action genre works to sustain neoliberal regimes of "new racisms," acquiescent to ever more conservative hegemonies of "victim blaming" and "self-help" (Reed 1999, 205) and particularizing white masculinity as the newly marginalized position within American culture.

Consistent with shifts in cinematic representations of white masculinity during the nineties, the disillusioned and frustrated protagonist of the affirmative action genre typically finds himself jobless, placeless, and alone. The narrative positions the white hero not as he was during the eighties, bashing through doors and plate-glass windows to bring wayward villains to justice (Jeffords 1993, 207), but instead as lost and frustrated in an alien landscape overrun by outsiders.[2] Clearing the space of cultural marginalization of its historical occupants, and reoccupying it with seemingly decentered masculine voices that no longer seem to hold sway in American culture, these texts reveal the contours of an "incipient crisis of whiteness" (Winant 1994, 283), what Richard Dyer refers to as a white backlash that manifests in a widespread and plaintive "me-too-ism" (1988, 44–65) that is markedly descriptive of the historical moment of the nineties.

Bewildered and bitter, the affirmative action hero reaches breaking point over the course of the narrative and is forced to reinvent himself to fit familiar tropes of all-American individualism and acuity. This hero's odyssey is not toward retribution or revenge but rather to comprehend his place in a new America and to position himself as benevolent overseer of the new cultural landscape. He is carefully constructed not as champion for a pre–civil rights white America but rather as introspective journeyman who seeks to restore common sense and prudence to racial and gender regimes that have gone awry.

Moreover, mirroring moves in the biracial buddy formula of the nineties, affirmative action films deploy sentimental portrayals of democratic brotherhood between white and black men. Smoothing over historical and cultural antagonisms between men of different races, these texts reiterate the fantasy of a nation freed from its hideous past and healed of its racial troubles. Consequently, racial conflict is rendered "unspeakable" in affirmative action films precisely because addressing it would necessitate acknowledgment of the hypocrisy of the white liberal agenda for racial reform and the paucity of its impact upon racial justice in contemporary America.

Here we might recall the tactic employed by Clarence Thomas, who, at the height of the media spectacle of the Senate confirmation hearings for his appointment to the U.S. Supreme Court in 1991, compellingly redirected the prejudicial impact of allegations of sexual harassment brought against him by Anita Hill as a "high-tech lynching." Redefining the gendered terms of the hearings, Thomas deliberately evoked the racialized imagery of lynching, retrieving a shameful past, so that *her* sexual oppression was obscured in the face of *his* racial subordination among members of the lily-white, all-male confirmation committee. The resultant brotherhood among men so constructed not only denied Hill her claims to sexual justice but also rendered "unspeakable" the continuing problem of racial inequality and injustice in America.[3]

Where Hollywood films of the nineties did address racial antagonisms, they did so either in civil rights nostalgia pictures or in light-hearted comedic features. Thus, reminiscent of Alan Parker's *Mississippi Burning* produced in 1988, Hollywood studios released a number of films over the course of the nineties that revisited the spectacular horrors of the pre–civil rights South. Notable among these were Richard Pearce's *A Long Walk Home* (1990), Joshua Brand's highly acclaimed television series *I'll Fly Away* (1991–93), Jonathan Kaplan's *Love Field* (1992), Jessie Nelson's *Corrina, Corrina* (1994), Carl Franklin's *Devil in a Blue Dress* (1995), Rob Reiner's *Ghosts of Mississippi* (1996), Kasi Lemmons's *Eve's Bayou* (1997), Norman Jewison's *The Hurricane* (1999), and Boaz Yakin's *Remember the Titans* (2000). Each dramatized boorish Southern recalcitrance against imminent social transformation in the cultural milieu of the American South of the fifties and sixties.[4]

Where movies of the nineties addressed contemporary issues of workplace equity, they did so through screwball comedies such as Kevin Hooks's *Strictly Business* (1991), Jonathan Lynn's *The Distinguished Gentleman* (1992), Peter MacDonald's *Mo' Money* (1992), Darnell Martin's *I Like It Like That* (1994), Donald Petrie's *The Associate* (1996), and so on. These films typically find black protagonists struggling and/or conniving to find their place in workplaces burdened with cronyism and old-fashioned racial favoritism. Utilizing farce as a means to subvert color and gender barriers, these texts celebrate plucky hero/heroines who appear in varying shades of "white face," orchestrating well-intentioned deceptions as a last resort to shame hoary patriarchs out of their racist habits of mind.

Like resourceful Tess McGill (Melanie Griffith), the personal assistant who comes armed with "a mind for business and a *bod* for sin" in Mike Nichols's *Working Girl* (1988), or Brantley Foster (Michael J. Fox), the mailroom clerk who impersonates a corporate executive in Herbert Ross's *The Secret of My Success* (1987), black protagonists of the workplace farce of the nineties do not demand stronger equal opportunity protections, nor do they critique neoliberal paeans to personal responsibility and individualism. Instead, like their forebears from the eighties, they scramble to secure their position in the corporate hierarchy through machinations, however absurd, of their own design.

Thus, films of the nineties dealt with race by either returning the audience to a historical moment long past or through variations on the theme of black Americans who, by some gaffe, find themselves in positions of high corporate or political power. The cinematic repertoire of the nineties, it will appear, addresses the question of race deliberately at either a historical or comedic distance. In the more proximal and quotidian milieu of the contemporary workplace, mainstream productions of the nineties steered clear of serious and dramatic attention to the implications of race and integrative reforms affecting the marketplace.

Echoing these silences, the affirmative action film predominantly recounts tales about women as they encounter the apparatus and institutions of the American workplace. The central narrative in affirmative action films revolves around the experiences of women, and particularly white women in the post–civil rights workforce, whether they are vilified as unqualified diversity hires or valorized as new messiahs of the mythic American meritocracy. The manifest content of the representative texts that this chapter focuses upon—*Disclosure, Courage under Fire, G.I. Jane,* and *The Contender*—is thus remarkably silent about racial dilemmas raised by workplace integration.

The gendered narratives of affirmative action films and the accompanying attenuation of the black threat may also suggest that the misogynist wrath that white women incur in these films is symptomatic of widespread anxieties that these women are perceived as a more likely threat in the post–affirmative action workplace. Given racist suspicions of black biological inferiority that remain undercover but entrenched, suspicions which occasionally bubble to the surface, as in the case of the Texaco "jelly beans" incident (Eichenwald 1996, 1) or the publication of works like *The Bell Curve* (Murray and Herrnstein 1994), the gendered focus of affirmative action films suggests that female co-workers pose a far more plausible and imminent threat of ousting white men from their positions of dominance than do black co-workers.

This may be in part because, despite disadvantages stemming from gender, white women share comparable race and class privileges with white men—access to decent schooling, job training, and the cultural capital to assimilate with relative ease into workplace culture. Nipping at the heels of male go-getters in the post–civil rights workplace, white women emerge as a hated threat, favored by affirmative action programs that have handed them unfair advantages over the past thirty years. Thus, while white males are reassured in their racist presumptions that black workers are too mediocre to pose a serious challenge to their dominance in the workplace, the affirmative action film portrays white women as bloodthirsty vixens or pious martyrs to assuage fears that they may be better at the job by the very standards of the meritocracy that liberal discourses champion. Offering pleasurable accounts of how white females take the fall or learn their place, these texts reassuringly deliver just deserts to those perceived as attempting to wrest control of the workplace away from the masculine lead.

We should recall, as the previous chapter has shown, that contrary to the cinematic emphasis on gender we find in the affirmative action genre, policy assaults on affirmative action over the decade of the nineties lingered on the villainies of black workers in the post–civil rights workplace. This comparison between cinematic and public policy discourses reveals that the valences of gender politics serve different strategic ends from racial appeals. Distancing white women as a constituency in electoral politics exacts a high price at the polls, particularly if, as a consequence, white women vote in solidarity with black and other non-white men and women. Instead, political campaigns strategically framed around racist assumptions about unqualified black hires consolidate the white voting bloc—men and women both—whipped into an electoral frenzy by the specter of black Americans getting ahead by unfair means.

The profoundly mythic arena of the cinematic, in contrast, makes room for male anxieties about "pushy broads" and "castrating bitches" who, more so than black co-workers, pose a plausible and imminent threat of ousting white men from their positions of dominance. Here the narrative inevitability of retributions for villainous females far greater than the discipline of wayward black workers provides visual evidence that men can, in fact, take back the office, the locker room, and the presidency from the fearsome competitive threat that white women pose.

Thus, a comparison between cinematic and public policy discourses reveals a range of interconnections and ventriloquisms between race and gender in cultural discourses and, simultaneously, crucial differences between these categories in terms of their service to hegemonic white male dominance. White anxieties about black defiance and guilt for the nation's racial past are relegated to history with a generic emphasis upon female troublemakers in the cinematic repertoire of the nineties as masculinist paranoia about the feminization of the workplace is assuaged in the public policy arena by recirculating tales of black mischief that can be relied upon to recruit white women as a sympathetic voting bloc.

Retracing what Susan Fraiman refers to as "geometries of race and gender" (1994, 67–84), the narrative device of disciplining or punishing women reworks white fixations over the "browning of America" in more palatable terms. As the fearsome black villain all but disappears from the cinematic repertoire of the nineties, a politically correct doppelganger emerges constituted in the form of the woman. This slippage from black villain to female vamp connects historical memories of troublesome blacks with the contemporary threat of white females. Thus, denunciations at the core of the affirmative action genre ventriloquize enduring concerns about black squatters in the workplace with dramatizations of the threat posed by white female upstarts. Such ventriloquisms illuminate the ways in which imbricating matrices of race and gender serve as euphemisms for each other, one doing the other's dirty work in a sense.

This, moreover, is not a simple matter of black absence, for black Americans retain a critical symbolic presence in the affirmative action genre. While they themselves make no claims to the mythic meritocracy, black characters of the affirmative action genre serve in critical ways to resuscitate whiteness out of dysfunctions it has lapsed into as a consequence of civil rights reforms of the sixties. Here blackness serves as a therapeutic restorative that revives white faith in cultural and social hegemonies, and that redeems white guilt for anti-black racisms by carefully locating such intolerances far in the nation's past.

Accordingly, the affirmative action film deploys the generic contrivance of black interlocutors with whose assistance fallen white protagonists find salvation and redemption. Within the cinematic repertoire of the nineties, we find white heroes and heroines of cinematic texts like Warren Beatty's *Bulworth* (1998), James Toback's *Black & White* (1999), and Thomas Carter's *Save the Last Dance* (2001) helping themselves to elements of blackness that reinvest heart and health in white protagonists who are broken or damaged by circumstance and history. Inscribing aesthetic and stylized elements of blackness on the bodies and speech patterns of white protagonists, these protagonists adopt a new blackface that restores them to wholeness and innocence.[5]

The positioning of black characters as "helpers" serving to rehabilitate white protagonists out of crisis and collapse, moreover, is a familiar trope. Noting both their "enabling and disenabling qualities," Toni Morrison reads these black nurses and helpers as "a useful, convenient, and sometimes welcome means for propping up and stabilizing the patriarchal and capitalist social order" (as quoted in Gooding-Williams 1993, 162). David Levering Lewis notes similarly that "the role of the African American as surrogate for the troubles and malefactions of white people is as old as the Republic, a part carefully scripted in the antebellum South and archetypally acted out in American literature from Harriet Beecher Stowe to William Faulkner and beyond" (2001, A21).

Cinematic representations followed in this tradition through the nineties when such portrayals became nearly typical. From Jerry Zucker's *Ghost* (1990) and John Sayles's *Passion Fish* (1992) onward through the close of the nineties, black characters in film typically played the role of caretaker or helper to the white lead. Thus, a young white hero who is fated to save the world from a postapocalyptic stupor orchestrated by a malevolent cyberintelligence relies upon the serene tutelage of a black caretaker in Andy and Larry Wachowski's *The Matrix* (1999). In Frank Darabont's *The Green Mile* (1999), a white death row guard, losing both faith and sanity, is miraculously restored after contact with a gentle black giant wrongly condemned for crimes he did not commit. And a disillusioned war veteran and golfer finds he is able to shed his psychic malaise and retrieve his "authentic swing" with help from a magical black caddy who enters his life in Robert Redford's *The Legend of Baggar Vance* (2000).

Constituting blackness as a magical antidote, these portrayals reiterate ideological categories of whiteness in crisis and blackness in servitude. Completing the essential triad of hero, villain, and helper in the cinematic "hero myth" (Seger 2000, 309–12), the soulful black healer is identified as repository of insights, cautions, and wisdoms that are all but lost in the maddening bustle of the worldly rat race. Dispensing remedies, restoratives, and, not coincidentally, black magic as needed, these black helpers are saved in ways as well, having been returned to familiar and recognizable roles of heroic servitude. So positioned, the black healers of cinematic texts are corralled within a remote and secluded enclave, uniquely endowed with cautionary insights about the "real world" but ultimately ill-equipped to fully participate in it themselves.

Black helpers in affirmative action films likewise perform key redemptive work, providing white protagonists and audiences a respite from their "unspeakable" yet ever-present racial guilt. Redirecting racial critiques of civil rights inheritances in more palatable gendered terms, black Americans facilitate the central didacticisms in these texts appearing primarily as de-fanged models of docility and discipline for feral females in the workplace.

Serving as the collective conscience of the meritocracy, black Americans are domesticated witnesses to American history whose insights into the nation's past equips them to proffer racially correct appraisals of sexist habits and racial secrets of today's meritocracy. Negotiating between white men and women, black interlocutors of the affirmative action genre preach, reprimand, and redeem as the scenario demands to log critical lessons about hegemonic color- and gender-blind ideals of the American worker and workplace.

The affirmative action genre, typified by the centrality of the female vamp and the relative marginalization of black helpers, serves up cautionary tales that reiterate the urgency of dismantling race- and gender-based affirmative action programs. Working their hegemonic discipline, these formulaic regurgitations bear critically on public consciousness. Sounding a unanimous chorus with mainstream network and cable news sources, the cinematic repertoire of the nineties moves apace with public policy assaults, one from the other, pilfering a mélange of silences and evocations about the changing American workplace. Inundated, thus, by a singular point of view on the merits and liabilities of social justice programs like affirmative action, the dominant discourses of our time register a churning discontent among Americans, relegating counterknowledges to the margins as laughable, odd, impossible.

Of Martyrs and Man-Eaters

Barry Levinson's 1994 release *Disclosure*, a film adaptation of Michael Crichton's best-selling novel of the same name, is a contemporary office drama that offers a twist on the typical sexual harassment scenario. The film recounts a series of dramatic events precipitated by Meredith Johnson (Demi Moore), a scheming, self-serving corporate shark who sexually harasses her male employee, Tom Sanders (Michael Douglas), edging him out of the promotion he covets and threatening his credibility and career at DigiCom, the high-tech computer firm where they both work.

Disclosure, like David Mamet's *Oleanna* (1988), the two earliest films to deal with sexual harassment in the workplace, inscribes a strategic role reversal that positions women as the aggressors and men their victims within the changing workplace. This role reversal is not coincidental. Rather, it makes manifest the terms of a social panic fanned by the media events of a series of sexual scandals over the early nineties—the Clarence Thomas/Anita Hill controversy, the Tailhook scandal, and the publication of Senator Robert Packwood's diaries.

Furthermore, the Supreme Court's sweeping decision in *Harris v. Forklift Systems, Inc.* (1993) recognized that "Title VII of the Civil Rights Act of 1964 is violated when the workplace is permeated with discriminatory behavior that is sufficiently severe or pervasive to create a hostile or abusive working environment." Sexual harassment, thus codified as a punishable offense, brought in its wake a power shift between men and women, "a shift accompanied by a great deal of anger as the rules of the office game change[d]" (James 1994, B1).

A paean to "an ordinary Joe pushed to the limits by a big bad, unreasonable world," the film's unspoken mantra is that women in power are "scary" (Maslin 1994, C1). Pandering to "raw male anxieties . . . from legitimate concerns over one's behavior being interpreted as harassment to nightmares of sexually castrating, scheming executrixes and rage at imagined injustices of affirmative action policies" (Bordo 1997, 51), cinematic texts like *Disclosure* tagged sexual harassment, like equal opportunity laws and affirmative action programs before it, as the newest bewildering shift affecting the corporate ranks.

The film opens with two short but instructive sequences that establish the protagonist, Tom Sanders, within a particular set of crises and constraints. We are first introduced to the morning bustle of the Sanders home, children dawdling and parents scurrying. As the camera pans the inside of the large, comfortable home, we find Eliza (Faryn Einhorn), a girl of about five, standing at her father's desk perusing the contents of an e-mail message that has just arrived for him. As she reads the message out loud, we learn that Sanders is an executive at a high-tech firm and that he is in line for a major promotion.

Anticipating the announcement of the promotion that morning, Sanders and his wife, Susan (Caroline Goodall), have been jittery and the morning has been chaotic. Unsupervised, their son Matt (Trevor Einhorn) has slopped toothpaste all over his shirt. Susan, a part-time lawyer, ends a phone conversation with a colleague, rushing to clean up the mess as she grumbles about her husband's ineptitude with the children. In a vain effort at asserting a paternal claim, Sanders explains to Eliza, "I'm the father. When the father says 'put your jacket on,' you put your jacket on." Offering a corrective to her father's old-fashioned notions, Eliza informs him that her friend "Marielle doesn't have a father. She has two mothers." Stumped for a response, Sanders mumbles, "That's interesting," hurrying the children out of the house.

A few minutes later, we find Sanders riding the morning ferry into the city engaged in a brief conversation with an older fellow passenger, asking how his job search is going. We learn that after twenty-eight years with IBM, the older man has been laid off in a move toward corporate downsizing. As the man puts it, he has been "surplused" in a "smaller, faster, cheaper, better" world. "If they wanted a euphemism, they should've said 'sodomized,'" the co-passenger laments. Seeking to help in some way, Sanders hands the man one of his business cards, suggesting he should give Cindy (Jacqueline Kim), Sanders's personal assistant, a call. Gazing at the card, the man muses, "Cindy—pretty name. Used to have fun with the girls. Nowadays, she probably wants your job."

Several key elements are introduced in these opening scenes. Sanders is an upper-middle-class white male facing typical burdens of contemporary American masculinity. His career forces him into the role of "absent father" to his children, hence his relative incompetence at parenting. He is a sensitive male of the nineties, however, for he makes an awkward but sincere effort at sharing child-care duties. He endures Susan's impatience, aware that he is in need of her tutelage. His futile efforts at preachy fatherhood are met by canny retorts from the children, reminders of how he has grown out of touch with the changing circumstances of the American family. Toward the end of the first scene of the film, then, we are introduced to a set of crises attending contemporary masculinities where the American family man is positioned as ineffective, overwhelmed, and, perhaps, disposable.

The disposability of the American male is reiterated in the ferry scene but in graver terms, for this time it is inscribed in the context of the workplace. The unnamed co-passenger who has been ousted from the corporate ranks after a lifetime of service offers living proof of circulating masculinist anxieties about shifts in the American workplace and the status of white men as an endangered species. Imperiled and resentful, the older man is a dinosaur in a rapidly changing workplace who gives voice to a secret nostalgia for times when "girls like Cindy" would not dare think of taking a man's job. As the "smaller, faster, cheaper, better" bottom line of contemporary commerce "sodomizes" the obsolescent patriarch, he is a hapless victim of social change. We are asked to indulge his chauvinisms as we would those of an elderly relative too set in his ways and against whom we are invited to assess the protagonist's progressiveness.[6]

Several contradictions are discernible here. For one, Sanders does in fact enjoy the services of Cindy Chang, his loyal personal assistant who is a woman in a position of obvious subservience to him. Despite the implausibility of her posing any real threat to Sanders or the older man, the exchange on the ferry fuels a ready suspicion of workers like her. Sanders is neither surprised nor offended by the older man's chauvinisms. Instead, imaginaries of the ideal worker—coded masculine—are reiterated in the threat posed by "girls like Cindy" on grounds that they "probably want your job." Thus, the exchange on the ferry makes keenly visible the enduring sexism of double standards that indulgently reserve for male upstarts the status of "mavericks" and "go-getters" while women in similar positions are branded "castrating bitches" and "pushy broads."

Ignoring the possibility that incompetence, obsolescence, or corruption may have spurred the older man's ouster, Sanders has assumed, with little evidence beyond the anecdotal, that the changing rules of the office game are to blame for his predicament. As the exchange on the ferry plays on unsubstantiated male anxieties about "girls like Cindy," by the end of the scene Sanders has chivalrously offered to help him find a new position and the older man, with unctuous ease, has accepted his offer of help. Unwittingly perhaps, both men have thus confirmed their privileged access to old-boy networks that remain stubbornly white and male.

As the audience is primed for a tale of heroic martyrdoms and narrow escapes for white men in today's workforce, we find Sanders, shocked and numb, riding the ferry home after his terrifying sexual encounter with his boss, Meredith Johnson. There he spots the unnamed older male sitting mutely on the other side of the deck. Averting his gaze and deliberately choosing a seat on the far end of the ferry, Sanders realizes, perhaps for the first time, that he and the co-passenger are both literally and figuratively in the same boat.[7] Like the unnamed Everyman on the ferry, Sanders faces dismissal and dishonor, and as if to confirm the older man's every resentful suspicion, Sanders's greatest challenge has come in the form of a conniving career woman.

From this point on, the film sets itself as a tale of dramatic conflict and intrigue as Sanders is located as the "great white hope" within a Darwinian fight for economic and sexual survival. Within the doomed downward spiral that threatens male workers young and old alike, Sanders is positioned at the cusp of an evolutionary turn, teetering between fanny-smacking boss and colorless, sexless worker. A tragic hero, Sanders logs critical lessons for white males in the new American workplace, for there is no doubt that he must learn new tricks if he is to survive.

It is this sense that *Disclosure* offers a redemptive response to Joel Schumacher's controversial 1993 film, *Falling Down*. Advertised as "the adventures of an ordinary man at war with the everyday world," *Falling Down* tells the nightmarish tale of William Foster (Michael Douglas), laid off from his job in the California defense industry and estranged from his family, who, over the course of a hot summer day in Los Angeles, transforms into the rampaging robo-citizen named D-Fens. Like the last straw on a camel's back, D-Fens's varied encounters with churlish "foreigners," wasteful city workers, and smug neo-Nazis cause him to snap. His responses reveal a seething anger beneath the seemingly tranquil surface of everyday life.

Mirroring incidents of "layoff rage" where disgruntled employees "arm themselves to the teeth and shoot up the office or the local branch of McDonald's" (Tahmincioglu 2001, C1), D-Fens "goes postal"[8] on his enemies. The Korean shopkeeper who fleeces his customers, the smirking, unhelpful staff at the fast food restaurant who refuse to serve him because it is a few seconds after the appointed breakfast hour, Puerto Rican gang members who threaten and bully him for trespassing their territory, and the neo-Nazi who grinningly reveals his basement stash of semi-automatic weapons—each adversary is "set straight" in episodes of spectacular Rambo-like violence.

For Robert Friedman, spokesperson for Warner Brothers, *Falling Down* "is a wake-up call" that serves to "show the viewer that society is out of control. Basically, no one is left untouched here" ("Minorities, Engineers Protest Depiction" 1993, B12). As the filmmaker Joel Schumacher explains, "there have been several movies in the US about anger in the street but they have all been by African-Americans. Well, they're not the only angry people in the United States" (Salisbury 1993, 76–78). Dramatizing white male rage at "things gone wrong," *Falling Down* is expressly a cautionary tale, a worst-case scenario of white men's responses to "everyday outrages" personified by immigrants, minimum wage workers, and big bureaucracy.

Despite its concern for what it perceives as a simmering rage among white males, however, *Falling Down* offers its protagonist no recourse. By

William Foster/D-Fens (Michael Douglas) directs his ire at others he encounters over the course of a daylong rampage in *Falling Down* (Joel Schumacher, 1993).

the end of the tale, D-Fens is a "perverted martyr," a victim of his own paranoias (Davies 1995, 224). Despite his start as sympathetic Everyman, by film's end he has devolved into a crazed vigilante, perishing in a blaze of monstrous and impotent rage, unfit as husband, father, or worker.

By contrast, the affirmative action hero in *Disclosure* is equipped with an enviable flexibility, a talent for morphing with changing times. Rectifying the bogus excesses of *Falling Down*, Sanders offers a model for action, a way out for white males in the workforce. Directing him away from reactionary critiques and the giddy rush of retribution, *Disclosure* offers its hero the means to escape the multicultural bog that threatens to engulf him. The dark fate that befalls D-Fens in *Falling Down* is, thus, rewritten in *Disclosure* with a protagonist who faces the frightening realities of the changing workplace by remaking himself rather than escaping them through wishful nostalgia or violent vigilantism.

Toward such a renewal, *Disclosure* focuses on Sanders's metamorphosis and retraining, his remarkable emergence as faltering hero of the new workplace. It is his dry-mouthed discovery and triumphant disclosure of the villainous secret that we are meant to identify with, his crossover from corporate outsider to adept insider, that the film centrally celebrates. By the end of the tale, Sanders has saved DigiCom and its shareholders from losing out on a lucrative merger deal. The technological innovations on which his team has been working are rescued from sabotage, and without any compromise on the "smaller, faster, cheaper, better" bottom line. He has himself triumphed over scandal and dishonor. The familiar heroic savior is thus recuperated and by the end has restored common sense to the post–civil rights excesses of the workplace.

Over the course of this remarkable renewal, Sanders emerges as an unlikely poster boy for feminism. When Sanders's wife learns about the harassment episode and that Johnson's allegations may cost Sanders his job, she reveals that, like many other women in the workplace, she too has encountered the unwanted advances of male colleagues. But rather than flying into a rage like him, she does what all women do. As she puts it, "We deal with it, we don't make a federal case out of it." Urging a reticent approach, she cajoles him to "just apologize and get [his] job back."

Sanders explodes in self-righteous indignation, and embodying feminist rage for the harassment he has endured, he screams, "Sexual harassment is about power! When did I have the power? When?"[9]

At a later point in the story, when the loyal Cindy Chang is called in to testify against Sanders in the quasi-legal mediation the company has arranged to settle Johnson's charge, we learn that Sanders frequently touches her, rubbing her shoulders and sometimes playfully smacking her on the buttocks. She reveals in her testimony that despite her discomfort, she has never reported this behavior. Both Susan, Sanders' wife, and Cindy, his personal assistant, are thus working women who, until they have Sanders's example, are poor warriors for feminism, for they have not responded with outrage at sexual harassment in the workplace.

Like the cross-dressing Dorothy Roberts (Dustin Hoffman) in Sydney Pollack's *Tootsie* (1982) and the outrageous but affable drag queens in Beeban Kidron's *To Wong Foo, Thanks for Everything, Julie Newmar* (1995), here, too, it is the male who offers women a model for feminist politics. Without him, the women have remained acquiescent, and it has fallen predictably on the white hero to open their eyes and show them the way to their emancipation.

Greater even than his gift to feminism is Sanders's service to the mythic meritocracy. Critical moments of ideological discipline are worked into the narrative by showcasing shifts in key individuals' attitudes about equal opportunity in the workplace. Take, for instance, Bob Garvin (Donald Sutherland), CEO of DigiCom, for whom Sanders works. Garvin, an opportunistic businessman who will scheme, connive, and cajole, whichever ensures him the largest returns, is seen addressing the DigiCom staff early in the narrative. "Every time I've wanted to break the glass ceiling," Garvin explains, "it's always been the same story, 'but Bob . . . but Bob . . .' I've thought about it often, since my daughter's death, that in today's climate, had she lived, it would be extremely rare that she ever got to run a company." The camera cuts to Meredith Johnson, and Garvin continues, "So it has a special meaning for me when I tell you that this Friday when we announce the merger, we will also announce that the new Vice President for Advanced Operations and Planning in Seattle will be Meredith Johnson."

As Garvin's decision to appoint Johnson is justified by the old guard's strategic, if ultimately disingenuous, alliance with liberal feminism, his choice is marred by traces of nepotism. As he makes explicit, it is Garvin's unfulfilled dream for his daughter to "get to run a company" that is realized by Johnson's appointment to the post of vice president. Efforts to break the glass ceiling and to provide equal opportunities for women in the workforce are, thus, gratuitously equated with nepotism in the post–affirmative action workplace.

Garvin addresses the staff a second time toward the end of the film, this time singing a different tune. "I have probably focused too much on breaking the glass ceiling," he confesses, "on finding a woman to run things up here, when what I should have been looking for, is the best person." The camera cuts to Sanders this time, and Garvin continues, "Someone whose long service with this company has established a record of creativity, sound judgment, and hands-on expertise. And that person is Stephanie Kaplan."

The clever last-minute turn to Stephanie Kaplan (Rosemary Forsythe), wiser and more stable than Johnson or Sanders, inoculates the film from being read as anti-woman. And as the quietly competent Kaplan takes her place at the podium, Garvin's discipline is complete, for, although he has found a woman for the job, it is unlikely he will ever again pander to the gender-conscious project of liberal feminism. With Johnson's ouster and Garvin's reformation, the wounded meritocracy is liberated from nefarious schemes of race and gender, its survival assured as long as merit is disentangled from flawed logics of color and sex.

By film's end, moreover, both Kaplan and Sanders have made it up closer to the "top guys" in the firm, and both have traded centrally on Meredith Johnson's spectacular deviance from the norm to get there. We are invited to cheer Johnson's fall from grace and to imagine the newly appointed cadre of diversity hires, who like her are keenly different from the normative white masculinity of the hero. Shifting in critical ways from the enterprising and inventive heroes of earlier cinematic texts like John Landis's *Trading Places* (1983) and Mike Nichols's *Working Girl* (1988), Johnson and her lot are unruly outsiders, symptomatic of an unstoppable dry rot at the core of affirmative action regimes.

Marked by their difference from the norm and their uneasy assimilation into the American workplace, these gendered others disrupt established workplace culture and are injurious to morale. They offer narrative evidence of the follies of race- and gender-conscious social justice programs. The contrast provided by white male heroes like Sanders who must clean up the mess the new entrants inevitably find themselves in works effectively to construct advocates for and beneficiaries of civil rights reforms as an unethical and conspiratorial special interest bloc who by the nineties have fallen victim to their own excesses.

The narrative underscores Johnson's difference, using a number of representational tactics. From her first moment on camera, Johnson is slickly sexual. Dressed in figure-hugging skirts and patent leather stilettos,

Corporate climber Meredith Johnson (Demi Moore) accepts her new appointment as vice president for advanced operations and planning at the high-tech computer firm DigiCom in *Disclosure* (Barry Levinson, 1994).

Johnson renews the classic femme fatale. She is seductive and sinister, a woman with such an obvious and debilitating sexual power that the men at DigiCom are reduced to adolescent locker-room banter, giggling in a huddle as they compare their "boners." Quite unlike any other woman they have encountered in the workplace, Johnson elicits a lustful ogle, a good long look that disrupts and distracts.

While she does temporarily serve the profit incentives of the corporation, Johnson is ultimately a liability for the company, repeatedly described by Garvin and his cronies as "changing the way we do things at DigiCom." Furthermore, despite her abilities to "hang with the guys," Johnson has little technical know-how of the products she is slated to supervise. As Sanders puts it, "she wouldn't know the difference between software and a cashmere sweater." If Johnson has arrived at her promotion at DigiCom after "a career of great achievement and distinction," as Garvin puts it, Sanders's contempt for her technical skills now taints her accomplishments with the suggestion of unearned special treatment. Thus, within a few minutes of appearing on screen, Johnson's highly sexualized look and her lack of technical know-how suggest in combination that she has finagled her place at the boardroom table through undeserved affirmative action favors, and perhaps, by "sleeping her way to the top."

Her technical ineptitude, moreover, combines with a toxic malevolence toward ethical and qualified workers like Sanders. As the narrative progresses, Johnson transforms visibly from steely, scheming executrix to snarling, rapacious beast. As the treacherous and sinister figure of the "Oriental" in early Hollywood productions gave voice to racist fears of the "yellow peril," representations of the woman in power of the affirmative action genre bespeak widespread apprehension over the influx of dangerous new entrants in the post–civil rights workplace. Where male villains of the affirmative action genre tend to be scripted as reactionary sexists, oafish leaders of the old guard, the enemy portrayed by Johnson is in a category all her own. She is a feral beast, a man-eater who is malicious, bloodthirsty, and out for your life/job.

So defined, the man-eater is reduced to her spectacular deviance from the norm. Such is the force of Johnson's sexual urge that she is unable to stop herself once the sexual encounter with Sanders begins. Eerily reminiscent of lingering stereotypes of the hypersexual Jezebel who cannot control her impulses, Johnson's advances are savage, her sexuality so wild that she is herself a victim of its demands. Likewise, she reacts with near-maniacal fury when Sanders rejects her advances, and at the dramatic climax she snarls liked an animal cornered, realizing that she can no longer evade disclosure. A deliberate "politics of Negroization" is discernible in these scenes, so that in the profoundly mythic arena of the cinematic, dangerous women like Johnson not only deserve ouster from the corporate ranks but they must also be representationally condensed with historical archetypes of hypersexed blackness.

Such indictments are not invented in filmic genres alone. Johnson's transformation from human to animal is comparable to the "blacking up" of African American villains in policy debates over affirmative action. Thus, the rapacious man-eater is an itinerant across discursive domains, pilfering elements of the venomous black racist and the lustful quota queen, categories that, as the previous chapter has shown, were excoriated in racially specific terms in public campaigns against affirmative action during the nineties. As women vamps and black supporters of affirmative action alike are "blackened" in their respective indictments, in the movies as in the policy arena, blackness emerges as the unwavering constant against which normality, functionality, and workplace virtue are defined.

By the film's denouement, we learn that Johnson acted in collusion with Garvin and several other men high in the corporate hierarchy in her efforts to sabotage Sanders. As she states with a pout at the end, "I'm only playing the game the way you guys set it up. And I'm being punished for it." Despite Sanders's derision for Johnson in this scene, she has in fact got it right this time, for at no point in the narrative are the men held responsible for their part in the scheme. The conniving, power-hungry woman is the only one disgraced, and she alone takes the fall.

At the end, then, we discern a petty double standard, which suggests not only that some corporate malefactors are more deserving of censure than others but, moreover, that the institutional structure of the American workplace is prone to oust only the most visibly disruptive others. As Garvin and his lackeys lap up the rewards that the corporate game has yielded, Johnson deserves her comeuppance, in large part because of her spectacular deviance from the norm.

In marked contrast, the most saintly of post–civil rights era heroes, whom the affirmative action film celebrates centrally, is the figure of the martyred white female. Laine Hanson (Joan Allen), the battered but victorious candidate for the vice presidency in Rod Lurie's *The Contender* (2000), is just such a figure, a politically correct doppelganger for white males and their particular burden of anxieties and frustrations.

Like the martyred heroines of Ridley Scott's *Thelma and Louise* (1991); the shadowy and anonymous No-Face who battles both cops and robbers in Warren Beatty's *Dick Tracy* (1990), who, we learn at film's end, is the alter ego of the cabaret temptress Breathless Mahoney (Madonna); and Ellie Arroway (Jodie Foster), the brilliant and dedicated astronomer who becomes a laughingstock among her peers by the end of Robert Zemeckis's *Contact* (1997), Laine Hanson poses a particularly feminist threat to male workers in the workplace. She bears witness to scandalous secrets of the American workforce and, as is typical in such cinematic scenarios, is martyred by silence, containment, and/or death by the end of the narrative.

Standards of the idealized worker take on mythic proportions as *The Contender* recounts the events of the first nomination of a woman to the vice presidency of the United States. The sitting vice president has died, and Jackson Evans (Jeff Bridges), the Democratic president, now serving a second term, wants to put a woman in office as his vice president. It is his chance to make it into the history books. As Kermit Newman (Sam Elliott), the White House chief of staff, puts it, "It is the President's swan song."

Wearing its liberal biases on its sleeve, *The Contender* sets up an old guard of archconservative politicians who orchestrate a viciously misogynist tone to the confirmation hearings that ensue. The film lingers on the contrast it establishes between the saintly Hanson and Shelley Runyon (Gary Oldman), the Republican senator from Illinois who opposes Hanson's nomination and actively sabotages her confirmation. In a blustery speech to a group of his aides gathered in his chamber a few hours before the start of the hearings, Runyon sets up the battle lines: "It is now up to us to light the spark which will result in a moral uprising so that we may have a new birth of national honesty and decency . . . Laine Hanson is a cancer, a cancer of liberalism, a cancer of disloyalty. Her nomination itself is the cancer of affirmative action . . . she is the cancer of virtuous decay."

Runyon's villainy is exemplified in his distress over Hanson's presence as a malignant outgrowth of the sixties, "a cancer of liberalism . . . of disloyalty . . . of affirmative action" as he puts it. The liberal feminist critique at the core of the film espouses clean distinctions between conservatives and liberals, old-fashioned sexists and modern men. The text focuses on Runyon's sexisms and consequently directs attention away from the gender-conscious project that the majority of men who appear in the film, including the president, the White House staff, and Hanson's own entourage of aides and assistants, are engaged in. After all, Evans has nominated Hanson to the vice presidency for the same reason that Runyon opposes her candidacy—because she is a woman.[10]

Like the David Duke advertisement aired by the Stop Prop 209 campaign in California in 1996 that was designed to attack anti–affirmative action voices as "racists of the worst order,"[11] *The Contender* proffers an outdated critique of old-fashioned sexisms, making no effort to challenge the vast edifice of systemic sexisms from which the majority of men, liberals and conservatives alike, continue to reap benefits.

In our first encounter with Hanson, a couple is engaged in noisy foreplay in a darkened bedroom. The phone rings, interrupting them, and a half-dressed man rises to take the call. "No, no, don't answer it," the woman implores playfully. She giggles and purrs, as the man takes the call, ignoring her protests. We learn that it is the president asking to speak with Senator Hanson. As the man hands the phone to the prone figure in bed, we realize that *she* is Senator Laine Hanson, Democrat of Ohio, Evans's first choice for vice president. The formulaic device of the midday sexual tryst, suggestive of extramarital temptation and clandestine passions, is the context for our first encounter with Hanson. Underneath the suit-clad, policy-talking senatorial exterior, Hanson is, at base, a woman, and, thus, defined by sexual difference.

In the limousine ride to the White House, we find Hanson, the nymph from the previous scene, dressed demurely in a suit. We learn that the man she has just had sex with is Will Hanson (Robin Thomas), her husband. She is noticeably giddy about the president's invitation, but she urges members of her campaign team riding with her to be calm. Coy and debutante-like, she murmurs, "I haven't even been asked yet." At the White House, Evans and his staff repeatedly comment on her appearance. "You look great," says the president. "That's a great suit," the chief of staff adds. Hanson's sexual escapade still fresh in the audience's mind, the narrative now makes a slow turn to recuperate her. In a series of such equivocations, Hanson will journey haltingly from the slut to the suit for the remainder of the film.

The narrative focuses on a series of dramatic events that are initiated when, over the course of the confirmation hearings, photographic evidence emerges that suggests that, as a college coed, Hanson participated in an evening of group sex at a drunken fraternity party. The senator is dismayed at the revelations, but she refuses to address them. As the cloud of suspicion grows, rumor and gossip hold sway, and Hanson's refusal to respond publicly is read increasingly as cowardice, and by Runyon's camp as an admission of guilt. When the president and his team urge her to make a public response to Runyon's accusations, she is resolute in her refusal, explaining, "If I answer their questions, that would mean it was okay for them to have been asked in the first place, and it isn't."

This is an important statement for the film, and it is repeated at a later point in the narrative. This time, it is the idealistic and inexperienced Reginald Webster (Christian Slater), Democrat from Delaware, who urges Hanson to come clean. One of the youngest members of the House of Representatives, Webster is unwilling to be sidetracked by party loyalties and dirty politics. He breaks ranks with the Democrats in the House, and, against the president's advice, volunteers himself to Runyon's team so that he may do his part to uncover the truth about Hanson. Positioned as the voice of the common man, Webster is a Capra-esque character, a modern-day Mr. Smith, who fearlessly puts his political career on the line for the sake of truth and ethical government.

He approaches Hanson at the height of the media events of the hearings, seeking to understand why she refuses to put the rumors and allegations to rest. When she demurs, explaining that "my personal life is just nobody's business," Webster counters, arguing, "that's not what the people will tell you. The people will tell you that it *is* their business. That you're setting the standards of morality for their children, especially their girls." Hanson, smiling wryly at Webster, asks him if he remembers a man by the name of Isaac Lamb. When Webster confesses that he does not, she explains that Lamb was the first person to come before the House Un-American Activities Committee hearings of the fifties. She continues: "He was the first one to name names, the first one to cooperate with the government. The dominoes fell from there, careers crashed, families destroyed. Just imagine, Mr. Webster, what if Mr. Lamb had just said 'Fuck you!' to the Committee. Imagine how much harder he would have made it for them." "Are you accusing the committee of sexual McCarthyism, Senator?" Webster exclaims, and Hanson replies: "I just can't respond to the Committee's lightly veiled accusations because it's not okay for them to be made. If I were a man, nobody would care how many sexual partners I had when I was in college. And if it's not relevant for a man, it's not relevant for a woman."

Hanson's private torture but public calm, her efforts to valiantly "stay above the fray, insisting her personal life is no one's business, and that a double standard exists for women" (Westbrook 2000, 1) locate her as a present day Joan of Arc willing to burn at the stake for her beliefs. She is ethical to a fault, a suffering martyr who will forsake political ambitions for principles. Reminiscent of scrupulously clean and ethically overendowed black characters from Hollywood texts of the sixties who contrasted sharply with vulgar white racists in films like Stanley Kramer's *Guess Who's Coming to Dinner* (1967) and Norman Jewison's *In the Heat of the Night* (1967), Hanson serves as a perfect foil for the reactionary excesses of dirty politicians like Shelley Runyon. Far from the "sex-crazed home-wrecking machine" that the confirmation hearings have made her out to be, Hanson even has a private sermon or two for the president. As she reminds him at the end of the film, "Principles only mean something if you stick by them when they're inconvenient."

However, Hanson's self-righteous silence takes its cues from liberal imperatives of color- and gender-blindness. Her promise as an effective vice president and her location as martyred heroine turn on her willingness to submit to "objective" standards of the mythic meritocracy. Thus, her resolute stand against sexist double standards exemplifies the burdens that working women bear, but it also serves effectively to vilify race- and gender-consciousness. The best, and perhaps only, way for women to receive equal treatment in the American workplace, Hanson suggests, is for them to align themselves with hegemonic standards of the genderless, colorless worker.

Consistent with the terms of contemporary policy assaults on affirmative action, then, Hanson and the "model majority" of women she represents position themselves in opposition to precisely those rationales of the sixties that gave rise to equal opportunity and affirmative action mandates. Offering a sexually correct affirmation of the fruits of a gender-blind meritocracy, Hanson provides living proof that continuing attachments to anachronistic gendered standards invented during the sixties are at cause for the sexist double standards of today's workplace.

When, at film's end, the House, in an unlikely show of open-mindedness, votes to confirm the president's morally impugned nominee, *The Contender* appears well on its way to affirming the sexual independence of women, as well as their right to aspire to the highest levels of political and economic power. In these sequences, the film ventures toward stunning indictments of sexist double standards in contemporary society and of the viciously misogynist old guard that perpetuates glass ceilings for women in the workforce.

But just as it appears that the film might deliver on its promise to coming generations of women,[12] we encounter key moments of abnegation in the film. For example, in a predictable turn of events, Hanson is rescued in the end by the mild-mannered but shrewd President Evans, who blindsides Runyon into a career-damaging ambush. Over a private steak and cigars dinner on the president's yacht, Evans uses the pretense of an old-boy deal with Runyon to manipulate him into a blunder that will become public in later scenes. Evans emerges as the able patriarch to the distressed Hanson, cannily trading his patronage for her loyalty. Thus, Hanson is recuperated at the end of the tale as a woman consigned to the protective custody of the male lead.

Similarly, late in the narrative, at the victorious close of the confirmation hearings, we find the president and Hanson taking an evening stroll on the back lawns of the White House. The two are engaged in an intimate, mutually confessional exchange. While the narrative has until this point celebrated Hanson's fierce individualism and her remarkable strength of character in the face of scandal and humiliation, in this final scene, we find her gratuitously answering all the questions that she has resolutely refused to answer for the whole of the film.

We now learn that the woman in the pictures engaging in the fraternity sex romp that Runyon has used to great effect in his attack against the nominee is not Hanson at all. Although the narrative has repeatedly implied her part in the lurid sexual encounter, the audience is now reassured that Hanson never was the sex-crazed nymph her detractors made her out to be. As Hanson successfully journeys once again from the slut to the suit, both the president and the audience are permitted a collective sigh of relief as Hanson is recuperated from disruptive sexual excess to virtuous sexual modesty. Reneging on its commitments to female independence and sexual autonomy, *The Contender* ends on a cautious note, containing the destabilizing threat of sexual difference and the toxic potential of sexual excess in the workplace.

Over the course of the narrative, Hanson's main competition comes from the soft-spoken and mild-mannered party loyalist Jack Hathaway (William L. Petersen), who is also the Democratic governor of Virginia. The opening scenes of the film find the governor on a fishing boat, being interviewed by a news reporter. As he discusses his support for abortion rights and flat taxes, a car careens off a bridge and into the lake nearby. Risking his own life, Hathaway dives into the lake in an attempt to rescue the unfortunate driver. As he recounts to the president a few days later, he finds a "pretty young woman, her face filled with terror" at the end of his descent into the frigid waters. The car door is jammed shut, he recalls, and he is unable to save the woman from drowning in her car. The incident propels Hathaway into the national spotlight, showered with accolades as an old-fashioned hero. Even the president confesses, "If it was me, I'm not sure I would have dove [*sic*] in there."

The Contender thus opens with a remarkable discrepancy in how it introduces Hanson in comparison to Hathaway. The narrative's gratuitous focus on her as sexual object and him as exceptional hero seems nevertheless to be a setup, and it is no surprise when, at film's end, it is revealed that Hathaway has in fact staged the drowning rescue. The doomed woman, a reservist in the army, was paid a sizable fee for agreeing to drive her car off the appointed bridge to allow Hathaway the opportunity to "save" her. As Hathaway is exposed as an opportunistic fraud and charged with negligent homicide, *The Contender* raises questions about contemporary heroism and its relation to hegemonic masculinity.

Beyond his glaring lapses of ethical judgment—his willingness to stage the scam rescue, the tragic and accidental murder of the reservist, and his disingenuous acceptance of praise for acts of bravery he did not commit—Hathaway is also positioned as an emasculated male in his privately tortured personal life. As the limousine delivers the governor from the Oval Office to his house on the outskirts of the city, Fiona (Kristen Shaw), Hathaway's sharp-tongued wife, is waiting on the steps of their home. Hathaway is returning from a much-anticipated meeting with the president, and Fiona is visibly agitated, for she has already learned from news reports on television that the president has passed up her husband for his vice presidential nominee.

Like Tom and Susan Sanders at the start of *Disclosure*, the Hathaways have anticipated the nomination for the past three weeks, and the disappointed Fiona now explodes with bilious rage: "You know, this is the second time they've fucked us over . . . Are you just going to take it up the ass? You want to bend over and make their job a little easier? Do you understand what is going on here? This is it. The whole fucking plan, Jack, everything we did to get to this point. We had one shot at this and it's gone, and you're just going to mope around like some fucking twelve-year-old girl who can't get a date to the dance." Tired and defeated, Hathaway asks, "What would you like me to do, Fiona?" "I'd like you to give a shit, Jack," she hisses. "I'd like you to call Shelley Runyon back, and I'd like you to get this fucking thing fixed."

Revisiting age-old stereotypes of the publicly demure but privately conniving "woman behind every successful man," Fiona Hathaway is an embittered and frustrated creature. She echoes shades of Meredith Johnson, venomously disparaging and doggedly ambitious, both excluded from the male fraternity. Hathaway is reduced to spineless excuses as Fiona's hissed accusations taunt him in specific terms for behaving like "a twelve-year-old girl who can't get a date to the dance," someone who is spinelessly "just going to take it up the ass." The homophobic assaults in this scene reveal that Hathaway's crime is not simply that he has bungled the staged rescue but, rather, that he falls far below hegemonic standards of masculinity.

Such narrative oppositions between the gutless, weak-willed man and the rapacious, beastly woman illuminate the ethical cadences of the saintly white woman worker. If Hanson is the newfangled hero of the post–civil rights era workforce, her victory is premised on calling out bloodthirsty women and blundering men alike. In other words, Hanson—representationally opposed to both Hathaway's craven ineptitude and Fiona's snarling malevolence—serves mainly to reiterate masculinist mythologies of conscience and courage. Her "favored son" status works to suggest that only those women—and men—who match up to such ready, "objective" standards deserve a place among the leadership of our time.

Rogue Feminists and the Figurative Phallus

Women workers most deserving of admiration and acceptance, as Laine Hanson demonstrates, are not merely those who survive the mudslinging and backstabbing of workplace games but those who emerge victorious, like favored sons in manhood rituals. Shape-shifters who perform in white male disguise, these characters submit themselves to the masculinist standards of the workplace. They pass for insiders at the white man's game even if it demands that they grow a metaphoric phallus to prove their mettle as one of the boys. The more authentic the performance, the greater the reward.

Stephanie Kaplan, the ethical choice for promotion at DigiCom, the high-tech computer firm in *Disclosure*, is a veteran of the corporate workplace. A woman quite unlike the scheming Meredith Johnson, Kaplan is older, plainer, and notably desexualized.[13] She keeps her ear to the ground and is as canny about digital technologies as cloak-and-dagger office games. Over the years, she has earned the moniker of "stealth bomber" among her staff and colleagues, a fitting handle, for as we learn at film's end, it is Kaplan who has been anonymously passing along key pieces of information that help Sanders expose Johnson in a series of mysterious e-mail messages.[14] If some battles in the corporate game demand forthrightness and showy heroics, Kaplan reminds us that others are won surreptitiously, through guile and cunning.

In her efforts to help the bungling Sanders, Kaplan has orchestrated the collusion of her son Spencer (David Drew Gallagher), who is a student at the nearby University of Washington. Spencer has access to the office and computer accounts of his faculty mentor, who is fortuitously traveling overseas, and it is from this account that Kaplan has been sending Sanders the anonymous e-mail messages. Thus, in an elaborate series of tactics, Kaplan has arranged the assistance of her son, the traveling professor, and Sanders in her bid for promotion in the corporate hierarchy. She has acted underhandedly, and perhaps with malice toward Johnson. But while Johnson is ousted as bad fruit of affirmative action, Kaplan, who uses much the same means—guile, secrecy, treachery—is rewarded with the promotion to vice president.

Kaplan's abilities and choices, therefore, spell out what are, for the narrative, key parameters of the ideal worker in the modern workforce. Having cracked open the muddy secret of the sabotage, Kaplan has nudged Sanders's transformation from naïve technical wonk to skillful corporate player. She has anonymously tipped off the insiders to betray

Johnson in uncompromising loyalty to workplace hierarchies. She performs the "dick in drag," as bell hooks puts it (1994, 22), carefully scripted as an indispensable operative in the misogynist culture of the workplace.

Women like Kaplan serve as liminal interlocutors who tirelessly police the borders of the mythic meritocracy, vigilant lookouts at corporate masts ferreting out sexual difference and deviance from the norm. Her oblique machinations force Johnson's betrayal and Garvin's reformation, and both are achieved without threat to the rules of the corporate game. In turn, Kaplan is welcomed with open arms into the corporate establishment, in no small measure because she guarantees that, unlike Johnson, she can be counted on to discipline, and when necessary excise, the disrupting form of the woman in the workplace.

While the men in *Disclosure* find themselves undone by Meredith Johnson's seductions, the women at DigiCom stay impervious to her designs. Thus, Katherine Alvarez (Roma Maffia), the tough-talking, celebrity-seeking lawyer whom Sanders hires in response to Johnson's allegations of sexual misconduct, and Mary Anne Hunter (Suzie Plakson), Sanders's plain Jane colleague in the Advanced Operations unit, "the only woman in her engineering classes in college," who, as she puts it, "had to work twice as hard at everything the men did," like Stephanie Kaplan, are unfazed by Johnson's wiles.

As Amy Robinson explains in her writing about "passing," these women may be read as "clairvoyant members of the in-group" (1994, 715–16) who by virtue of biological closeness with Johnson are able to see through her charms. Like black doormen posted outside lavish hotels during the period of Jim Crow who were expected to detect and turn away blacks who tried to pass for whites in their attempts to enter exclusive spaces of white privilege, white women workers in contemporary workplaces serve as biologically endowed sentries posted at the gates of corporate hierarchies. Robinson explains:

> There is an indescribable something, which enables a Negro to spot a passer sometimes at a glance, and no doubt this accounts for the large number of colored doormen at theaters, dining rooms and other exclusive places.

> In the context of Jim Crow, the "indescribable something" that endows Negroes with a unique racial clairvoyance leads to their employment as optic sensors in whites-only establishments. (719)

Workers like Kaplan may, likewise, be positioned as gatekeepers patrolling the margins of white male-dominated workplaces to ensure that troublesome new entrants are excised. Akin to representatives of the model majority, successful women positioned at the forefront of public campaigns against affirmative action over the decade of the nineties, these voices lend credence to white male anxieties about reverse discrimination. Kaplan and her compatriots in the public policy arena serve the mythic meritocracy as no white male could. These figures impact on public consciousness, distilling anecdotes and cultural archetypes into authorized truths. Hence, in policy assaults as in cinematic genres, a familiar category of model women emerges, women who play by the rules, for whom gender is irrelevant, and who can be counted on deny their debts to social justice programs.

The paradoxical figure of Stephanie Kaplan is mirrored in key respects by the character of Lillian DeHaven (Anne Bancroft) in Ridley Scott's *G.I. Jane* (1996). The dramatic story of the first female to successfully make it through the harrowing training program for the elite Navy SEAL commando force, *G.I. Jane* opens at the scene of confirmation hearings for Theodore Hayes (Daniel von Bargen), secretary of the Navy designate. DeHaven is the formidable Democratic senator from Texas who presides crustily over the hearings.

We join the hearings already in progress and find Hayes making his statement to the committee. "Of course, women have always been a vital link in the lifeline that supplies combat units," he states. "The last few years have brought real progress in the interests of women in all aspects of naval service. What's more, the Navy has instituted special sensitivity courses for all its male recruits demonstrating even more progress in the area of . . ." DeHaven, sitting at the center of the podium and flanked on both sides by white men, interrupts the nominee impatiently. "Whoa, Whoa, Whoa! Mr. Hayes! If a cannibal used a fork and knife would you call that progress?" she asks derisively.[15] When the laughter that follows dies down, DeHaven continues, "I'm deeply concerned over the Navy's seemingly incontrovertible attitude about women in the military."

As a case in point, she reveals the contents of an internal document prepared by the Navy that reports on the circumstances of a recent crash involving a female aviator. Outraged at the ill-spirited tenor of the report, DeHaven points to degrading remarks by other aviators and innuendo in the report about the downed aviator's performance in unrelated situations. "There's even reference here to her sexual activity the weekend prior," DeHaven continues. "In my seven years on this committee, I have never seen a downed aviator treated like this," she barks, shaking the report at Hayes. With a subtle threat in her words, she concludes, "I'm deeply disturbed by this report, Mr. Hayes, not just for what it bodes for the future of women in the Navy but for your future as well."

Scrambling in response, the "defense boys" request a private meeting with DeHaven to propose a contingency program for "full gender-integration of the Navy." "If female candidates measure up in a series of test cases," the men explain, "the DOD [Department of Defense] will support full integration within three years' time." In a perfect quid pro quo, the Department of Defense gets their man, and DeHaven, "the ruthless barracuda," has won the promise of a gender-blind Navy.[16] Lillian DeHaven is thus introduced in the opening sequences of the film as a masterful politician, an old hand at the obligatory wheeling and dealing of the political arena.

We find the senator in her office, a few scenes later, perusing dossiers of potential candidates for the unprecedented gender-integration test case. An aide lists the qualifications of one candidate: "Top scores in marksmanship, distance runner, took fifth place in some inter-service marathon. Age: twenty-seven." The accompanying photograph shows a muscular, androgynous woman running track. "Perfect!" remarks DeHaven sarcastically. "Only, do a chromosome check." She rejects another, asking, "Is this the face you want to see on the cover of *Newsweek?* She looks like the wife of a Russian beet farmer." Finally, she spots the winning file and, smiling approvingly, remarks, "This is really top drawer, with silk stockings inside."

The senator's sexist scrutiny of the candidates' photographs is echoed in her probing questions a few days later at her first meeting with the "top drawer" recruit. Sizing up the young woman, DeHaven asks, "Have you got a man? A fiancé? Steady beau? You know, some kind of solvent heterosexual?" Reading confusion on the woman's face, she explains: "I hate to ask, but I don't want this thing blowing up in our faces if you happen to be backing for the other side."

DeHaven's focus on the recruit's physical appearance and sexual preferences are at odds with her public persona as the vociferous liberal feminist committed to dismantling the entrenched misogyny of the armed forces. In the privacy of her chambers, the senator is revealed as a political opportunist, handpicking the poster girl for her reelection campaign. DeHaven, it will appear, has taken on the integration of the military for its promise as a public relations venture. With it, she ensures herself a place in the history books, and just enough notoriety as a trailblazer to ensure success in the coming elections. Midway through the tale, when the military top brass secretly threaten her with multiple military base closings in her home state of Texas unless she finds a way of terminating the G.I. Jane venture, DeHaven folds, trading in the recruit she has hand-selected for votes in the coming elections. As she explains to the recruit, late in the film, "I never expected you to do so damn well. I thought you would ring out in two weeks. Bing, bang, it's over, and we're popular."

Like Stephanie Kaplan, the "stealth bomber" in *Disclosure*, the "barracuda" DeHaven is savvy about how the game is played. The behind-the-scenes machinations of these career women highlight the pitiful returns of the feminist agenda of the sixties, for neither Kaplan nor DeHaven shows any genuine commitment to the advancement of women other than themselves. Instead, these portrayals suggest that established old dames of the workforce self-indulgently reap the benefits of the social movements of the sixties while they renege on their responsibilities to future generations of women.

We first encountered the older, more established woman in mean-spirited competition with younger women with Katherine Parker (Sigourney Weaver), the plagiarizing boss in Mike Nichols's *Working Girl* (1988) who underhandedly passes off her secretary's ideas as her own. This portrayal of the liberal feminist of previous generations recurs in cinematic texts of recent years: for example, the aging beauty queen Kathy Morningside (Candice Bergen) in Donald Petrie's *Miss Congeniality* (2000) protests her ouster from the position of pageant organizer by plotting the murder of the new Miss United States, and a well-preserved fallen angel, Madison Lee (Demi Moore), attempts to trounce her father/boss and his fresh-faced team of luscious crime fighters in a spectacular Oedipal revival in McG's *Charlie's Angels: Full Throttle* (2003).

Each of these portrayals retraces the archetype of the rogue feminist, scripted with deliberate consistency as modern but malicious, empowered but unethical. Ironically, the murderous pageant organizer's motive in *Miss Congeniality* is ageism prompted by the Miss United States organization's announcement that it will soon replace her with a "younger model" despite her twenty-one years of diligent service. Likewise, the trigger-happy ex-angel in *Charlie's Angels: Full Throttle* orchestrates murder and mayhem as a form of "Amazon retribution" for what she perceives as her ex-employer Charles Townsend's sexist and patronizing habits. Nevertheless, these women take shape in cinematic texts simultaneously as poor soldiers for feminism and serve to impugn the feminist agenda as opportunistic sham. In this way, cinematic texts of the nineties plot an inescapable devolution for women who espouse feminist ideals of the sixties. Their feminisms at cause, these women are mired inexorably in crime and corruption. Like *G.I. Jane*'s Lillian DeHaven, they occupy the space of the dreaded feminist, their belligerent demands for gender equity and fairness recalling the cultural archetype of the "feminazi."[17] Feminists, by these accounts, are inherently unethical, and feminism, by extension, is intrinsically unprincipled.

Feeding circulating apprehensions, particularly among young women, that feminists hate men, that they are anti-sex, that they are all lesbians, and so on, cinematic portrayals of the rogue feminist are reinforced within the cultural environment of contemporary postfeminism. Celebrating heteronormative family values where teen superstars like Jessica Simpson and Britney Spears preach premarital abstinence and where reality television shows like *The Bachelorette* are proclaimed "a big win for feminists" (Holbrook 2003) on grounds that the harem of potential spouses is male instead of female, the postfeminist exhortation for "wonder bras not burning bras" finds a ready audience among moviegoers and voters alike.

Cinematic denouncements of the rogue feminist pilfer from cultural imaginaries of the dreaded feminazi whose motives are always already suspect. Thus, for example, female chief executives of small businesses who appeared in campaign commercials in Washington in 1998 and testified to being shut out of old-boy networks of privilege, like the cast of single mothers and lesbians who called out the "enemies of women's rights" in radio commercials of the Stop Prop 209 campaign in 1996 California, were drowned out with characteristic ease by hyperbolic accounts of rogue feminists that circulated on talk radio, network news, and in Hollywood films of the nineties. In contrast, women who distanced themselves from the legacies of feminism, those who expressed disavowal through the familiar refrain "I'm not a feminist, but . . . " curried favor in policy campaigns and affirmative action films alike.

Lieutenant Jordan "L.T." O'Neil (Demi Moore), the protagonist of *G.I. Jane*, is the first female to successfully make it through the punishing training program for the elite Navy SEAL commando force. Like Laine Hanson in *The Contender*, O'Neil presents an idealized representation of women workers in the post–civil rights workplace. Both heroines break new ground as they batter through the gendered glass ceiling, and both enjoy the prestige of being pioneers in previously all-male bastions. Despite their remarkable potential as poster women for feminism and affirmative action, however, each is carefully scripted away from such a disposition.

In a key scene soon after she has received DeHaven's invitation to train with the SEALs, O'Neil discovers that Royce (Jason Beghe), her boyfriend, is skeptical about her making it through the training program.

We find the couple sharing a bubble bath at the end of the day, discussing their options. As Royce sees it, the Navy's invitation is nothing more than a publicity stunt that will prove that integrating the armed services is unwise. "To tell you the truth, I don't get it," he confesses. "You're doing shit-hot at Intel. What do you want to go off and play soldier girl for?" Exasperated, he continues, "The SEALs, babe? These guys are world class warriors . . . They will eat cornflakes out of your skull."

Irritated by his patronizing tone, O'Neil responds: "Royce, we're the same age, we entered the Navy the same month and which one of us is wearing more ribbons? Operational experience is the key to advancement yet anyone with tits can't be on a sub, can't be a SEAL." If she did take DeHaven up on her invitation, she explains, it would not be to serve the senator's integrationist agenda. As she puts it, "this is just a career opportunity. The only thing that scares me are the sexual politics. I'm just not interested in being a poster girl for women's rights." Her interest in the training opportunity is thus carefully scripted away from structural change in the patriarchal standards of the armed services. Instead, O'Neil wants to try her hand at SEAL training because it would enable individual gain and, in particular, opportunities that she deserves but that have evaded her to this point.

Suspicious and fearful of feminists and the feminist agenda, O'Neil will neither found her politics on her gender nor reap unfair rewards from her identity as a woman. She will temporarily join forces with Lillian DeHaven, but only because lingering inequities force women to either be excluded from essential operational experience or to "sleep their way to the top." Subtly analogizing the performance of sexual favors in the workplace with the gender-conscious project of liberal feminism, O'Neil collapses key ethical distinctions. Equating the office feminist with the office slut, she finds both contemptible because they trade centrally on gender identity and difference in the workplace.

O'Neil's idealized and heroic gender blindness is contrasted with a persistent gender-consciousness among those with whom she interacts. DeHaven chooses her because she is a woman—and particularly a good-looking woman suitable for photo-ops. Royce doubts her abilities to make it through SEAL training because she is a mere woman. The men of her cohort are clearly uncomfortable; some joke and whistle, others simply leer. Theodore Hayes, the secretary of the Navy, who received his confirmation in exchange for supporting the G.I. Jane experiment, refers to her as "Joan of Arc meets Super Girl," for he cannot otherwise fathom how a woman has survived weeks of intensive test exercises. John Urgayle (Viggo Mortensen), the command master chief who is directly charged with O'Neil's training, nurtures a variety of responses to her—from contempt to admiration as the narrative progresses—and each is premised on the fact that she is a woman.

Commanding officer Salem (Scott Wilson), a sympathizer with the old guard, is resentful of meddlesome politicians and women like O'Neil who have forced the previously all-male bastion of the armed forces to endure bewildering changes in procedure and protocol. Unsure of himself at their first meeting, he holds out a chair for O'Neil as he invites her to sit down. He offers her a beverage and stubs out his cigar in a show of old-fashioned chivalry. When O'Neil asserts that she is not looking for any special treatment, the commanding officer replies condescendingly, "We're not trying to change your sex, Lieutenant." The only way a woman would avoid special treatment in the military, the commanding officer seems to suggest, is if she changed her sex. "Things may not always be smooth," he tells her, "but we are trying to make things as painless as possible." O'Neil tries once again to state her position. "I'm not here to make some kind of statement," she tells the officer. "All I care about is completing the training and getting some operational experience. Just like everyone else, I suspect." This time the commanding officer responds wryly: "If you were like everyone else, Lieutenant, I suspect we wouldn't be making statements about not making statements, would we?"

From the start, then, O'Neil's difference from the norm is visible and marked, a given in the testosterone-driven context of the armed services. Her difference necessitates adjustments to the routine. The training program must take steps to incorporate her into their program—separate quarters, separate medical facilities, and preferential access to the commanding officer. Her presence muddles military protocol, and the double standard that sets her up as an outsider ensures that she will never fit in with the rest of the recruits.

Mirroring real-life controversies over the place of women in the armed forces, *G.I. Jane* was released in the wake of highly publicized efforts by women to enter elite military academies like the Citadel and the Virginia Military Institute, both previously all-male colleges that fought a six-year battle in the courts to prevent women from being granted admission (Manegold 2000; Rein 2001, B1). As Stephen Hunter, writing for the *Washington Post*, puts it, "the closed men's locker room rife with the stench of sweat, gun lube and bourbon has been penetrated by the one thing to which it is vulnerable"—the powerful, disorienting presence of a woman (1997, D1).

Reinforced by its cultural context, the men in O'Neil's cohort are resentful and belligerent. At their first encounter in the mess tent, the male recruits gawk as she makes her entrance for the evening meal. Commenting on O'Neil's nipples, which are visible through her shirt as she comes in from the cold, one of them shouts lecherously, "Oh man!" Doesn't she know it's rude to point?" Through the whistles and catcalls that follow, one of them complains, "Look, I don't know what she did to get in here, I hate to speculate, but I know I petitioned for two years to get into this program. That's two years of letter writing! Two years of pulling strings! And now I finally get here, and it's gone co-ed?"

O'Neil's presence in the training unit is not simply disruptive. It is also potentially lethal. She is the weak link, the Achilles heel of the unit, and as command master chief Urgayle puts it, "her presence makes us all vulnerable." It is this sexist double standard—the male recruits are immune from endangering the unit but O'Neil is biologically prone to do so—that O'Neil seeks to dislodge. Unlike the ways that Meredith Johnson exploits her differences for personal gain, O'Neil wants nothing more than to erase those differences. She rejects the separate quarters and the thirty-point advantage she is offered on the physical endurance course. "One standard," she demands. "Treat me the same, no better, no worse."

As O'Neil attempts to assimilate, we are witness to her physical transformation from feminine other to masculine norm. Like the "toughening up" that Sherrie Inness (1999) has shown of Clarice Starling (Jodie Foster) in Jonathan Demme's *The Silence of the Lambs* (1991) and Dana Scully (Gillian Anderson) from Chris Cooper's cult-favorite television series *The X-Files* (1993–2001) where "toughness" equates to masculinization, here the camera lingers voyeuristically on O'Neil's taut, glistening muscles and sweaty torso. She sheds her earrings and shaves off her hair. The strenuous physical training interrupts her menstrual cycle. As each day passes, she sports facial abrasions and skin rashes from the rigors of combat training. Like warrior marks, each wound draws her closer to the elusive androgyny that is her ticket to acceptance among her cohort.

At a key moment of climax in the film, O'Neil and her team are engaged in a training exercise that requires them to play out an elaborate fictional raid on an enemy installation. They fail in their mission, and Urgayle, playing the part of enemy captain, takes O'Neil and her team prisoner. In an attempt to recreate authentic conditions of combat,

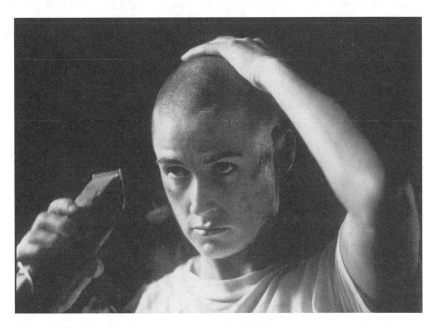

Lieutenant Jordan O'Neil (Demi Moore) shaves off her hair as she transforms to match her male Navy Seals compatriots in *G.I. Jane* (Ridley Scott, 1996).

Urgayle subjects O'Neil and her team to vicious beatings aimed at extracting information from the prisoners. As the torture continues, Urgayle focuses his assault on O'Neil, beating her severely. Urgayle is playing on masculine ideologies of chivalry, hopeful that the men on her team will end their silence to put an end to O'Neil's beating. Just when it appears that O'Neil has been clobbered into submission, Urgayle begins to cut open her pants in a mock rape, a routine tactic of wartime retribution. O'Neil uses this moment to slam her head into Urgayle's face, breaking his nose and reengaging the fight. As Urgayle finally knocks O'Neil down, he walks away, telling her contemptuously to "seek life elsewhere." And it is here that O'Neil, turning the final corner in her evolution to the masculine, staggers to her feet and barks back, "Suck my dick!"

O'Neil's claim to a phallus is received with cheers and chants from her hitherto surly teammates. The heterosexist challenge inscribed in the exhortation "Suck my dick" bestows O'Neil with a figurative phallus. Urgayle is stunned, and O'Neil, bloody and near collapse, breaks into a satisfied smile. Her metamorphosis is complete and the cohort finally accepts her as one of its own. As Judi Addelston explains, the penis is the "ultimate insignia" of masculinity, and "individuals who are on the margins of masculinity [by virtue of class, race, and other subordinations] must publicly show their penis (real or metaphorical) in order either to achieve or reify masculinity" (1999, 338). O'Neil's entrance into the Navy SEAL training program reveals the terms of the latest crisis for national masculinity, for "if women could be soldiers too then what was there left for a man to do that was manly; where and how was virility to show its mettle?" (Simpson 1994, 2). *G.I. Jane* affords this crisis a moment of relief by restoring the phallus to the status of indomitable organ of power—even Jordan O'Neil needs one to make it as a Navy SEAL.

This is a moment of triumph for O'Neil within the narrative, for she has finally made her way into the hypermasculine, heterosexual fraternity. It is an ironic victory, however, for she has not made it through the training program by posing as genderless. She has made it in instead by perfectly honing her performance of masculinity. At the end, then, O'Neil has perfected the "cock-in-the-head" (Cordova 1997, 34), which means that although she cannot physically grow a penis, O'Neil has made all of the performative and ideological adjustments that the mythic meritocracy demands of her. Possessing a figurative phallus, O'Neil is less a celebration of liberal feminism and more a dismal showing of its lost potential. As the threat she poses is contained and defanged, she performs "masculinity in drag." Abdicating every trace of gender blindness that she started with, O'Neil ultimately reinforces the hegemonic, masculinist ideal of the American worker.

Such cinematic accounts of meritorious workers bear critically on neoliberal discourses of ideal workers and workplaces. In neat packages, these portrayals distill within the cultural imaginary, advancing notably gendered standards of the meritocratic ideal as they leave their mark on our view of the "normal," the "objective." Rather than a putatively neutral baseline, then, the idea of merit takes its cues from hegemonic standards of masculinity, so that qualifications that are pegged as "meritorious" tend to be specifically masculine. Tracing the porous boundaries between the cinematic and the policy arena, we find that in public campaigns against affirmative action as in the affirmative action genre of mainstream cinema, the meritorious ideal of the workplace is premised upon a vast field of accepted knowledges that are gendered rather than gender-blind and, as we will discover in the next section, racial rather than race-blind.

Black Interlocutors and Ventriloquisms of Race and Gender

Key to the semiotics of Jordan O'Neil's transformation in *G.I. Jane* is the recurring analogy the narrative builds between the crises her sexual difference foments and those precipitated decades ago by racial difference. In a key scene midway through the film, O'Neil's unit is forced to swim several yards back to shore during a training exercise after she is unable to hoist herself out of the water into a waiting rescue raft. The men are resentful and O'Neil is furious with herself for having failed the exercise. Swimming back in the quiet of the water, Lieutenant McCool (Morris Chestnut), the sole African American in the group, who has in previous scenes offered the lone voice of accommodation for O'Neil in the face of petulant objections from the cohort, recounts the story of his grandfather, who faced significant hurdles in his ambitions to join the Navy.

"He wanted to fight with them big guns off them big-ass battle-ships," McCool begins. "Navy says to him, 'No. You can only do one thing on a battleship and that is cook.' And I'm not talking a hundred years ago either. I'm talking the United States Navy in the middle of World War Two. You know the reason they gave him? The reason they told my grandfather he couldn't fight for his country? Because Negroes can't see at night. Bad night vision." When one of the white recruits swimming nearby reacts, saying, "Damn! That's unbelievable! Thank God, times have changed," McCool asks, "Have they?" Then, turning back to O'Neil, he reassures her, "So you see, O'Neil, I know where you're coming from. Because to them, you're just the new nigger on the block."

Memories of indignities his grandfather endured sixty years ago are vivid in McCool's mind and unite him and O'Neil in historical solidarity. Articulating what John Fiske has referred to as "blackstream knowledge" (1994, 192), repressed counterknowledges, which like hidden transcripts emerge out of black lived vernaculars and in specific relief to dominant white discourses, McCool speaks from a position of vicarious knowledge, for although he no longer endures these exclusions himself, he knows through his grandfather how O'Neil must feel. Their exclusion has, more-over, turned on dominant perceptions of physical deficiency—bad night vision among blacks and inadequate strength among women. The racisms embedded in the former, now starkly visible sixty years after the fact, confirm sexisms inherent in the latter as the sole black male is enlisted in authenticating claims about discrimination against white women.

Performing the archetypal sagacious black helper, McCool serves primarily to reassure O'Neil that despite its glacial pace, the white male establishment of the armed services will make the necessary adjustments to accommodate her. Mirroring moves in contemporary Hollywood texts that locate racial conflict in a historical moment long past, McCool's tes-timony is forcefully optimistic. Echoing the interracial buddy formula of the nineties, the affirmative action film assures its audience of McCool's standing in the color-blind democratic fraternity of the unit, his presence proof that, by its own standards, the mythic meritocracy will discipline workplace chauvinists much as it did workplace bigots of previous decades.

Serving as the conscience of the mythic meritocracy, black interlocutors of the affirmative action genre issue pithy didacticisms that work to restore faith in dominant truths—that anti-black racisms no longer taint the American workplace, that women must bide their time as black Americans did in the past to find acceptance, that objective standards of merit are a sufficient guarantee of success, and that workplace sexisms, like workplace racisms of the past, are aberrations in the ethical norms of the meritocracy. Vouching for the unassailable logics of a color- and gender-blind meritocracy, thus, black voices cheer on the "new niggers on the block," issuing judicious reminders about the true character of the American meritocracy.

At the end of the film, we see O'Neil at her locker surprised to find intimate tokens of admiration—a dog-eared book of poetry by D. H. Lawrence and one of his own medals of honor—left for her by the hitherto hard-nosed Urgayle. Magnanimously accepting O'Neil's triumph, as if on cue, Urgayle has made a remarkable evolution from workplace chauvinist to champion of gender equity, and his gifts, like keepsakes exchanged by clandestine lovers, move O'Neil to tears. Completing the necessarily paradoxical matrix of nineties masculinity, *G.I. Jane* concludes with Urgayle emerging as the formulaic tough guy with a soft heart. Their marshmallow insides trembling with sympathy and admiration, white males in O'Neil's workplace are a far cry from the heartless "them" that McCool had earlier described.

As things turn out, O'Neil is, in fact, forced to "ring out" of the training program, but not because she fails the training exercises. Instead, she is removed by the rogue feminist Lillian DeHaven while the mostly male and white cohort, including the punishing Urgayle, having experienced a remarkable change of heart, are now rooting for her. Likewise, O'Neil's final confrontation with DeHaven and her triumphant reentry into the training program are only possible with the assistance of her hitherto begrudging boyfriend, Royce. Thus, by the end of tale, white men have lined up like noble heroes to assist the deserving O'Neil, and the black helper's cautionary insights are rendered irrelevant as the white female, having learned perfectly how to "do it for daddy" (hooks 1996, 84), recedes away from the margins occupied by "niggers on the block."[18]

The silent but meaningful locker room exchange between O'Neil and Urgayle comes in the wake of an emergency mission to the coast of Libya into which the novice Navy SEALS crew is hurriedly recruited. The mission quickly goes awry when a Libyan border patrol unit stops to inspect a ramshackle lookout post at which O'Neil is trapped, hidden from view. As the tension mounts with each step the swarthy gunman takes toward her, Urgayle, who heads the crew, panics and fires at him. Having announced their presence to the enemy thus, a shoot-out ensues in which Urgayle is wounded, and the fresh-faced team, now under O'Neil's command, pulls off a daring rescue of their fallen comrade.

Despite the gratuitous positioning of the sole woman as team leader in the final rescue, the impulse to shield white women from the threat of dark, alien forces prompts and justifies American aggression against the racial Other (Fraiman 1994, 71–72). Race is thus accorded its hegemonic place by film's end as Americans work in unison to allay the menacing threat posed by racial Others. Now the unit repairs its internal fissions and, returning the white woman to her position of cherished possession, closes ranks to protect her from the threat of penetration by dark and foreign forces.[19]

Edward Zwick's 1996 release *Courage under Fire* improvises on these representational strategies and offers keen insights into the role reserved for blackness in the affirmative action genre. Set against the backdrop of the Persian Gulf War of the early nineties, the film recounts the events surrounding the death of Army captain Karen Emma Walden (Meg Ryan), killed on duty while serving as a Medevac helicopter pilot. Several months have elapsed since the end of the war, and the Army, urged on by officials in the White House, has commissioned a review of Walden's career in the hopes of honoring her posthumously with the Medal of Honor. If approved, Walden will be the first woman ever to receive the coveted award, and the media events of such a bestowal promise high public relations returns for the White House.

Walden fits the figure of the workplace martyr, an obligatory figure in the affirmative action formula. Her competence at the job poses a grave feminist threat in the masculinist enclave of the armed services, which only her absence or demise can relieve. For Ilario (Matt Damon), the rookie medic on Walden's team, the captain showed neither doubt nor fear while making life and death decisions. "She had this quality," he remembers, "the heavier the pressure, the calmer she got." He idolizes Walden, stating: "You know, she put up with a lot of shit to become an officer. You know, she had to work twice as hard as everybody else, be twice as good. She never let her guard down or showed any sign of weakness. She was tough, she could handle it."

Likewise, Walden's parents, living a quiet life in rural Texas, remember how stubborn their daughter had been in her decision to fly helicopters for the Army after she graduated from college. Divorced after only a year or so of marriage, Walden had nevertheless managed to be "a really good mom" to her daughter Anne Marie (Christina Stojanovich) and "never asked for help unless she really needed it." Endowing Walden with the

Army Captain Karen Emma Walden (Meg Ryan) tries to keep it together as she fires on approaching Iraqis in *Courage under Fire* (Edward Zwick, 1996).

elusive twin capacities of supermom and superworker, her bereaved father continues, "You can't imagine how hard it was for her to leave that little girl and go fight in the war, but it was important to Karen to do her duty."

As the internal inquiry presses into the details of Walden's final mission, *Courage* uncovers the truth about the events Rashomon-style, each surviving member of her team narrating the events of their harrowing encounter with hostile forces at Al Kufan in the Iraqi desert. One by one, the men on Walden's team offer partial retellings of the incident. Discrepancies abound until we learn, at film's end, that Walden did not die from enemy fire as the men have maintained. Rather, as Ilario confesses, sobbing at the end, the men have been guarding the horrible secret that they themselves are responsible for Walden's death.

As we meet the men on Walden's team, each appears debilitated and haunted by the episode. Rady (Tim Guinee), the radio operator on the crew, has retreated into himself and is stridently protective of the

Lieutenant Colonel Nate Serling (Denzel Washington) closes in on answers from Sergeant Johnny Monfriez (Lou Diamond Phillips) in *Courage under Fire*.

dead Walden. Altameyer (Seth Gilliam), the crew chief, whom we find hospitalized with terminal cancer, cannot muster words. He screams in anguish, praying for death as he relives the incident in his mind. In contrast, the gunner on the team, Sergeant Johnny Monfriez (Lou Diamond Phillips), is a mixture of boastful bravado and vitriolic rage. In his version, Walden was "afraid . . . she was a fucking coward." He is a combustible mix of threats, boasts, and pleas, and with each step we take toward the truth about Al Kufan, Monfriez responds as a ticking bomb climaxing to a violent suicide. Ultimately, we learn that it is Monfriez's sexist refusal of Walden's leadership and his insubordination and mutinous confrontation with her that sparked the chain of events leading to her death, and that forced the subsequent cover-up.

The audience makes its tortuous journey through these retellings together with Lieutenant Colonel Nathaniel Serling (Denzel Washington), a highly decorated African American officer who has been enlisted to prepare the internal review on Walden. An armored tank commander who served in the Persian Gulf, Serling is a tragic figure in his own right. During an intense nighttime struggle at Al Bathra in Iraq, Serling ordered an attack on what he believed were enemy tanks. But as the team quickly discovers, Serling has accidentally fired on his own men, killing several of them, and consequently, he himself is now the subject of a hushed internal inquiry into this incident of friendly fire.

Thus *Courage* narrates parallel tales of conscience and consequences. The men in Walden's unit have committed the same crime as Serling, and like him, they are collapsing under the weight of their guilt. For his part, Serling is tormented by his culpability in the Al Bathra incident. Slowly spiraling out of control, Serling has taken to drinking heavily and has withdrawn from his wife and children. He harbors a growing contempt for the bureaucratic machinations of the Army in their efforts at a cover-up, and wants nothing more than to come clean about his deadly blunder at Al Bathra.

At the start of the film, we find Serling at an in camera deposition that the Army has arranged to uncover the events of the incident. The investigator feeds Serling his lines, tacitly urging him to stick to the story that under the circumstances at the battlefield—with their thermal night vision equipment confused by burning tanks and smoke obscuring visual identification—there was no way to tell the difference between an "enemy" and a "friendly." Serling insists to the contrary that he "should have been able to tell the difference," but the investigator brushes his admissions aside.

It is no comfort when his supervisor, Brigadier General Hershberg (Michael Moriarty), in his attempts to reassure Serling, confirms that the Army will protect him. "Nat, nobody's going to hang you out to dry. I won't let 'em." Hershberg thinks of himself a friend to Serling who, as he puts it, has nursed him, patted his back, and pushed promotions for him. He explains to Serling: "Now, losing a man like your friend Boylar,[20] I've been there. And this whole mess, it's my ass on the line right there beside yours. I can feel the chill in the air as well as you can." Thus, Serling, reading between the lines, is left with the empty consolation of Hershberg's "I won't tell if you won't" pledge that invidiously hints at the possibility that Serling has been a beneficiary of other instances of such protection over his seventeen-year career in the Army.

Reading these elements of *Courage* against the crisis precipitated by Jayson Blair, the African American star reporter at the *New York Times* who was found out as having plagiarized and fabricated scores of news stories over a four-year period (Barry et al. 2003, 1), it is possible to see how the Blair scandal echoes shades of the dilemma that Serling poses for the Army. Disclosures of the Blair scandal spurred a brief and predictable national dialogue about whether by overlooking "warning signs," the editorial top brass at the *Times*, succumbing to specious elements of white guilt, had conferred unearned racial preferences upon the undeserving Blair (Duke and Fears 2003, C1). Raising the specter of nepotism, protectionism, and unearned advancement in the workforce, Serling poses a similar dilemma for the Army. The hushed tones of the inquiry and the Army's insistent and gratuitous protectiveness deliberately toy with the possibility that Serling, a black officer, may have been promoted beyond his abilities by white supervisors, and that such unearned favors may be conferred routinely in the workplace.

Compromised in various ways, Serling is nevertheless endowed with an ethical conscience, and as the narrative progresses, we find him devolving into self-destruction. His impatience growing by the day, Serling refuses the Army's tacit pledge of protection and, late one drunken evening, confesses to a snooping *Washington Post* reporter, Tony Gartner (Scott Glenn): "You know they told Boylar's parents that he died from enemy fire. I told them that. I carried the message. I went to the funeral and watched his mother cry her eyes out. I stood there and looked his father in the eye and told him his son died brave under fire. And I was the one who gave the order. I did it. Then the Army gave me a medal for bravery and valor. Then they buried me . . . in medals." With a dry chuckle, Serling continues, "Got a sense of humor, don't they?" Rather than hiding behind the protection the bureaucracy affords him, we find Serling acting out, trying to sabotage himself in an effort to be found out.

Serling's crisis is precipitated not only by the fact that he has accidentally killed his own men but also by mounting suspicions that the meritocracy may be systemically corrupt. Contrary to the ethical norm he has assumed, his experiences now hint at the possibility that the Army confers unearned honors upon cowardly soldiers and, worse, covers up their deadly blunders. Proof of Walden's innocence, the truth about her abilities for "courage under fire," thus, holds the key that will free Serling from his nightmares. It is the only way that Serling can prove that despite the disingenuous honors and undeserved medals it has conferred upon him, the meritocracy is nevertheless authentic and that he is not an imposter in it. Thus, Serling explains to Gartner that despite pressures from the Army and the White House to complete his report as quickly as possible, he cannot overlook the discrepancies surrounding Walden's death. "I just want to get something clear, you know," he states. "I just want *somebody* to be a hero."

Midway through the narrative, having identified a series of inconsistencies in testimony collected from Walden's team, Serling reports to Hershberg that he will not rush the report on Walden. The general responds sharply: "Should I remind you who recommended you for this posting when no one else would touch you?" Realizing for the first time that he has been volunteered into a tacit quid pro quo—a rubber stamp of approval on the Walden nomination in exchange for the Army's protection for Al Bathra—his worst fears are confirmed. "Are you saying that you chose me because I wouldn't rock the boat?" Serling demands. And Hershberg responds: "Dereliction of duty, drunken and disorderly, conduct unbecoming. At best, a dishonorable discharge, at worst, Al Bathra alone would give us plenty of grounds if we want." Stunned by Hershberg's uncharacteristic candor, Serling observes wryly, "Well, at least someone is finally willing to come out and say it." When Hershberg removes the defiant Serling from the Walden inquiry, Serling digs his heels in and promises that he "will complete this report. On my own if I have to. I'm going to get *this* one right."

Thus, *Courage* recounts a paradoxical tale of black racial consciousness as Serling, forced outside the system for the first time, is finally able to grasp the prejudices of the faltering meritocracy. A circumscribed and guarded racial consciousness is foregrounded, however, for Serling's defiance against Hershberg and the Army top brass remains within the protective custody of white hegemonic ideals. Rebuffed by Hershberg, he turns to the *Washington Post* reporter, Gartner, in his efforts to complete his report on Walden. Shifting from the protection of one "great white father" to another,[21] Serling remains securely in the service of hegemonic didacticisms, as he works for the remainder of film to restore the meritocracy to its ethical norms.

At film's end, Serling, dressed in his military best, is seated before Boylar's parents in the living room of their well-appointed plantation style home in Virginia. As he tearfully confesses and begs their forgiveness, the film cuts from the Boylar home to the film's other critical moment of redemption—the poignant conferral ceremony in the sunny environs of the White House grounds, where Walden's angelic young daughter, Anne Marie, receives the Medal of Honor on her mother's behalf. Both moments afford Serling key opportunities to clear his conscience and prove himself an ethical soldier for the Army and the meritocracy. These moments serve to clean out the workplace, as both unearned racial advantage and misogynist secrets among the boys are cast out as aberrations.

As things play out in *Courage*, despite fierce ambition and dogged effort, despite how "butch" she was, Walden is ultimately reduced to the status of currency exchanged between male partners, her martyrdom the "occasion for mediation, transaction, transition, transference, between man and his fellow man" (Fraiman 1994, 67). Occupying familiar positions, white women serve as facilitators of male brotherhoods as they ease relations of reciprocity and kinship between black men and their white cohort (Fraiman 1994, 67–84; Linville 2000, 100–120). The affirmative action film thus remains forcefully about racial relations between men, as ethically overendowed black voices ease white racial guilt by laboring to correct sexist erasures of white women.

As the African American Serling takes on the mantle of conscience of the mythic meritocracy—as he puts it to Hershberg, "someone has to be accountable for this"—it appears he has little access to black history, showing neither cynicism nor discontent about the unethical propensities of the white establishment. While McCool in *G.I. Jane* is afforded a moment of jaded sarcasm in response to the young white recruit who is blissfully unaware about the continuing struggles of those on the margins of the workforce, Serling's abilities to read systemic inequities that mar the meritocracy are notably blunted. Rather, the narrative takes some pains to locate Serling as fully assimilated and consequently blind to racial imperfections in the American workforce. Thus, for instance, positioned as just one of the guys, Serling shares in the humor of xenophobic in-jokes when American soldiers refer to Iraqi enemies as "ragheads" and "fuckers," and he chuckles obligingly when the misogynist Monfriez brags about "humping" Army nurses.

Serling's nod-and-wink approval of workplace bigots and sexists, his naiveté concerning systemic flaws in the mythic meritocracy, offers a strategic representation of black middle-class complicity with the hegemonic racial order of things. In clear contrast to *Die Hard with a Vengeance*'s troublesome Zeus Carver, Serling's racial point of view is innocuous and in several ways identical to that of the average white male with whom he works. Unlike Carver, Serling does not think racially, he does not needlessly make things about race, and he does not tediously anticipate racisms at every turn.

Instead, he epitomizes hegemonic political truths with which elite black discourses have kept pace. Deploying the formulaic device of individual dint against systemic apathy, *Courage* positions the black middle class as allies within the practices of "new racisms," which as early as the decade of the eighties were no longer the sole province of avowed conservatives (Bonilla-Silva 2003; Goldberg 2002). Rather, as Adolph Reed Jr. explains, "black liberals, even leftists, and of course nationalists of all stripes embraced this line, as it became the era's common sense" (1999, 205). Continuing into the nineties, black middle-class consent to the hegemonic racial order of things worked to define any other stance as illegitimate, as Zeus Carver in *Vengeance* aptly demonstrates, and, moreover, to paint the payoffs generated by black hegemonic conformance as significant and optimal.

Thus, epitomizing the black middle class of the nineties, Serling seeks neither radical activism nor popular mobilization to fight his battles. He neither confides in nor does he solicit the assistance of others on the margins. Rather, the racial innocence of these characters rewrites the history of black defiance, scripted instead toward an obsequious attachment to hegemonic standards—merit, hierarchy, and loyalty—as they labor to restore rather than raze the proverbial master's house. The effectiveness of such racially correct interlocutors vouching for the meritocracy cannot be underestimated, for, as recent policy campaigns against affirmative action confirm, they are unrivaled in terms of their credibility, their "superstanding," as Derrick Bell refers to it, before a wider audience.

Having been invited, even if as tokens, into the mythic meritocracy, black interlocutors of the affirmative action genre aptly demonstrate the genuflections required of these workers in the post–affirmative action workforce. Their assimilation into the democratic fraternity hinges on their disavowal of historical black defiance along with their acquiescence to neoliberal scripts of personal responsibilization. Moreover, while the discipline of feral females in the workplace remains the province of the white hero, black workers like Serling in *Courage* and McCool in *G.I. Jane* are scripted as dutiful helpers called upon to authenticate sexisms and deadly sexist violence against white women.

These labors serve a number of critical hegemonic ends. For one, the narrative emphasis on unmasking gendered secrets of the meritocracy clears the discursive field of analogous racial crimes. The resultant generic silence on the sticky and persistent dilemma of race sustains the fantasy of a nation freed from its racial past and offers the audience a respite from its "unspeakable" yet ever-present racial guilt.

Furthermore, membership in the biracial brotherhood is made contingent upon black men assuming a sizable burden of responsibility for systemic flaws in the meritocracy. The parallels between Serling's crime and the one committed by Walden's team serve to indict white males for their sexist secrets in much the same terms as black men for their unearned racial benefits. Thus, white males are taken to task for their sexisms in these texts but on the condition that black men accept responsibility for unfair racial advantages accruing to them. Partners in secret crimes, showy retributions for the sexist sins of whiteness compel concomitant disclosures of the racial sins of blackness. The formulaic coupling of black male redemption with white female martyrdom serves to clinch these equivalences, as admissions of white culpability for sexist secrets of the meritocracy are made contingent upon confessions of black guilt for racial advantage in the post–affirmative action workplace.

Such recruitments of the black middle class in service of the mythic meritocracy proceed apace in policy campaigns against social justice programs like affirmative action. Thus, middle-class and wealthier African Americans emerge as integral players in the cast of characters paraded as campaign spokespersons in racist policy attacks on affirmative action. Their "superstanding" hinges on their abilities to confirm suspicions about "dusky Donald Trumps and brown-skinned Bill Gateses who [it is assumed] have grown rich from affirmative action programs" (Varner 1998, B1). In step with Hollywood productions, public campaigns of the nineties dwelled on the suggestion of affirmative action preferences using blacks themselves. Authenticating circulating nightmares about reverse discrimination, these voices, together with the imagined category of the model majority, were enlisted in normalizing the quotidian practices of "new racisms" and "new sexisms" alike.

By the end of the nineties, then, the profoundly mythic stage of mainstream cinema constructed formulaic figures of white women to disclose the sexist secrets of the workplace as a necessary condition for confirmations of racial preferences accruing to black Americans. Permeating the porous boundaries between the cinematic and the policy arena, these constructions worked to inoculate moviegoers and voters alike from lingering guilt for the nation's racial past as well as to authenticate racist claims that hold "quota-addicted" African Americans responsible for the twin burdens of reverse discrimination and political correctness.

Hollywood Cinema as Racial Regime

The narrative and figural strategies of the affirmative action genre of the nineties reveal the ways in which mainstream Hollywood productions reproduce the dominant racial order of things to celebrate hegemonic paradigms of racial progress. As deviations in the ethical norms of the workplace are scripted onto sexual and racial difference, crises in the meritocracy, the genre reveals, are always occasioned by the introduction of nontraditional workers. White women, performing in various shades of drag, highlight nagging dilemmas raised by policy inheritances of the sixties and ease fantasies of black inclusion into multiracial, democratic brotherhoods of men. Likewise, a de-fanged and docile black racial consciousness is celebrated as the genre serves up self-congratulatory parables of ethical white masculinity. Reworking assimilation narratives of earlier social problem films, the affirmative action genre works to enlist black men and white women in containing the threat the other poses in white male bastions of the workplace.

Narrow hegemonic categories abound—conniving career women who oust oldtimers from old-boy networks of privilege and prestige, and bungling male upstarts who resist at first but with heroic adaptability refashion themselves as champions of the multicultural meritocracy. Likewise, ethically overendowed superwomen who trade career opportunities to call out systemic inequities in the meritocracy work in step with sagacious black helpers who take on the burden of cleaning up aberrations in the workplace by purging themselves of their melanin merit. Each figure enables trenchant critiques of the legacies of the sixties and preaches hegemonic ideals of color and gender blindness.

These allegorical meanings are not necessarily invented in the mythic arena of the cinematic. Instead, the martyr, the man-eater, the phallicized female, and the black helper are itinerants across discursive terrains, lending themselves to versatile refashioning as they cross between the cinematic and public policy and back again. This complex repertoire of cultural meanings worked over, transformed, and recirculated within contemporary cinematic texts permeates the divisive and racialized semiotics of contemporary conservative hegemonies and leaves its mark on policy assaults on affirmative action, multiculturalism, the welfare state, immigration, and so on.

Thus, for instance, the model majority of the policy arena is tweaked to workplace martyrdom in cinematic texts in analogous ways as the genuflections of black helpers in the affirmative action genre are reworked into the racially correct voice-overs of superblack sellouts within contemporary public policy assaults. Circulating tales of white male frustration over reverse discrimination and lingering attention to the racial and gendered deviance of new workers play stereophonically for overlapping audiences of cinematic productions and political campaigns. Producing dappled fields of voice and silence, filmic and public policy texts each exaggerate some anxieties and allay others. Ethical claims circulating in one domain percolate through, pointing to a range of cross-pollinations between public policy assaults and cinematic discourses.

White anxieties about black defiance and guilt for the nation's racial past are relegated to history in the cinematic repertoire of the nineties with a generic emphasis upon female troublemakers, as male anxieties about the fearsome threat that white women pose in the workforce are mollified in the public policy arena by circulating tales of black misconduct. Whether race is deployed as an effective stratagem of divisiveness in policy assaults or gendered cinematic scripts work to cloud persevering national dilemmas about race, these generic combinations of silence and evocation perform key hegemonic work. Making and remaking ethical claims about merit and objectivity, they naturalize white male control over the post–civil rights workplace, and variously sort white women and black men into a range of collusions with the hegemonic mainstream.

CHAPTER 3

Civil Rights, Affirmative Action, and the American South: Eyewitnesses to the Racial Past

> Once memory enters into our consciousness, it is hard to
> circumvent, harder to stop, and impossible to run from . . .
> Memory does something else besides telling us how we got
> here from there: it reminds us of the causes of difference
> between popular memory and official versions of history.
>
> —Teshome H. Gabriel, *Questions of Third Cinema*

In January 2000, the United States Catholic bishops announced their decision to nominate the slain civil rights leader Martin Luther King Jr. to be "declared a martyr by the Roman Catholic Church" ("Bishops Want Vatican" 2000, 7; Nolan 2000, A1; Paulson 2000, A1). Martyrs for the Christian faith, according to Vatican practice, include individuals who are inspired by and die for their faith, men and women who "maintain their religious principles in the face of opposition from the world around them" (C. Murphy 2000, B3).[1]

Disagreements followed in the wake of the announcement over whether King qualified for martyrdom. Monsignor Peter Dora, spokesperson for the Roman Catholic Archdiocese of Atlanta, explained, "In the Catholic Church, a martyr is traditionally someone who has died for the faith or died for Christ. Dr. King, in the popular mind, gave his life for civil rights or human rights, which is not quite the same thing" (G. White 2000, 10A). Others pointed out that King was a Southern Baptist minister, not a Catholic, and that he was killed not while preaching but while advocating labor rights (Paulson 2000, A1). In contrast, the Reverend Terry Wingate, pastor of the Purity Baptist Church in northeast Washington, found the nomination "fitting because King is looked upon in the Black community as a martyr who gave his life that others might

145

be free" (C. Murphy 2000, B3). Likewise, the Reverend Joseph Roberts, senior pastor of Ebenezer Baptist Church in Atlanta, where King had served as associate pastor, argued:

> King is the closest thing we have to a modern-day martyr. When you look at his life and think about the fact that martyrs in the early church were thrown to the lions because of their beliefs, you can certainly draw lines with what he was doing . . . The man went in unarmed. He stood on principle. In the face of opposition and violence, he stood nonviolently, as did his Lord. (G. White 2000, 10A)

As it turned out, King did not ultimately qualify as Catholic martyr. Viewed in isolation, the nomination and the public dialogue that ensued point to the uniquely venerated place that King occupies in American public discourse. But King's nomination to martyrdom did not emerge out of the blue. These events are located instead within a larger discourse of sanitized nostalgia within which chosen leaders of the civil rights movement survive in national memory.

The contours of such national memory have been sculpted over the course of decades by press accounts and cinematic narratives, by rituals of public memorialization, and by a concomitant selective amnesia about aspects of the racial past. Within these discourses, civil rights leaders have emerged as beatified figures and market commodities alike, just as the social unrests of the sixties are found hollowed out and co-opted into the mainstream.

Indeed, when the King family commissioned the release of a cartoon video entitled *My Friend, Martin* in celebration of his seventieth birthday in January 1999, a video that featured a multiracial group of children who get transported back in time to meet a teenaged King, the Reverend Joseph Lowery, a former King associate and past president of the Southern Christian Leadership Conference, lamented, "I stand in fear and am trembling that Martin is going to be Mickey Moused and Fat Albertized" (quoted in Shepard 1999, 7). Likewise, when portions of King's historic "I Have a Dream" speech appeared sandwiched between the voices of

Homer Simpson and Kermit the Frog in a television commercial for a cellular phone company, critics accused the King family of having "relinquished their roles as keepers of the flame to become merchants of the dream" (Staples 2001, A26; Tucker 1999, 7Q).[2]

Adolph Reed Jr. has commented on the analogous emergence of a commodity market for trinkets and other memorabilia featuring the radical black nationalist Malcolm X that arose in the wake of Spike Lee's controversial biopic *Malcolm X* in 1992. Reed notes the rise of a fraught "Malcolmania" among African American youth that he describes as "Malcolm's incorporation into the logic of merchandising" (1999, 200–201). Here, Reverend Lowery's fears about a Mickey Moused and Fat Albertized Martin are of a piece with concerns voiced by African Americans reacting to the bowdlerization of Malcolm in that both laments are betrayed by a nostalgic self-righteousness. As Reed explains, "What is being bowdlerized is an already romanticized image, a hero larger than—and therefore outside of—life, an *object* of reverence" (1999, 201, emphasis in original).

Marked for and by objectification, the civil rights movement and its leaders—Martin and Malcolm alike—have ossified into static national icons, sanctified and distorted. Immortalized in animated cartoons and in the shape of action figures,[3] these "objects of reverence" privilege some recollections and not others. Such reconstructions canonize a tidy history of civil rights, located safely in the distant past, privileging what Lance Hill and others have referred to as the "myth of nonviolence" (2004, 2), and enabling national claims of "justice done" on the issue of civil rights in America.

The history of the struggle for black civil rights, in other words, is inseparable from a romantic nostalgia about black-white solidarities that coalesced around strategies of nonviolent direct action, about the character of American liberalism, and about a pathological intransigence attributed to the American South. Each aspect of this nostalgia is epistemic, that is, each has served to construct the "true story" of the civil rights struggle. Each has compellingly shaped authorized knowledges of racial battles of the past and, consequently, each bears forcefully upon racial truths of the moment.

The epistemic strength and vulnerabilities of such national memory become keenly visible when debates over affirmative action are witness to strategic appropriations of civil rights appeals. For example, we see anti–affirmative action organizers naming themselves "true heirs to the revolution" (Pashler 1996) and staking a claim in historic struggles of the sixties. These maneuvers point to the ways that recent assaults on affirmative action strategically marshaled the ethical reserves of the civil rights movement to vilify affirmative action as mutant progeny of that struggle.

During the 1996 campaign to end affirmative action programs in California, Republicans excerpted portions of King's "I Have a Dream" speech for use in a series of television advertisements that positioned race-conscious affirmative action as anathema to King's historic appeal to "the content of our character not the color our skin." The King estate immediately brought an injunction to block the advertisements from airing (Lesher 1996, A20; Lesher and Boxall 1996, A3; "State GOP Pulls TV Ads" 1996, A3), and Coretta Scott King issued a strongly worded editorial to right the record on her husband's views:

> Who would have thought, 33 years after my husband, Martin Luther King Jr., uttered those words that their meaning would be distorted by supporters of the California Civil Rights Initiative, which would eliminate state affirmative action plans. My husband unequivocally supported such programs. He did indeed dream of a day when his children would be judged by the content of their character, instead of the color of their skin. But he often said that programs and reforms were needed to hasten the day when his dream of genuine equality—reflected in reality, not just theory—would be fulfilled. (1996, 15)

Admonishing campaign organizers for distorting King's position on affirmative action, Coretta Scott King expresses concern that the King who is being resurrected in the Proposition 209 campaign misrepresents the "real Martin." In the same vein, the Reverend Jesse Jackson referred to the advertisements as "blasphemy" ("GOP Backs Off King Speech"

1996, 5B), likening right-wing appropriations of King's words to "intellectual terrorism" (Woodson and Bennett 1994). In response, William Bennett, a distinguished fellow with the Heritage Foundation, a right-wing think tank based in Washington, D.C., suggested:

> If you said in 1968 that you should judge people by the content of their character, not the color of their skin, you should be color-blind, you were a liberal. If you say it now, you are a conservative. It is in this sense that Martin Luther King today is a conservative. (Woodson and Bennett 1994)

Bennett's claim drawing King into the "conservative" fold, like fears that Martin Luther King Jr. is being Mickey Moused and Fat Albertized, reflects the ways in which, almost forty years after his death, collective memory of the civil rights struggle in America coalesces around nettled claims over which representations of the civil rights past and its leaders are "accurate" as well as who has control over recollections of this historical past.

Recent debates over affirmative action are replete with references to and recollections of the "black struggle" in America so that contemporary public knowledge of affirmative action is animated in precise ways by what we as a nation collectively remember about the sixties, about the black grassroots movement that arose in the American South, and the remarkable legal and cultural transformations it spurred. Engaging a wistful nostalgia and a willful amnesia about aspects of this racial past, contemporary assaults on affirmative action offer us a critical window into the politics of public memory, highlighting how social power privileges dominant versions of historical pasts, how one version edges out another in successive retellings, and how some versions are mangled or lost over time.

Civil rights historians and biographers have in recent years issued a number of works preoccupied with excavating the "true" and "authentic" story of the civil rights movement and the lives of its leaders (Bermanzohn 2003; Dyson 2000; Haskins 2002; Oates 1994; Tyson 2004). This chapter leans away from such a preoccupation, offering instead an analysis of cinematic imaginations of this past. If filmic representations are telling of cultural predispositions, of national desires and cautionary nightmares, the epistemic work of cinematic memories is critical to understanding how iconic images of the American South and of the black sixties emerge in public discourses of the present as well as the policy implications of such dominant collective memories for racial battles of the moment.

I offer a single comparative analysis that underscores the relations between affirmative action battles of the nineties and their appropriations of the civil rights past. I focus on three related media texts—Joel Schumacher's *A Time to Kill* (1996), a Hollywood film that dramatizes racial conflict in a small town in present-day Mississippi; an independent documentary, *Waking in Mississippi* (Christine Herring and Andre Alexis Robinson, 1998), which chronicles the making of Schumacher's film on location in the small town of Canton, Mississippi; and *Lights, Camera, Canton* (1995), a network news program that aired on CBS's *48 Hours* and focused on the impact of Schumacher's production on the residents of Canton.

Together, Schumacher's *A Time to Kill*, Herring and Robinson's *Waking in Mississippi*, and CBS's *Lights, Camera, Canton* reveal dappled surfaces of memory and amnesia—canonized versions of events and icons of the sixties and others that have been relegated to obscurity. Pursuing overlaps and divergences between dominant and less familiar versions of the racial past, my analysis is geared centrally to exploring what George Lipsitz refers to as the "roads not taken" in dominant constructions of the past (1990, 30). Such analysis illuminates the cadences of "countermemory," residual or resistant strains that are ever present, lurking in the shadows of what becomes accepted public knowledge. Such analysis allows us to take stock of the implications of the selective and circumscribed boundaries of authorized truths of our time.

Mythic Mississippi

Critiquing the mood in California over the course of its recent battles over affirmative action, George Lipsitz refers to the Golden State as "the Mississippi of the 1990s" (1998, 211–33). "Mississippi," he suggests, "is not the only state with ghosts from its past and skeletons in its closet" (231). Rather, racialized appeals advanced by neoconservatives in California "have far more in common with the defense of white supremacy in Mississippi in the past and present than they recognize" (229). Californian leaders, he explains, "deploy the same combination of racism and disavowal that proved so poisonous in Mississippi during the 1960s." They may seem more benign than the "Ross Barnetts and James Eastlands of yesterday . . . because their speeches rarely contain direct racist epithets," but the "suffering and strife [they have] engendered in California today is greater in both quantity and quality than anything Mississippi's white supremacists did to their citizens thirty years ago (228–29).[4]

A provocative indictment in many respects, Lipsitz's critique nevertheless relies crucially upon the symbolic importance of Mississippi in the national imagination as a place that is connected more to the past than the present. It reasserts a familiar distinction, accepting without question the dominant racial narrative that locates the North as victor and the South as vanquished in a narrative of national rehabilitation and redemption.

Bearing critically on authorized truths about anti-racist struggle and the telos of American racial reform, dominant accounts of the racial past are escorted by a myopic and enduring fascination with the American South as mythic "scene of the crime." Markers of difference that position the South at a distance from the rest of America, these constructions bear critically on authorized truths about the problem of race at the present moment. So entrenched are these truths that even critiques of these assaults, like Lipsitz's claim, work predictably to indict Californian neoconservatism as Mississippian, as if the South stands alone, the sole measure of racial crimes past and present.

Likewise, we find anti–affirmative action voices in public policy debates deliberately setting themselves apart from "bigots of yesteryear" (Connerly 1996a) by reiterating such ready cultural imaginations of the South. Thus, reminding his audience that "in our time, we have discredited them [David Duke and his cadre of Southern white supremacists] and their brand of racism," Ward Connerly, spokesperson for California's

Proposition 209 effectively checked off the ways in which the 1996 state-wide campaign against affirmative action was keenly not Southern, and as a consequence, clearly not racist. Cultural imaginaries of the American South thus emerge as a critical epistemic element in absolving current assaults and their spokespersons of racism or anti-black discrimination.

The constitution of the South as anomaly, as mythic scene of the crime, is traced back to news accounts from the sixties that reveal how the hegemonic Northern agenda for civil rights reforms emerged as a national claim to rehabilitate an anachronistic American South. The consonance of Northern voices with "the Great Emancipator" and visions of a guiltless America emerged in contrast to the South analogized to South African apartheid and fascist Germany. Southern voices provided grist for this mill as they were heard over and over in news accounts of the sixties constructing segregation as innocuous "local custom" and as "rational social order that made it possible for blacks and whites to live side by side." Pronouncements like Alabama governor George C. Wallace's infamous "Segregation now, segregation tomorrow, segregation forever" slogan played repeatedly in Northern news reports to portray the Southern bigot as outmoded and unrepresentative of Americans as a whole.

In the weeks following passage of the historic Civil Rights Act in July 1964, news reports were crowded with stories logging popular reactions to the end of segregation in the South. In an article entitled "And the Walls Came Tumbling Down," *Time* offered vignettes from a number of Southern towns. The article described incidents of peaceful desegregation as in the case of J. L. Meadows, a seventy-year-old "Negro chauffeur" who strolled into the Dinkler-Tutwiler Hotel's Town and Country restaurant in Birmingham, Alabama, "sat down amid a roomful of staring white diners, ordered, and was served without incident" ("And the Walls Came" 1964, 25). "Even in Mississippi, land of violence," the article continued, "there was quiet compliance. Negroes played golf on Jackson's municipal course, ate at a Vicksburg whites-only lunch counter, and, drawing scarcely a disapproving glance, checked into and ate at Jackson's two leading hotels and a motel" (25).

However, other stories described "holdouts" where state officials in a variety of Southern states had publicly denounced the newly passed civil rights law as "unconstitutional." Governor Paul B. Johnson Jr. of Mississippi, for instance, urged businessmen to refuse to comply with the law until it had been tested in the courts, arguing that "integrationists should move with caution or we're going to have some chaotic days" ("South's Leaders Hold Bill" 1964, 9). In other instances, news reports addressed "trouble spots" where fistfights and other confrontations between blacks and whites were reported. "In Atlanta, Georgia, perhaps the most moderate of the South's big cities," one story reported, "some of the worst flare-ups took place" ("And the Walls Came" 1964, 26). The article continued:

> One [such flare-up] occurred when three Negro ministerial students sought to test a fried-chicken joint owned by Lester Maddox, an unsuccessful Georgia office seeker and a loud racist. Maddox was waiting for them in the parking lot of his place, waving a snub-nosed pistol. "You ain't never gonna eat here!" he shouted, shoving against the car door as the Negroes started to get out. When the students persisted, Maddox and another white man grabbed ax handles from a stockpile Maddox had laid in for just such an occasion. "Git, git," Maddox ordered. The Negroes did, with a crowd of angry Maddox patrons at their heels. Among them was a small boy dragging a three-foot ax handle and squealing: "I'm gonna kill me a nigger!" ("And the Walls Came" 1964, 26)

The Lester Maddox story made it to the front page of the *New York Times*, complete with a photograph of the bullish Maddox wielding his pistol at one of the retreating black students (Millones 1964, 1). Similarly, a restaurant owner, R. W. Glover, appeared prominently in a photograph in the *New York Times* as he pulled shut the front door to his restaurant near the University of Virginia in Charlottesville on July 4, 1964. Glover, looking directly at the camera, was quoted saying that he was closing permanently because of the passage of the civil rights bill ("Closing Up" 1964, 4). Reflecting Southern capitulation and anxiety, Cy Shiap, owner of a steakhouse in Danville, Virginia, asserted: "Last year we fought them because they were breaking the law. This year, I'd be breaking the law if I refused to serve them. I'm a law-abiding citizen. If the law says feed them, I feed them. While I don't like it, I'm not going to break the law" (Millones 1964, 1).

Thus, news accounts of the sixties etched figures like George Wallace as "advocates of evil" (Wehrwein 1964a, 25), and Southern intransigence as a mulish inflexibility, a deliberate and unyielding obstinacy that simply required renewed discipline. These portrayals worked to condemn the racial politics of the American South and, by extension, to normalize Northern liberal attitudes about race. Reiterating quotidian differences between "reasonable" white Americans and Southern zealots, these reports substantiated public memory of an unremorseful South grudgingly tolerating the forced federal mandates of civil rights reforms.

Searing themselves into public consciousness, iconic visual images corroborated story after story in news reports that located the "American race problem" in the South and in the deviant minds of Southern bigots. The photojournalist Will Counts produced electrifying images of Elizabeth Eckford, one of the "Little Rock Nine," being yelled at and spat upon by an angry white mob as she made her way to attend her first day at Central High School in Little Rock, Arkansas, on Labor Day 1957 after federal mandates for integration had admitted Eckford and eight other African American students to the previously all-white school (Spencer 1999).

Similarly, in the famous Norman Rockwell painting *The Problem We All Live With* that appeared in *Look* magazine in 1964, the focus is on a six-year-old African American girl's walk to a newly integrated elementary school in New Orleans, escorted by towering, suit-clad U.S. marshals. As the girl, dressed in her Sunday best, makes her way in front of a wall— smeared with racist graffiti and the stain of a tomato lobbed by someone in an angry unseen mob—Rockwell's iconography graphically gestures to aberrant Southern hate.

Discursive inheritances of these constructions of the American South as national Other have remained hegemonic over past decades, a reserve of anecdotal evidence of the contrasts between the South and the rest of the nation. Nearly forty years later, iconic images of Southern intransigence remain authorized in the national imagination as cinematic texts serve critically to mark the American South of the sixties as the preeminent site of the nation's racial dilemmas.

Thus, from the decade of the eighties through the nineties, Hollywood studios released a number of nostalgia films that returned the audience to the oppressive milieu of racial intolerance and anti-black violence in the American South of the fifties and sixties.[5] Together with the "civil rights biopic," a genre that included Spike Lee's *Malcolm X* (1992), Mario Van Peebles's *Panther* (1995), Rob Reiner's *Ghosts of Mississippi* (1996), Norman Jewison's *The Hurricane* (1999), and Michael Mann's *Ali* (2001), these texts "return to the sixties" to depict Southern torpor and resistance in the face of imminent racial transformation.

Mark Golub refers to such films as "Hollywood redemption history" (1998, 23),[6] explaining that these are "generic tales marking a self-conscious departure from Eurocentrist narratives . . . explicitly intended as [an] anti-racist narrative" that give marginalized groups a "chance to have 'their own story told'" (23). Dramatizing "upheavals and transformations of white racial consciousness in intimate personal encounters with the 'black' experience" (Willis 2001, 99), these films nevertheless emerge as de-fanged excursions into the historical past, centrally celebrating the distance the nation has traveled since the sixties. Thus, as Golub notes, although these narratives begin with a focus on the fight against racial oppression, the point-of-identification character eventually turns out to be a charismatic white man with whom the audience identifies (23). Offering a conservative revisionism that indulges the showy heroics of white Southerners positioned as "men before their time," redeemed FBI agents (*Mississippi Burning*, 1988) and maverick small-town Southern lawyers (*A Time to Kill*, 1996; *Ghosts of Mississippi*, 1996; *The Chamber*, 1996) alike emerge as lead characters within the narrative. In turn, the tale shifts focus from the marginalized group's history to the salvation of this central white male character.

Nostalgia films serve centrally as a celebration of distance. Underscoring public memories of an anomalous and anachronistic American

South, these narratives proffer images of the South as "a place apart." As Mimi White explains, these texts "enable viewers to declare . . . 'But that was then, this is now,' . . . that problems . . . were worse 'back then'" (1998, 121). Marking out the distance separating today's audiences from the nation's racial past, anti-black racisms are defined "Southern," located safely far back in time. These markers of distance serve keenly to render Southern civil rights claims irrelevant in the contemporary North and to suggest, in the context of recent assaults on affirmative action, that solutions invented in the sixties to address peculiarly Southern dilemmas have outlived their purpose, surviving only as obsolete remedies for exotic ailments.

Joel Schumacher's screen adaptation of John Grisham's first novel, *A Time to Kill*, stands apart from such Hollywood redemption histories in that it does not return to some horrific moment in the past. Instead, the characters we find center-stage and the ethical dilemmas they confront play out in present-day Mississippi. What is key, however, is that the drama transpiring on screen is aesthetically suspended in time, and the South represented in the film is sluggish and unchanging. Like John Sayles's *Passion Fish* (1992), James Foley's *The Chamber* (1996), and Clint Eastwood's *Midnight in the Garden of Good and Evil* (1997), the contemporary South constructed in *A Time to Kill* serves to reassure mainstream audiences not only that "that was then, this is now" (White 1998, 121) but, moreover, that "things are different here," reminders of the ways in which racial problems are always "worse down there."

Filmic representations of the American racial nightmare, then, typically either return the audience to the spectacular horrors of the South of long ago or they transport viewers to specifically rural backwaters of the contemporary South. Positioned thus, as either safely far back in time or sufficiently far away in space, cinematic portrayals of the South build and emphasize distance—temporal as well as spatial—between the mythic South and its imagined converse, the "American North." As Allison Graham suggests, even those texts that attempt to make a statement about contemporary Mississippi nevertheless take their cues from the past (2001, 181), from far away in time and space.

These dichotomies focus national attention on lingering dilemmas of race, but in highly circumscribed ways. That is, while these texts focus on racial violence and oppression, the action is located far away in the backwater South. Such an abiding focus on Southern aberrance ontologically connects issues of race with the American South. Authorized definitions of racism, likewise, are contained by the logics of overt displays of violence and repression that are located at a safe distance. These constructions offer proof that such racial disorders are exotic and bizarre in the everyday context of life in the contemporary United States. They perform key resuscitative work within the national imaginary, absolving the imagined North of its lingering racial crimes.

Highlighting these connotative labors of the mythic South, the narrative of Schumacher's *A Time to Kill* opens with a hideous crime. Walking home from the local provisions store on a hazy summer afternoon, Tonya Hailey (RaéVen Larrymore Kelly), a ten-year-old African American girl, is beaten, raped, and left for dead by two local white thugs, Billy Ray Cobb (Nicky Katt) and James Louis Willard (Doug Hutchison). The men have been on a boorish drunken rampage, veering about town in a dusty yellow pickup truck, a Confederate flag sticker conspicuously adorning the rear window. Sweaty, beer-bellied, and foul-mouthed, the men yell racial epithets as they lob beer bottles at black teenagers playing basketball in makeshift, streetside play yards. They hoot and howl, driving recklessly by black residents sitting silently on ramshackle verandas, who watch them go by without surprise or recourse.

Vulgar, working-class brutes, Billy Ray and James Louis are villains with "dark racial motives" (Ainslie and Brabeck 2003, 43). Replaying the cinematic archetype of the Southern villain as "hick" and "redneck" (Graham 2001, 147–93), these portrayals resonate within public consciousness. Uncannily prefiguring the gruesome dragging death of James Byrd in Jasper, Texas, in the early morning hours of June 7, 1998 (Burka 1998, 9; Chua-Eoan 1998, 34–35), the brutal, racist assault in *A Time to Kill* is a crime from another time. Billy Ray's and James Louis's actions elicit a gasp not only because they are savage but also because they disrupt the authorized response: "But that was then, this is now." Serving to smooth over such disruptions, the cinematic narrative is deliberately located in the rural South. Technology, urbanity, and industry are strategically absent as the rural quiet of a hazy afternoon and the ambient melody of a blues guitar offer assurances that this place is keenly different from everywhere else, that things are always "worse down there."

The Jasper, Texas, incident enjoyed prolonged media attention with dozens of reporters and journalists stationed for weeks in the small east Texas town as the sensational trial progressed. Beyond hard news, stories about Jasper proliferated in a variety of media genres. Among the journalists who covered the racially charged trial of the three men indicted for Byrd's murder, two published their experiences in paperback memoirs (J. King 2002; Temple-Raston 2002). The pay cable network *Showtime* produced a television movie, *Jasper, Texas* (Jeff Byrd, 2003), dramatizing the story, and long-time friends Whitney Dow and Marco Williams brought a white and a black perspective to their highly acclaimed documentary feature *Two Towns of Jasper* (2002).

Each of these retellings emphasizes the anachronisms of Jasper, Texas, and underscores the enduring place of the South within the national imaginary of race. As one journalist put it, "the American South believed it was finally repairing the deep burns to its social fabric left by the flames of racial hatred that swept across the region through the 1950s and 1960s. And then came Jasper, Texas" ("Uneasiness in South" 1999, 25). Abiding logics that construct the lingering racial wounds of the South as keenly different are thus reproduced by endless regurgitations of horrific Southern crimes, reminders of the ways in which the American South remains a hostage to its racial past and thus keenly opposed to the North.

As they emerge in the context of contemporary affirmative action debates, such authorized imaginaries serve critically to delimit what counts as racial oppression, the din of such dominant versions drowning out opposing conceptualizations and categories. Structural reform of political and economic inequity and its attendant institutional racisms and sexisms disappear from view as policy assaults on affirmative action, enabled by these distillations of public consciousness, foreground Southern deficiency as leitmotif of the national racial narrative.

Southern Simulacra

As the gruesome crime that opens Schumacher's *A Time to Kill* merges in the national imaginary with hideous secrets of the South, a series of simulacral ironies emerge. For one, the narrative universe of the film is located in a fictional small town in the Deep South presented as cinematic simulacrum of the actual Southern town of Canton, Mississippi, where Schumacher and his crew shot the entirety of the film over the summer of 1995.

The real-life Canton is a predominantly black, Southern town, its current population around twelve thousand. Located in central Mississippi, twenty miles north of the state capital, Canton is the seat of Madison County. The local economy combines farming, poultry processing, and paper production. In 2003, the automobile giant Nissan opened the world's largest automobile manufacturing plant on the southern edges of the town, which for local officials transformed Canton "from cotton center of Madison County to auto center of the world" (Canton Convention and Visitors Bureau 2003). Despite the optimism of the town's newly appointed slogan, "Rich history, bright future," Canton has suffered unrelenting economic depression for much of its post-Reconstruction history. Typical of rural Southern towns scratching together meager revenues from stagnant economies, roughly 40 percent of the population lives below the poverty line.

While the official Web site of the City of Canton makes no mention of it, Canton is roughly 70 percent black (Chen 1997; Herring 1997, 24; Robertson 1997, 14). The town remains sharply segregated. Ninety-nine percent of those attending Canton Public High School are African American, while Canton Academy, the local private school founded in 1967, serves an overwhelmingly white constituency.[7] Asked what he thought would happen if black students enrolled in the all-white private school, Mike Coggins, the headmaster, volunteered, "There may be some people who still hold those old attitudes, that [it] would infuriate them enough that I'm sure they would let me know or [it could get] to the point where maybe they'd take their child out" (*Waking in Mississippi*). Forty years after federal courts integrated public schools, when asked about the odds of an integrated high school in Canton, County Supervisor Louise

Spivey replied, "probably . . . not very likely." Then, changing her mind, Spivey continued, ". . . in time . . . ten years. Yes, I don't think it could be much sooner" (*Waking in Mississippi*).

Under the watchful eye of the white minority, zoning regulations and economic incentives emerged strategically over the years to ensure white political governance of the town. Canton enjoyed an uninterrupted history of white male mayoral and municipal control until 1995, when for the first time in the town's history, an African American, Alice Scott, won the mayoral race, ousting fifteen-year incumbent Sidney Runnels from office. Scott was not the first black candidate to run in a local mayoral race. However, her campaign emerged as the first ever to pose a serious challenge to the white incumbent. As a local radio personality, Jerry Lousteau of WMGO, explained:

> I don't think some of the white power structure realized that this was about to happen. And I think some of them may have been a little too secure in the fact that we've had the majority of the aldermen and mayors—since aldermen and mayors started work here, and the town's always been seventy to seventy-two percent black—why would that change now? And I think it may have snuck up on some of them, and that may have added to the tension. It was an event whose time had come but some folks were still a little surprised that it had come then. (*Waking in Mississippi*)

The mayoral race as it played out between Scott and Runnels polarized residents. As Runnels characterized it:

> It became a very racial election to be honest with you, and I'm sorry that it turned around like that. You know, I've said this to many groups before while I was campaigning, "If I'm a racist why have I not had anybody run against me that was black since 1989?" And this was 1994 . . . You know, I've been called a lot of things but . . . when they called me racist, that was wrong. But that's politics. (*Waking in Mississippi*)

When Scott was asked why it had taken Canton, a town with a 70 percent black population, until 1995 to elect a black mayor, she responded:

You had to find someone with enough backbone, enough fortitude, enough stamina to stand up and look a white, fifteen-year male incumbent in the face and say, "I'm not satisfied, and I want to try and do something about it." You don't find that every day. And I wouldn't have done it eight years prior to doing it because if I were to run and not win, I would not know how people would take me. And I could possibly be fired from my job working in a town where I fought against someone to do this. (*Waking in Mississippi*)

When the votes were counted, local officials announced that the election had resulted in a tie between the candidates. Tensions soared as locals, both black and white, expressed incredulity and suspicion over the unprecedented tie vote. A federally monitored runoff was scheduled, as opposing camps orchestrated vicious, racially charged attacks against each other. White organizers issued "every vote counts" appeals, urging local whites to cast their ballots in solidarity with the white incumbent. They contacted town residents who had moved away, urging them to send in absentee votes to guarantee a white victory in the runoff. And black residents, unconvinced that the first election had in fact produced a tie vote, threatened a riot if "the white man steals another election" (*Waking in Mississippi*). Mayor Runnels's office, perceiving the threatened riot as a likely possibility, requested that National Guardsmen be sent to Canton, and in a matter of hours dozens of armed guards appeared in Canton's town square. For Runnels, blacks were trying "scare tactics of the sixties," which included

Telling people they knew how they were voting, telling people that they would come down and harass them at their house, or possibly if they could do that they would burn their house down. Supposedly some of the same things that they said whites did during the sixties, some of the blacks turned around on people and tried it. And I couldn't overcome that. (*Waking in Mississippi*)

In the summer of 1995, after Alice Scott had decisively won the runoff election,[8] production crews from Warner Brothers studios arrived in Canton to shoot *A Time to Kill*. A few years earlier, town officials had pushed for a new public face to reinvent Canton as the quintessential Southern small town ideal for Hollywood studios with scripts requiring the "idyllic background of a quaint Southern square."

As small towns in Mississippi began to compete for Hollywood location revenues, town officials in Canton approved a series of preservation projects to restore the Canton Square District located in the heart of the old town. Refashioning the town into a "major force in the film industry," city officials redesigned Canton's tourism Web site, advertising its "turn of the century town square," "the great columned mansions," and "majestic Greek Revival Courthouse," and offering the City of Canton as a "great location for any shoot" (Web site for the City of Canton, Mississippi). Between 1994 and 1995, a new courthouse was built a block north of the town square, and the old courthouse, originally constructed in the mid-1800s, underwent a two-million-dollar renovation. By the mid-nineties, when production crews on *A Time to Kill* arrived in Canton, more than twenty million dollars in public and private funds had been invested toward beautification and renovation of the Canton Square District (Web site for the City of Canton, Mississippi).

As cinematic productions of the nineties refashioned backwater towns into bustling back lots, Southern towns collaborated opportunistically to reconstruct themselves in specific ways. Producing an image tailor-made for buyers in Hollywood, a deliberate commercial negotiation of Southern spaces emerges for the consumption of film audiences across the United States and overseas. Reminiscent of the tourism efforts of state officials in other Southern states, the transformation of Canton, Mississippi, trades on a particular Southern identity.

A strategic simulacrum of the American South emerges thus, offering twin assurances of distance and familiarity for the consumption of film audiences. These portrayals combine markers of distance measured in time and space from the North as well as familiarity in the sense that such portrayals recycle an identifiable range of Southern aberrations. Hollywood demand for a cookie-cutter South, a "colorful place steeped in mystery, home to timeless tradition," together with Southern municipal officials focused on raising local revenues, produced hyperreal Southern spaces that were frozen in time. Such self-conscious displays turn on a particular brand of cultural arrested development that remains emblematic of the American South.

The Warner Brothers production team remained in Canton for five months over the summer of 1995, shooting at several of the newly renovated historic buildings. Their presence was an economic windfall for Canton, generating eight million dollars in revenues, with nearly ten thousand Mississippians drawing a paycheck from the production (*Lights, Camera, Canton*). The production recruited local craftsmen to supplement the studio crew and cast hundreds of local residents as extras. Members of the National Guard, some of whom had been brought to Canton a year earlier to contain the threat of riots over the mayoral elections, were now rehired to play themselves in scenes where angry mobs of whites and blacks clashed in front of the historic courthouse.

Like the circus coming to town, Schumacher's presence disrupted local routine. By the time the production rolled its wagons out of town, the first "cappuccino bar" had opened downtown. Samuel L. Jackson, one of the stars of the production, became the first African American to play golf at the local country club. The Canton Film Museum opened a year later, documenting props, costumes, and set memorabilia that the production had brought to town. And in the next few years, other Hollywood productions followed, including Joel and Ethan Coen's *O Brother, Where Art Thou* (2000) and Jay Russell's *My Dog Skip* (2000), which like *A Time to Kill* was shot almost entirely in the small town. Documentaries, commercials, and smaller budget films followed, including Martha Coolidge's production of Eudora Welty's *The Ponder Heart* (2001) for PBS's Masterpiece Theater, and the Jackson-based independent filmmaker Tim Rice's *The Rising Place* (2001).

Moreover, the production of *A Time to Kill* focused national media attention on Canton and residents of the small town. Christine Herring was a graduate student studying film at Duke University in 1995 when she began receiving phone calls from her hometown, Canton, urging her to send in her absentee ballot in the mayoral runoff between Alice Scott and Sidney Runnels. When Schumacher's crew arrived in Canton, she decided to team up with fellow Duke student Andre Alexis Robinson and return home to document "Warner Brother's ironic fabrication of a race riot in 1995 for *A Time To Kill*, only one year after the threat of actual rioting brought dozens of armed guards to Canton's town square" (Gone South 1995).

Robinson, an African American who earlier had graduated from Central High School in Little Rock, Arkansas, and Herring, who had attended the private all-white Canton Academy, drove into the Mississippi Delta to collect over eighty hours of footage of community leaders, elected officials, residents, and class valedictorians from both the predominantly black public high school and the local all-white private academy (Robertson 1997, 14). Combining these voices with interviews with Hollywood star Samuel L. Jackson, director Joel Schumacher, and Warner Brothers publicist Michael Singer, Herring and Robinson produced the documentary feature *Waking in Mississippi*, which offers a complex look at "how a town can seem to forget that the same tensions they are play-acting had been all too real just one year before" (Chen 1997).

Media fascination with Schumacher's presence in the small town reached a national audience when the CBS news magazine *48 Hours* arrived in Canton on "the biggest day of shooting" on *A Time to Kill* to capture the action of the explosive riot scenes of the climax of the film. With anchor Dan Rather at the helm, the CBS team interviewed cast, crew, and local residents to produce *Lights, Camera, Canton*. In a series of six-to-eight-minute segments, the hour-long program sought to document "Hollywood's takeover of a small Southern town" as a "healing moment in the town's history" (Azrael 1997, 48).[9]

Lights, Camera, Canton begins with a montage of establishing shots—the historic courthouse, a rusty cotton harvester idle in the fields, horses grazing lazily in nearby meadows, a quiet barbershop on Main Street. The accompanying voice-over by the journalist Bill Lagattuta begins: "Canton, Mississippi. Population: eleven thousand. A sleepy Southern town about to be rudely awakened." Heralding a "time to think and a time to talk," Dan Rather announces in the same vein: "In the next forty-eight hours, racial tensions will boil over, passions will flare, and a riot will break out . . . providing, of course, everyone follows the script."

Lauding Schumacher's production for digging up long-seated and thorny racial dilemmas, *Lights, Camera, Canton* is framed as "a story about race in America." With cameras trained on the elaborately choreographed riotous confrontations of Schumacher's climactic scenes, the news program combines its portrayal of the small Southern town as lethargic and "sleepy," roused from its slumber by the traveling ruckus of a Hollywood production, with regurgitations of the American South as racial hold-out. Delivering distance between a valorized America contrasting with a recidivist South, Schumacher and Rather, like tourists visiting the past from the present, variously orchestrate a Southern spectacle, ready-made and recognizable for the national audience.

Herring's and Robinson's *Waking in Mississippi* similarly introduces a sleepy and forgotten Canton. Cameras pointing out of the window of a moving car, the documentary begins with a video montage of streets lined with crumbling storefronts long closed. Desolate, abandoned homes go by, their windows boarded up and yards overrun by weeds. The sound track plays a languid blues guitar but here there are no grazing horses in open meadows. No one naps on a lazy front porch. The midday silence of these streets does not evoke the quaint romance of the Deep South. Instead, this is a town comatose from economic stagnation, forgotten by municipal and business leaders alike. This is black Canton.

Herring and Robinson describe a Canton, Mississippi, that is in marked contrast to both Schumacher's and Rather's versions. Traveling what George Lipsitz refers to as "roads not taken" (1990, 30), *Waking in Mississippi* challenges the verisimilitude of Southern simulacra sold to Hollywood executives and film audiences. In contrast with abiding logics of Southern deficiency as emblematic of the national racial narrative, Herring's and Robinson's film disentangles dilemmas of race from an imagined anomalous South and, as a consequence, denaturalizes the selective and circumscribed boundaries of what counts as true.

Framed as a tale of dysfunction and disaffection, *Waking in Mississippi* proffers a South that has much in common with the urban North. Here, visible markers of economic deprivation and political apathy in the Canton, Mississippi, of this film combine to indict structural inequities— unequal investment, uneven development, and inadequate basic resources. Dilemmas about race, as they fester in such places, are not easily explained by the peculiarities of the American South. Rather, this framing suggests that racial antagonisms are fueled by chronic structural failures, by collapsing public services, by economic opportunism and political corruption.

Where Schumacher's riot scenes orchestrated the irony, unselfconsciously perhaps, of "playacting the same tensions that had been all too real just one year before," the hour-long *Lights, Camera, Canton*, despite its predictable focus on racial secrets of the Deep South, is remarkable for its utter silence on the fractious mayoral race in Canton that had, only months earlier, brought the National Guard to the small Southern town. Instead, *Lights, Camera, Canton* is crowded with testimonies from town residents that proffer an idealized image of the South as racially rehabilitated, an emerging model of interracial harmony. Thus, Joanne Gordon, director of Canton's visitor bureau, a white woman, is giddily enthusiastic in one scene. Beaming at the camera, she states, "I think that this is great! . . . It's been a great partnership among the company and among the local citizens of Canton . . . I . . . asked Joel Schumacher yesterday if he could please slow down because the people don't want it to end. It's been wonderful."

Scuttling evidence of racial antagonisms, the program is, on the one hand, typical of the contemporary repertoire of mainstream network news shows—circumscribed and superficial. But if racial confrontations in the South make for entertaining cinema, and if the spectacle of such make-believe racial violence is sufficiently newsworthy for an hour-long prime-time news program, the absence of any mention of the near riot in Canton's town square a year earlier deserves a careful regard. For one thing, acknowledging the events of the Scott-Runnels mayoral contest would necessitate attention to the racial present rather than the past. Such attention, moreover, would narrow the imagined gap between the South and the North. In contrast, eliding the threat of actual rioting that had brought dozens of armed guards to Canton's town square less than a year earlier maintains Southern distance, both temporal and spatial. It reiterates hegemonic truths that the racial past is more troublesome than the present, and that racial dilemmas in the South remain worse than those in the North.

Lights, Camera, Canton includes a single voice, that of Dr. William Truly Jr., a local black resident and NAACP member, to suggest that some locals may have had reservations about the transformative impact of Schumacher's production. "It has basically been like two worlds here—a black world and a white world," Truly explains. "We had people who simply didn't talk to each other. But we find ourselves now talking to each other about the movie. I think the movie has served as a bridge." Then he adds cautiously, "I would like to think that we will continue to build bridges between blacks and whites. But that is only a hope."

Where Truly is an exception within the giddy celebration of *Lights, Camera, Canton*, Herring's and Robinson's *Waking in Mississippi* showcases skepticism, featuring a complex mix of responses ranging from hope to jaded cynicism.[10] Speaking as a weathered veteran of enduring racial wars, an African American community activist, the Reverend Jasper Bacon, states: "In one sense [racial integration] cannot be forced . . . You can make segregation unlawful, but you cannot legalize or force integration." In a later sequence, Bacon continues,

> I was told that both local news and national news indicated that this movie had really impacted race relations in a positive way. I question that. In my mind, it appears to have allowed for some interaction between blacks and whites. But to allow for some interaction doesn't necessarily mean that some real changes or some real coming-together has taken place. On the other hand, it appears that the movie, in some cases, could have even aggravated wounds that have always been there, some sores that have always been there. In some cases, the movie could have even been a reminder of what Grandmother, what Mom and Dad faced.

Testifying to "sores that have always been there," Lonnie Hamlin-April, another African American community activist, suggested she had not found any evidence that Schumacher's production had spurred interracial dialogue. "I've never participated in any of it," she stated. "I don't know anyone who did. So, you know, I don't know where all of this is." Jerry Lousteau, a white resident, agreed: "Whether you got involved with it [the production] just to make a few bucks or whether you were dazzled that big-time Hollywood was here, it was a wonderful distraction. But I think that folks are fooling themselves if they think it put aside any issues for long . . . because the election issues lasted a year after the election. And still are issues. And will probably be issues for some time."

These testimonies from *Waking in Mississippi* articulate lived experiences of racial realities in the contemporary South. What is remarkable about them is not simply their candor but rather the ways in which they describe racial estrangement as an everyday American dilemma. These testimonies are not peculiarly Southern, nor do they register as isolated and anomalous. Instead, the entrenched racial rifts described in *Waking in Mississippi* are of a piece with social critiques at the core of other independent documentaries that focus on Northern and urban racial contexts—*Hoop Dreams* (Steve James, 1994), *The Promised Land* (Edmund Coulthard and Nick Godwin, 1995), *Two Nations of Black America* (June Cross, 1998), and others—which suggests that Southern dilemmas, far from aberrant, instead bear a striking resemblance to contemporary racial issues elsewhere in the contemporary United States.

These parallels between South and North are underscored in scenes from *Waking in Mississippi* where the actor Samuel L. Jackson, the first African American to gain membership at the Canton Country Club, recalls the hubbub on the links the first day he went in for a game of golf.[11] As he explains it, while "there was a definite air of racism around here during the [fifties and sixties] I'm sure, I've actually felt it since I've been here. So I know it's [still] present." Jackson continues, "And these are people that are over fifty years old whom I've encountered in various places [who] have treated me in a very different kind of way until they found out that I'm in a movie and then it's like, 'You're not . . .'" For the Canton radio personality Jerry Lousteau, Jackson's presence at the country club should have served "as some sort of benchmark like the [Scott-Runnels] election." Lousteau explains, "You know, I don't know the membership rules at the Canton Country Club but I would venture there are not many people like Samuel Jackson out there playing golf every day."

For Jackson, the local response is not simply a matter of Southern anachronism, of Southerners being out of touch. Instead, he explains, "It's kind of like the *Do the Right Thing* syndrome with [the] John Turturro [character] . . . where he talks about Michael Jackson or Michael Jordan [to say], 'Oh . . . you're not a nigger, you're a movie star. That's different.' So I get treated differently because of that." Here Jackson explains rural Southern attitudes about African Americans with an analogy from the urban North. In this moment, as fifty-year-old white Mississippians are seen indulging the same anti-black racisms as young Italian American New Yorkers in Spike Lee's *Do the Right Thing*, it becomes difficult to sustain clear logics of distance between North and South.

Jackson's observation is one example of the ways that *Waking in Mississippi* gives voice to resistant accounts of the South, versions that demand a reevaluation of the tidy history of civil rights and its assumptions about Southern aberrance. These testimonies highlight the extent to which the Southern struggle for racial equality remains in step with the work of Northern civil rights advocates. They underscore the commonalities rather than differences between Northern and Southern race struggles. Thus, hinting at the propinquities rather than distance between the North and the South, these testimonies offers us a second example of the "roads not taken" in dominant accounts of racial history, another glimpse of the elusive category of countermemory.

Eyewitnesses to the Racial Past

The cinematic narrative of *A Time to Kill* convenes a pageant of eyewitnesses, each straddling the racial past and present to subtle and strategic effect. Building upon the circulating repertoire of anecdotes and experience that ontologically connect race with the American South, these characters offer critical insights into the epistemic work of the mythic South within contemporary assaults on racialized social justice.

Carl Lee Hailey (Samuel L. Jackson), the father of the young rape victim, balances two sets of emotions as he processes Billy Ray's and James

Louis's brutal crime. He is racked with grief at the viciousness of the attack and at his failure as a father to protect his daughter from the men. "I called for you, Daddy," he recalls her saying to him. "When them men was hurting me, I called for you . . . over and over . . . but you didn't never come." But beyond his grief, Carl Lee is besieged by doubts about the Southern criminal justice system. Recalling how, only a year ago, four white men who had raped an African American girl in the Delta had been unfairly acquitted by a Southern jury, Carl Lee fears that, like them, Billy Ray and James Louis will escape conviction, given racisms endemic to Southern courtrooms.

For Carl Lee, vengeful and desperate, it is "a time to kill," and while the prisoners endure Sheriff Ozzie Walls's (Charles S. Dutton) interrogations in the precinct office, Carl Lee steals into the courthouse armed with a rifle, to wait in hiding through the night. The next morning, a crowd of onlookers gathers in the halls of the courthouse to watch as the shackled Billy Ray and James Louis are led up the main stairs to their arraignment. As they begin their ascent, the hushed silence of the courthouse halls is shattered as Carl Lee rushes at them with a guttural scream. The crowd of witnesses watches in mute horror as Carl Lee shoots repeatedly, killing both prisoners and accidentally injuring Deputy Dwayne Looney (Chris Cooper), a police guard escorting them up to the hearing.

In keeping with genre conventions of the Hollywood nostalgia film, *A Time to Kill* switches focus at this point to develop the character of Jake Tyler Brigance (Matthew McConaughey), a Southern white lawyer who serves as defense counsel for Carl Lee in the murder trial that ensues. Jake is the "charismatic white man who fights (or comes to fight) against the oppression that is the central issue of the film" (Golub 1998, 23), and the tale—though it began as an anti-racist narrative that sets out to consider "if a black man can receive a fair trial in the South"—turns into a saga about Jake's salvation and triumph over white supremacists and complicit Southern women.

Old-fashioned male chivalry constructs fathers as virtuous defenders of their daughters, as the paternal instinct to protect is presented as universal. As John Grisham, the author of the story, explains:

It was something I saw in a courtroom. I watched a little girl testify one day—she was about twelve years old, I guess—and she'd been brutally raped and almost killed by a man. I remember thinking, "that poor child." You know, if that was my little girl, I'd somehow get a gun and this guy would be dead . . . Everybody can connect with that dad. Every dad can connect, every parent can connect . . . I wanted to explore what an all-white jury would do to a black father who did what every juror would want to do. (*Lights, Camera, Canton*)

Thus, Jake's motivation for taking the case and pleading Carl Lee's innocence is that he knows instinctually how he would feel if Billy Ray and James Louis had unleashed their murderous lust upon Hannah, his own daughter (Alexandra Kyle).[12] Likewise, Jake's summation at the end of the trial is premised centrally on the presumption of universal fatherly instincts. And when Jake cannily drives the jury to consider how they would feel if Carl Lee's brutalized daughter were their own, white instead

Defense counsel Jake Brigance (Matthew McConaughey) questions defendant Carl Lee Hailey (Samuel L. Jackson), charged with the double murder of Southern thugs who beat and raped his ten-year-old daughter, in *A Time to Kill* (Joel Schumacher, 1996).

of black, the racist all-white jury that has had its mind set on convicting Carl Lee for much of the trial experiences a stunning about-face. Jake's summation literally opens the racist jurors' eyes, as Carl Lee's vigilante outburst is rendered palatable—even heroic—with appeals to an old-fashioned ethic of chivalry, presumed universal among men.

As the narrative progresses, Southern femininity emerges unhampered by time. The film sets up a deliberate contrast between the sexual self-confidence that empowers Ellen Roark (Sandra Bullock), the plucky law student from Boston who is attending law school at nearby Ole Miss, and Southern women like Ethel Twitty (Brenda Fricker), who is Jake's straight-arrow, small-town secretary. Ellen is the aggressor in her relationship with Jake—she approaches him, pursues him, and helps him out in crucial ways as the trial proceeds. Jake's ambitions for working to "change the world, one case at a time" are matched by Ellen's gutsy intentions "to spend a glorious career stomping out the death penalty."[13] In contrast, when Jake and his colleague Harry Rex Vonner (Oliver Platt) inquire playfully about the possibility of a clandestine romantic history between Ethel and the rakish alcoholic Lucien Wilbanks (Donald Sutherland) for whom Ethel worked for twenty years, the old dame responds with coquettish indignance, insisting, "I'm an upstanding, God-fearing, respectable Southern woman with unimpeachable morals who has been happily married for twenty-seven years. And I never had nor ever will have any boyfriend!"

Like Ethel, Jake's wife, Carla (Ashley Judd), performs timid, modest, old-fashioned femininity. She is disapproving of Jake's decision to represent Carl Lee and does not stay by his side when the stakes rise. When the "good, God-fearing Klan" convenes in the small town in an attempt to intimidate Jake and his family with threatening phone calls and by burning crosses in their front yard, Carla explodes in frustration, demanding:

[Sorry] about what? That you weren't home when someone practically burned our house down? That you missed supper and didn't even bother to call? Or that lately you've become much more interested in getting your face on the news than what's going on with your own family? Or that Hannah comes home every day bawling because of other kids calling her a "nigger lover"? What exactly are you sorry about, Jake?

Shaken by an attempted bombing at their home, Carla leaves town with their daughter for a temporary stay with her parents in Gulfport, and shortly thereafter Ethel leaves as well, after her husband, Bud (Danny Nelson), is severely beaten by Klansmen in another attempt at intimidation. As she bids Jake farewell, Ethel's words are disapproving:

> There's nothing you can say. I know you didn't want any of this to happen. But it happened all the same. You wagered all our lives on this. You just went ahead and did what you felt you had to do, no matter what the cost. Some folks think that's brave. Not me, Jake. Now, you may win. But I think we've all lost here.

These Southern women, in strategic contrast with Ellen, make traditional choices of self-interest over sacrifice, safety over heroism, and the pretense of civility over rude upheaval. They acquiesce to Southern customs and social mores and thwart the Southern male's progressiveness with disapproval and desertion.

As white Southern women occupy positions of complicity with the "Southern way of life," working-class Southern men appear as members of the hastily convened local Ku Klux Klan and racist courtroom jurors. Others emerge as rogues with a conscience, including Klan defectors who secretly inform on and foil the organization's clandestine efforts. Still others like Deputy Looney serve the African American Sheriff Walls without a trace of racial resentment, choosing to support Carl Lee during the sensational trial at significant personal cost.[14]

In contrast, wealthy "plantation racists" like Judge Omar Noose (Patrick McGoohan), who presides over Carl Lee's trial, the ruthless district attorney Rufus Buckley (Kevin Spacey), who is charged with prosecuting him, and the narcissistic Harry Rex Vonner, who pursues a dilettantish range of superficial pleasures, are men embroiled in networks of Southern white male privilege. Enjoying particularly Southern dividends of racio-economic prestige, these are men of substantial means for whom articulations of race matters are tedious and vulgar.

Southern liberals are set apart from the foregoing archetypes as characters with whom the audience is meant to identity. Thus, we have Jake Brigance who, reminiscent of Atticus Finch, the heroic Southern lawyer in Harper Lee's prize-winning novel *To Kill a Mockingbird*, agrees to defend the African American Carl Lee despite harassment and alienation from his neighbors and family. This hero emerges in stark contrast to vulgar Southern racists against whom he is positioned as exceptional not simply because he opposes anti-black racisms but because he stands against them in the cultural milieu of the South.

Further, Jake asserts a vehement and unapologetic Southernness, harboring scorn and ridicule for what he refers to as "Northern, liberal, cry-me-a-river, we-are-the-only-enlightened-ones-in-the-Northern-hemisphere bullshit." He eschews the reviled logics of multicultural political correctness, instead typifying an old-fashioned but ethical pragmatism on questions of racial justice. He is, for example, "very much in support of the death penalty." "I'd like to go back to hangings in the courthouse lawns if we could," he states, explaining that "the problem with the death penalty . . . is that we do not use it enough." Likewise, he shows no discomfort when Carla, "a sweet little sorority girl from Ole Miss," chooses the old-fashioned security of established gender roles, content with her position as wife and mother in the domestic sphere of the home. And he is sufficiently reconciled with gentlemanly norms of sexual propriety to arrange meetings with Ellen, the Northern law student, in black-owned diners on the black side of town so no one in his circle will catch him fraternizing with "a woman like her."

Lucien Wilbanks embodies an older generation of this Southern liberal archetype, described in the narrative as "the third white man in Mississippi to join the NAACP, permanently disbarred by the Superior Court for attacking police who busted a picket line during [an oil workers'] strike." Wilbanks serves the narrative as a conscientious but impotent objector to abiding racisms of the South.[15] Jake has learned the tricks of the trade from his mentor Wilbanks, but times have changed since Wilbanks and his NAACP comrades tried to change the world. Now Southern white heroes must chart a new course of social transformation, one that pointedly excludes the agenda that Wilbanks and his cohorts championed.

Thus, a new generation of Southern heroes offers a rational response to the bleeding heart excesses of the sixties, demanding a tempering of doctrinaire liberalisms. While Northern whites who make such demands suffer excoriation as "racists," Southerners like Jake survive instead as heroic voices of plebeian reason. Their critiques of civil rights excesses are positioned in contrast to Southern supremacists and Northern liberals alike as the "no-nonsense" heroism of the Southern male gives implicit support to neoconservative critics of racialized social justice. Contemporary discursive investments in white male victimhood and earnest avowals of color and gender blindness are thus rendered palatable, even heroic, as Southern male voices articulate uniquely credible critiques of Northern excess.

These efforts to position Southern men as "voices of reason" who moderate the "heady excesses of the armies of liberalism" are traced back to civil rights debates of the mid-sixties when Southern leaders sought to contrast Northern hypocrisies about race with Southern pragmatism. Thus, during congressional hearings on the landmark civil rights bill in early 1964, Southern leaders made several attempts to draw attention to hidden patterns of Northern racisms. For example, Senator Richard B. Russell (D-Ga.) proposed a "Voluntary Racial Relocation Program to adjust the imbalance of the Negro population between the eleven states of the old Confederacy and the rest of the Union" (Kenworthy 1964e, 1). Russell explained:

> If the people of the Southern states are to be forced to conform to some federally dictated social order, which is wholly alien to them, then I think it is only fair and right that the Negro population be spread more evenly over all sections of the country. This would afford those who support these so-called civil rights proposals an opportunity to put into practice in their own areas the social order that they find so desirable and which they are

attempting to force upon the people of the South. In other words, they ought to have the opportunity to practice what they preach. (1)

These arguments posed rhetorical challenges to Northern white commitments to racial equality. Russell hinted provocatively that faced with the prospect of blacks in every private club and rooming house, Northern reactions would not be unlike those of whites in the South. Likewise, Alabama governor George C. Wallace, on his presidential campaign in Wisconsin in early 1964, attempted to "out" Northern racisms as he taunted the audience: "before you go on a moral crusade, you ought to look at your Indian reservations" (Wehrwein 1964b, 40). Emphasizing his "respect for Alabama Negroes," Wallace often recounted anecdotes to emphasize patterns of residential segregation that were widespread in the North. "When I moved into the Governor's mansion in Montgomery in 1963, there were six Negro families on the same block, and not a one of them moved out because I moved in" (Franklin 1964, 23). Highlighting the commonplace of whites in the "liberal North who often flee to suburbs when Negroes move in," Wallace had Northern white audiences chuckling at their own veiled double standards on these occasions.

In April 1964 Wallace received nearly 25 percent of the total votes cast in the Democratic presidential primary in Wisconsin. When, a month later, he won nearly 30 percent of the vote in the Indiana primary and more than 40 percent in Maryland, Southern segregationists hailed these victories as "the Great Awakening," as "evidence of widespread Northern support for their beliefs" (Sitton 1964d, E5), and as a "demonstration of their contention that the North as well as the South was opposed to racial change" (Sitton 1964c, 19). In the same vein, Arthur Krock, in a letter to the editor of the *New York Times*, referred to the primary election results as a "protest vote," contending that "this protest is considerable and continental rather than merely Southern in scope" (1964, 30). These articulations did not simply serve to impugn the North. They worked to create a recurring role for Southern voices in calling out white racisms in the North, to articulate particularly Southern reproaches against Northern hypocrisies.

Like veterans of wars recounting battlefront experiences, Southern voices offer a range of eyewitness testimonies that are authentic and reliable. However hideous, these accounts suggest, racial relations in the South reflect a lived history of struggle and compromise, an interracial codependence that is markedly absent in the North. Here, the uniquely tortured history of race in the American South paradoxically ascribes a matchless credibility to Southerners on matters of race. Mythic scene of the crime, and simultaneously remarkable site of racial resistance, the South emerges through these constructions as a place where, despite the odds, meaningful norms of racial coexistence, however tentative, have been brokered.

Such accounts, moreover, enable particular indictments of the liberal North suggesting that whereas the South claims its racial dilemmas, the North, in contrast, denies its own. Authorized memories of the South as "a place apart," then, are keenly productive of a uniquely Southern legitimacy on questions of race in America. Whereas, in the sixties, the Northern agenda for civil rights reform managed to condemn Southern voices as un-American and unethical, by the nineties, Southern liberals, it will appear, had won a reprieve in terms of credibility and common sense on race matters. Within the narrative universe of *A Time to Kill*, white heroes like Jake and the quintessentially Southern critiques they proffered were invested with a renewed ethical pragmatism, which by the nineties reflected authorized truths about multicultural excess and its mutant progeny of civil rights reforms as having overstayed their welcome.

Racial Crimes Past and Present

The pragmatist Southern critique that Jake presents, merging as it does with analogous critiques leveled by neoconservatives elsewhere in the nineties, is rendered unimpeachable with a complement of conscientious African American voices that echo the white hero's complaints. Midway through the narrative, Jake is called in to the precinct offices, where he finds Carl Lee in a meeting with Reverend Agee (Thomas Merdis), the pastor of the local black church, and out-of-towners Reverend Isaiah Street (Joe Seneca), a representative of the NAACP who "marched with Dr.

King," and Norman Reinfeld (Jonathan Hadary), a high-powered litiga-tor—coded Jewish and Northern—with significant experience with cap-ital murder cases.

Reverend Street had earlier expressed his concerns about Carl Lee's choice of attorney as "a man who is not sensitive to the needs of the movement." Now Street explains: "Mr. Hailey's case has far-reaching ram-ifications. Carl Lee's acquittal for the killings of two white men would do more for the black people of Mississippi than any event since we inte-grated the schools. His conviction, on the other hand, will be a slap at us. A symbol of deep-seated racism, perhaps enough to ignite a nation. See how important this case is?"

But as the conversation proceeds, we discover that the NAACP's concern for Carl Lee is feigned. The big-name, media-savvy litigator they have recruited for Carl Lee's defense will serve the NAACP more than he will Carl Lee, and Street is revealed as an opportunistic instiga-tor, seeking to sensationalize Carl Lee's trial to make a national media event out of a racially charged Southern murder case. We learn also that, having raised a small collection from local churches to help Carl Lee's family with their household expenses, Reverend Agee has been manipu-lated by the NAACP into pooling the church collection toward Carl Lee's legal defense instead. Reminding the NAACP that the legal defense fund they have arranged should properly be sent to Jake, and that the church collection must be passed in full to his wife as promised, Carl Lee dis-misses the out-of-towners. "I think I'll take my chances with Jake here," he announces, declining the NAACP's self-serving offer and calling the meeting to an end.

Alone in his cell with Jake, Carl Lee admits that he did set the NAACP up, embarrassing them into paying his overdue litigation ex-penses and compelling Agee to support his family as he had promised. He tells Jake that he could not have done it without him, but when Jake suggests giddily that they "make one hell of a team," Carl Lee douses his enthusiasm, saying, "You out there, Jake. I'm in here. We ain't no team." Although Carl Lee chooses the small town Southern white male as his ally in a move that indicts civil rights organizations like the NAACP for their wasteful self-indulgence, his choices are shrewd and strategic. He does not reward the Southern male with Uncle Tom obsequiousness and neither does he abide by doctrinaire racial loyalties. Rather, Carl Lee personifies the canny resilience of poor Southern blacks who have learned, through bitter experience perhaps, that they must rely upon any means necessary for their own survival.

In a later scene, Carl Lee explains to the white lawyer that "America is a war, and you [Jake] are on the other side. We ain't no friends, Jake. We're on different sides of the line. I ain't never seen you in my part of town. I bet you don't even know where I live. Our daughters, Jake, they ain't never going to play together." No presumption of fairness or justice softens his indictment of contemporary race relations. The solution to his problem is the Southern white male, not because Carl Lee expects Jake to work ethically toward his defense but because he is "one of the bad guys." He explains:

> You're my secret weapon. You think just like them. That's why I picked you. You're one of them, don't you see? . . . You don't mean to be, but you are. It's how you's raised . . . Oh, you think you ain't cause you eat in Claude's and you're out there trying to get me off on TV talking about black and white. But the fact is you're just like all the rest of them. When you look at me, you don't see a man. You see a black man. "Nigger." "Negro." "Black." "African American." No matter how you see me, you see me as different. You see me like that jury sees me. You are them. Now, throw out your points of law, Jake. If you was on that jury, what would it take to convince you to set me free? That's how you save my ass. That's how you save us both.

A damning critique of civil rights struggles of the sixties is advanced in these scenes. For one, the racial recidivisms of the contemporary South, the primitive circumstances in which we find African Americans living on the outskirts of town, "all of the rapin' and killin' [that] people are tired of" combine to indict the civil rights movement of the sixties as having done little to transform the politico-economic circumstances of African Americans living in the Deep South. Further, if Carl Lee expects the Southern courtroom to function as obsolescent arena of favoritism and corruption, thirty years after the fact, he is also firmly aware that he cannot count on the civil rights establishment to "save his ass." Not only has the Northern civil rights establishment proved itself utterly ineffective in dislodging entrenched racisms; it has also collapsed, bit by ignominious bit, into self-serving hypocrisy.

By the end of the tale, thus, Jake and Carl Lee have issued nearly identical critiques of the civil rights revolution of the sixties even as they bring diametrically opposing life experiences to their assessments. Such Southern testimonies, rich with authenticity and credibility, perform unparalleled service in assessing contemporary racial dilemmas and in privileging particular solutions to them.

Eschewing civil rights reforms and racial solidarities, black and white Southerners reveal guile and cunning as effective responses to the institutional racisms of the South. Celebrating the potential for alliances between African Americans and Southern white males, Schumacher's text allows black Southerners a single option out of their racial predicaments—the neoliberal imperative that popular struggle and organizing is misguided and that each man must instead look out for himself. Black protagonists, the text asserts, must hitch their proverbial wagons onto neoliberal dicta of self-reliance and individualist dint.

Providing a racially correct voice-over to the strategies of new racisms of the nineties, cinematic texts like *A Time to Kill* participate in what Stephen Steinberg (1995) has referred to as the "liberal retreat from racial justice." Here, liberal whites give cover to vigilante violence on the logic that black residents have few other options. Thus, Jake is Carl Lee's secret weapon who must shelter him from the consequences of his violent vigilantism because they—liberal whites and poor blacks alike—have no recourse. Institutional reform, systemic accountability, grassroots resistance, these options never emerge as real possibilities. Instead, Carl Lee's problem and his chosen solution are of a piece in that they serve to indict vulgar white racists and an opportunistic and ineffective civil rights establishment. These are the racial criminals of the present, and they each justly deserve rehabilitation.

Remembering Saints and Demons

A particular pageant of iconic saints and demons is resurrected in these portrayals to impeach civil rights reforms born of the South. Here, specific accounts of black organizations and individuals remembered as "fighting for all America" emerge in contrast with others scripted as "agitators" and "troublemakers." These reconstructions circulate particular images of those who "won" and others who "lost," of how the civil rights struggle and the American South can and should be remembered.

Such authorized memories take their cues from narratives of the sixties that celebrated moderate black leaders and appointed Northern white liberals as allies in the fight for civil rights forty years ago. Returning to news accounts of the sixties, we find that "rational" and "reasonable" civil rights reforms were promoted while Southern whites and militant blacks, fierce opponents in the civil rights struggle, were portrayed alike as rabid ideologues. Blunting deeper challenges to the hegemonic order, these authorized narratives transformed "militancy into constituency," revealing, as Michael Omi and Howard Winant have argued, "tactics of absorption and insulation" in the civil rights agenda of the sixties (1994, 106).

Northern leaders separated militant black voices and "subversives on college campuses" from "established civil rights organizations" (Herbers 1964c, 48). Highlighting their departures from "established" and "reasonable" civil rights leaders, radical blacks were seen to pose dangers to "the American way," vilified in much the same way as Southern segregationists. Blacks identified with "established" civil rights organizations, on the other hand, were relentlessly sanctified and valorized (Terte 1964, 22). Repeated exaltations of Rosa Parks as the spark for the Montgomery bus boycott in 1955, the tragic martyrdom of four young girls in September 1963 who were killed in a bomb attack on the Sixteenth Street Baptist Church in Birmingham, the televised attacks in March 1965 against nonviolent marchers on the Edmund Pettus Bridge in Selma— each account imagines a constituency of terrorized but tenacious African Americans. Authorized memories of these events reconstruct a singular Southern civil rights movement that is premised on Northern magnanimity and Southern rehabilitation.

In contrast, the Congress of Racial Equality, whose members staged a rush-hour traffic-stopping demonstration on the TriBorough Bridge in New York City in March 1964, was the target of a volley of harsh criticism from Northern liberal whites who complained that such "inflammations of the public peace" elicited "outrage from the middle-class community" (Gilhool et al. 1964, 8; Hechinger 1964, 7). Similarly, two highly successful school boycotts in New York in early 1964 organized by the Reverend Milton A. Galamison, who headed the Citywide Committee for Integrated Schools, spurred the response that "extreme elements representing the center of the deprived ghettoes are resorting to action which repels middle-class citizens including the more city-wide and nationally oriented Negro leadership" (Hechinger 1964, 7).

As these criticisms acknowledged the line between "continuing demands for total integration on the part of those speaking for the deprived, non-middle-class population and the biracial middle-class drive for moderate integration," they simultaneously revealed "the raw nerve of middle-class fears about integration—the threat of having children from 'good neighborhoods' transported by bus into slum areas" (Hechinger 1964, 7). Like Southern officials who unsurprisingly took a hard line approach to these strategies—as Allen Thompson, mayor of Jackson, Mississippi, stated, "any demonstration or assembly by Negroes, peaceful or not, [is] an unlawful demonstration" ("Police Fear Crisis" 1964, 52)—the Northern response was inhospitable to black demands that did not match standards of "moderation."

Thus, the Northern agenda opposed "sane and reasonable" black leaders recognized as "men of intelligence, stature, and good judgment" (Perlmutter 1964, 1) against "agitators," "extremists," and "intimidators" who condoned "illegal and extremist violence" ("Extremism Loses" 1964, 34; Krock 1964, 30). Charging militant black leaders with "belligerent emotionalism," a "lust for power," and other "sinister motives," the mainstream white civil rights agenda relentlessly policed the boundaries of black resistance. As Northern newspaper editorials warned, blacks who continued to engage in "illegal" and "inconvenient" street demonstrations risked alienating the support of "the vast sympathetic liberal community"

(Gilhool et al. 1964, 8). Serving warning in patronizing tones, these voices reminded readers that "when the hard question of the priority of public spending arises, the Negroes, a minority after all, must have the electoral assistance of the rest of us" (8).

Scuttling inconvenient public statements by Martin Luther King Jr. that "Negroes must continue to press for equal rights at the risk of being called immoderate," for "if moderation means slowing up in our fight then moderation is a tragic vice which members of our race must condemn" (Herbers 1964b, 27), the mainstream press and many Northern whites condemned black leaders like Malcolm X rather than eloquent negotiators like King for irresponsibly stirring up blacks. Speaking to an audience of Harvard faculty and students, Malcolm responded:

> When we [black leaders] warn you [whites] how angry the Negro is becoming, you, instead of thanking us for giving you a little warning, try to accuse us of stirring up the Negro. Don't you know that if your house is on fire and I come to warn you that your house is burning, you shouldn't accuse me of setting the fire. (1964/1991, 136–37)

Thus, black leaders who invited liberal whites to join their quest were hailed as civil rights heroes. Those who identified whites as enemies and instead urged their followers to "do whatever is necessary by any means necessary to protect [them]selves" remained outsiders, worthy of contempt and censure (Malcolm X 1963; 1964/1991, 173).

By the nineties, a time when radical black leaders like Malcolm X were enjoying a merchandised cultural renewal, we find cinematic texts like *A Time to Kill* issuing damning critiques of the NAACP, an organization that would have been counted among the "sane and reasonable" leadership of the civil rights establishment of the sixties. A particular assessment of authorized memories of the civil rights revolution of the sixties is at hand here. On the one hand, we are witness to a romantic nostalgia that incorporates chosen figures from the Southern civil rights movement into the logics of cinematic and commodity merchandising. As these bowdlerized icons of reverence are co-opted into the catalogs of the cultural marketplace, their threat is duly contained. On the other hand, elements of the civil rights agenda of the sixties—legal reforms for racial justice, the meticulous work of civil rights enforcement and monitoring, the celebration of racial consciousness and solidarity—have remained willfully independent of the armies of appropriation, and it is these elements that we find condemned in contemporary cinematic texts.

One among a number of Hollywood texts of the nineties, *A Time to Kill* is not alone in its choice of saints and demons from the sixties. Here, nostalgia films join a chorus of filmic genres to spurn specific discursive inheritances from the South of the sixties. By the logic of these portrayals, the civil rights movement survives as a carefully culled all-American episode of social transformation and, crucially, as a singular and tidy historical fact. Appropriation, co-optation, and silence stand guard at the borders of these public memories to offer contemporary assessments of the Southern civil rights struggle as a mission long accomplished. And by the logic of these cinematic reconstructions, racial recidivisms, where they are not explained by vulgar Southern attitudes, are recounted as misbegotten fruit of the sixties.

CBS's *Lights, Camera, Canton* and Herring's and Robinson's *Waking in Mississippi* offer us critical insights into this mix of reverence and condemnation as local residents and visiting celebrities alike offer a series of trenchant testimonials that articulate an eerie sense of déjà vu as residents of the small town of Canton watch hooded Klansmen gather in the town square in preparation for the climactic scenes of Schumacher's film. One black resident, a woman, declares solemnly in *Lights, Camera, Canton*, "It's almost too real, almost too real. Some of this really has happened in real life in this town." Likewise, an NAACP activist, William Truly, states, "It may appear to be fantasy. And it may appear to be make-believe. But in the minds of many of us, this movie is real." And yet another black resident, watching from a street corner, smiles warily at the sight of extras dressed as Klansmen. "Got the Klan marching in Canton," he observes quietly. "That's strange. I know it's just a movie, but it's strange. That is a sight to see, ain't it?"

Where these voices articulate a flash of recognition, underscoring a lingering proximity with racist brutalities of the past, for others like County Supervisor Louise Spivey, a white woman, the sight of Klansmen in the town square elicits a uneasy chuckle: "I was, sort of, astonished, you know," she explains in a scene from *Waking in Mississippi*. "Sort of takes you back . . . Then someone yelled, 'Cut! Cut! Cut!' and everybody took off their hoods. And my goodness gracious! It was people from the Baptist Church . . . deacons from the Church . . . my good friends from the city." Similarly, African Americans who appeared as part of the raucous crowd in the climactic riot scenes recall in *Waking in Mississippi* how funny it was that whites dressed up as Klansmen pleaded off-screen with blacks posing as protestors not to hit hard because "this was just acting, you're not really fighting." Another local extra recalled, laughing, how one Klansman who had his hood pulled off by a black protestor exclaimed, "No, not the hair. Please don't pull my hair."

Each time Schumacher's cameras stopped rolling, eyewitness testimonies note how the scene transformed from riotous "sixties footage" to whites and blacks congenially helping each to their feet, joking and patting each other on the back. A local white dressed in Klan regalia points self-consciously to his white robes, saying, "Hopefully, everyone remembers it's just a costume," while a black extra chuckles as he tries on a Klan hood, exclaiming, "See, I don't even know how this thing goes on."

These accounts portray the fictional racial confrontation as a moment of release and levity for black and white residents of Canton. Revealing a willed amnesia about the near riots of the mayoral election of 1995, the fabricated riot enables black and white extras to clash with childlike glee. Playacting racial vengeance that delivers therapeutic relief, the fraternal merriment of the shoot analogizes Schumacher's staged confrontation to harmless street theater. Much of its entertainment value lies in the suggestion of distance from real life, in its improbability.

Balancing this semblance of levity, Herring's and Robinson's *Waking in Mississippi* takes the embattled 1995 mayoral elections in Canton as its starting point through interviews with black residents as they reveal their commitments to elusive integration ideals through lawful advocacy and social reform. Theirs is not a spectacular struggle. There are no sensational trials, no fiery speeches, and no sense of relief or justice. Theirs is a story of quotidian oppression, of silence and resignation, of everyday slights and subversions. Whereas the showy heroics of Southern males and the corroborating testimonies of Southern blacks impugn racial reforms of the sixties in *A Time to Kill*, *Waking in Mississippi* reminds us that African Americans in the South, much like their counterparts in the North, continue to struggle toward civil rights by dint of tactics invented in the South of the sixties.

In contrast, one segment of *Lights, Camera, Canton* focuses on Elizabeth Omilami, an African American cast in the role of a protestor, who recalls in a moment of rest between shoots that her father, Josiah Williams, led the "Forsythe County march when we were attacked by two hundred Klansmen." "There were only sixteen of us," she remembers, "and I was there." The only difference for Omilami between Schumacher's staged race riot and her experiences as a civil rights protestor during the sixties is that "in real life, because of the nonviolent philosophies of Martin Luther King, we couldn't yell back. We had to say, 'I love you.'" The make-believe riot of Schumacher's production thus offers Omilami a long-awaited chance to "do what I've been wanting to do all my life."

By the end of Schumacher's tale, moreover, black men have committed the murders of three Southern whites—Billy Ray Cobb and James Louis Willard at the hands of Carl Lee Hailey, and the Klan Grand Dragon, Stump Sisson (Kurtwood Smith), killed in the frenzy of the riot when a militant black teenager (Patrick Sutton) lobs a firebomb at him. These black killers slip by unscathed: by the end of the film Carl Lee is acquitted of the murder charges, while the unnamed teenager is never discovered as Sisson's killer. Given the numbers of African American men who suffered lynching and court-sanctioned murder in the South of the Jim Crow era, given that these men routinely suffer punishments for crimes they do not commit, the giddy celebration of vengeance that black men and women enjoy in these texts hints at the contours of liberal white guilt and its tendencies toward overcompensation.

Together, Omilami's gleeful pretense of racial vengeance and the acquittals—fortuitous or otherwise—that spare the black killers of

Schumacher's narrative deliver a peculiar racial comeuppance. In the South, these narratives suggest, liberal standards of color blindness remain elusive. Vigilantism and guile survive as the only plausible courses of action for black Southerners in the context of draconian racial mores. Black residents of the real-life town of Canton and their simulacral doubles are offered the means to cathartic racial vengeance in ways that underscore the force of individual action over structural reform.

Placing the burden of racial justice on the shoulders of individual Southerners, both *Lights, Camera, Canton* and *A Time to Kill* peg civil rights reforms of the sixties as ineffective. Here, Omilami's confessions of delight in *Lights, Camera, Canton*, like the desperate homicides of *A Time to Kill*, serve to reiterate neoliberal dicta of self-help and individualism. As black Southerners are called upon to articulate critiques of strategies of the sixties, these texts offer these disenfranchised individuals the chance, however fleeting, to bash Southern white supremacy with their bare hands. As hapless and desperate African Americans are celebrated as heroes for taking matters into their own hands, the nonviolent agenda of the Southern civil rights movement survives as frustrated and disappointing. Southern voices perform key ideological work here, positioned forcefully as "individuals" negotiating predicaments arising from race. Eschewing historical legacies of racial solidarity and grassroots organizing, these black voices serve to indict the American South in precise terms and simultaneously to spurn the civil rights legacy of the sixties.

As dominant discourses variously sanctify and commodify chosen leaders of the civil rights movement, vast networks of grassroots organizations of the sixties and the reforms they forced into place emerge as part of the problem. Credible eyewitnesses from the South, in filmic and news texts alike, echo these critiques of sixties discourses and tactics. Blacks and whites join in the chorus to argue that liberal individualism is far more reliable as a solution to lingering problems of race than reformist inventions of the sixties. Southern voices chime in, making earnest claims about the continuing salience of race in contemporary culture and the utter ineffectiveness of race remedies traced genealogically to the American South of the sixties.

Cinematic regurgitations of these "lessons from the sixties" work effectively to evacuate the expediency of racialized reforms invented in the sixties. Authorized memories of the American South contribute to a peculiar double jeopardy in that they excoriate reforms of the sixties as having outlived their usefulness in the North and simultaneously as hopelessly ineffective in the South. Within the context of neoliberal assaults on social justice in the nineties, such authorized memories serve in at least three ways. First, they reassure mainstream audiences and voters of distance, both spatial and temporal, between the tortured dilemmas of the South and the liberal milieu of the contemporary North. Second, they reserve a unique position of unmatched credibility for Southern voices that work to open up the logics of civil rights to incredulity and contestation. And finally, they underscore distinctions between moral imperatives for racial reform in the sixties that are genealogically traced to the South of that moment and the continuing exigencies of those reforms within social justice debates of the present.

By the decade of the nineties, cinematic constructions of the contemporary South served effectively to blunt particularly Southern and racialized modes of black resistance as either unnecessary or racist or both. This is their central and particular contribution to the discursive assaults of the nineties. Preferred memories of the American South and its civil rights past highlight a particular and strategic teleology for the national racial narrative, carving out a selective version of the past that celebrates a narrative of racial progress, within which continuing demands for racialized social justice emerge as ineffective, opportunistic, and racist.

CHAPTER 4

Of Heroism and Healing, Racism and Redemption: Tall Tales and Short Lists

> It is no fallacy when a story flourishes in the heart of a folklore,
> it is because in one way or another it expresses an aspect of
> "the spirit of the group."
>
> —Frantz Fanon, *The Wretched of the Earth*

It would have been hard to miss Ward Connerly, chairman of the campaign for California's Proposition 209, during the months that preceded the general elections in 1996. In a media blitz of carefully scheduled performances that reached a crescendo during the fall of 1996, Connerly appeared on national television and radio programs, at commencement ceremonies and public forums on the future of race in America. Microphone in hand, Connerly told remarkable stories about the human costs of affirmation action—accounts of vicious imbalances fostered by affirmative action mandates, of individual resilience and tenacity in the face of unfair exclusions, of human kindness and compassion in contrast with state apathy and corruption.

At the same time, a cottage industry of reportage arranged a parade of Connerly's business partners, Delta Phi Omega fraternity brothers, and estranged family members who would variously add to the public record on Connerly. Details about the soft-spoken and self-made businessman from Sacramento, his wife of nearly forty years, Eileen, and their spacious home in Arden Oaks, an upscale suburb of Sacramento, appeared in popular magazines and journals (Bearak 1997, 1; Pooley 1997, 32–36; Watters 1997). Here, tragic tales of the father who "ran out" on the family when Connerly was a child of two, the "racist" maternal grandmother who raised him during his early childhood in Leesville, Louisiana, and the sister whom he denounced as a "welfare addict," as well as stories about what some referred to as the regent's "female trouble" (Anson 1996, 15), all offered crucial insights into Connerly's personal convictions and political choices. Hailed variously as "race traitor," "strange fruit," and "the bravest black man in America," Connerly arrived on the national scene as gifted storyteller and himself the subject of contentious tales of principle and promise.

Connerly's emerging life story played out in the public sphere, offering what Kathy Abrams refers to as "a striking union of the revelatory with the corporeal" (1991, 975). Recounting everyday stories about hardship and human resilience, these narratives turned poignant anecdotes into potent political messages. Turning its focus on the form and force of such narratives, this chapter examines the implications of recurring stories, what Hayden White has referred to as "encodations of experience [that] pervade our structures of consciousness" (1978, 4), which, as this analysis will show, bear critically on the racial and gendered truths of our time.

A rich repertoire of such stories, of *petit* and *grand récits*, in Jean Baudrillard's words, is discernible in policy debates over affirmative action that played out over the decade of the nineties. The impact of such narrative encodations in public policy debate is not unusual. Rather, as critical race theorists have shown, narrative commonplaces perpetuate their particular order of coherence in the public affairs of the state much as they do in the private everyday lives of people (Delgado 1989, 2411–41; Scheppele 1989, 2082–83). By these accounts, in law as in public policy,

> No set of legal institutions or prescriptions exists apart from the narratives that locate it and give it meaning. For every constitution there is an epic, for each decalogue a scripture. Once understood in the context of the narratives that give it meaning, law becomes not merely a system of rules to be observed, but a world in which we live. (Cover 1983, 4–5)

This analysis focuses centrally on the ways in which state-sanctioned narratives—tales recounted by political authorities that organize woes and frustrations into an authorized hierarchy—command intense emotional legitimacy. What is at stake here is not the fallible or fictional in stories,

OF HEROISM AND HEALING, RACISM AND REDEMPTION – 191

nor the difference between factual and narrative knowledge. Rather, as Sanford Schram and Paul Neisser remind us, facts, along with everything else, are constructed through stories (1997, 7). Each version is escorted by its own perspectival blindness: every narrative simultaneously building "structures of attention and inattention" (Schram and Neisser 1997, 8) and each manifesting "assumed boundaries for what is thinkable, doable, possible, and valued" (Nakagawa 1993, 145).

Narratives, as they perform in the public sphere, are consequently interested rather than disinterested, potent rather than innocuous. Each shaped by its ideological investments, they ensure that both authorized and subjugated knowledges are always partial, always silent on some aspects. These silences are brought into relief by "unreading stories," that is, by highlighting remainders of narratives and reading what they have left out. Attending to such silences and the possibilities for "unreading" that lurk therein, this analysis offers an account of how and why, despite their vulnerabilities, some narratives endure and others wither.

Beyond the work of stories in terms of details they mute and others they amplify, this approach allows us to think through the implications of the state itself as "storied site," as Slavoj Žižek (1989) has argued, to understand how stories secure, if not state legitimacy, then the state's political affectivity. Constructed through a range of accounts—as oppressor and benefactor, as vulnerable and valiant, as heroic and villainous— the modern state has a powerful existence in cultural discourses and popular imaginations, and public debates over civil rights and affirmative action have been witness to powerful articulations and rearticulations of these stories of the state. Greater even than their service to one or another political agenda, such stories—whether they recount parables of a state "hijacked by special interests" or serving a "liberal cabal in Washington"—work ultimately to fill out the contours of mythic spaces occupied by the state.

I locate this analysis at two distinct points in time: the first, during the period surrounding the passage of the Civil Rights Act of 1964, and the second, in the context of ballot initiatives that eliminated affirmative action programs during the decade of the nineties. The Civil Rights Act, like Proposition 209 in California in 1996 and Initiative 200 in Washington in 1998, spurred dramatic reversals in entrenched legal standards and highlighted shifting cultural habits. These are "great transformations," as Michael Omi and Howard Winant have argued, in that racial meanings and truths established during these periods have forcefully shaped the dominant knowledges and cultural politics of their time (1994, 97).

Moreover, the intensity of public debates that erupted over the Civil Rights Act remains unmatched but for contests over affirmative action that came to a head in the nineties. Escorted by a profusion of articulations about race, gender, equality, and discrimination, each of these events gave rise to intense battles over intersecting and overlapping narratives of heroism and resistance, of bigotry and redemption. Attention to these moments in time illuminates the workings of power in narratives, and the ways in which narrative practices are implicated in the production of dominant knowledges about race and gender in the public policy process.

Returning to news coverage and legislative records of the mid-sixties, I present a comparative reading of authoritative and authorized narratives. The analysis pursues the ways in which culturally resonant narratives have operated within public debates on affirmative action and civil rights across time. Strategically deployed metanarratives of mythic American individualism, therapeutic motifs of national healing and recovery, and integrative petit récits that contain and co-opt oppositional voices are revealed in impassioned appeals for civil rights during the sixties as well as within recent attacks against them. Together, these comparisons lead us to consider the multiplicity of ideological accents that signifiers speak in, to examine how opposing points of view come to speak in the same narrative tongue. Such comparisons allow us to reveal the work of narrative reversal and renewal in the racial logics of our time and, thus, to open up to scrutiny knowledge regimes that operate as naturalized and transparent.

The Grammar of Liberalism

Remarkable parallels are discernible between the narrative strategies of recent campaigns to eliminate affirmative action and those that dominated civil rights debates during the mid-sixties. Weeks of impassioned debate in both houses of Congress from February to June of 1964 circulated a range of stock stories of individual humiliation and oppression, of human resilience and courage. Opening debate on the civil rights bill in the Senate in March 1964, Senator Hubert H. Humphrey (D-Minn.) asked, "Suppose you attempted to go into Rock Creek Park with your loved ones on Sunday, but discovered you first had to go to court for authority to use these public facilities? How long would most white citizens tolerate such a state of affairs?" (*Congressional Record* 1964, 6542).

Likewise, referring to "thousands of pages of testimony . . . taken in field hearings all over our land . . . by the U.S. Commission on Civil Rights," Senator Thomas H. Kuchel (R-Calif.), co-sponsor of the civil rights bill in the Senate with Senator Humphrey, argued that "discrimination has been demonstrated and documented in a long and sordid series of illegal and unconstitutional denials of equal treatment under law in almost every activity of many of our fellowmen" (*Congressional Record* 1964, 6554). Although "every American has read of Negro citizens and African diplomats being refused the opportunity to sit at a lunch counter, and eat a noonday meal as they travel an interstate highway" (6556), Kuchel asked, "should the shading of a man's skin determine whether or not he can eat a sandwich or secure a room for himself and his family after a drive of hundreds of miles?" (6558). He continued:

> Recently, I learned of a group of Catholic nuns who, last autumn, were visiting some of the historic battlefields of Virginia, a very short distance from the nation's capital. About 3 o'clock in the afternoon these nuns thought they would eat a late lunch before returning to Washington. They entered a roadside restaurant and were refused service. Why? Because two of the five nuns happened to be Negro. That this could happen in 20th century America is outrageous. (6558)

Senator Philip A. Hart (D-Mich.) narrated events from Dallas County, Alabama, to highlight irregularities in voter registration protocols. In one instance, Hart explained, voter registration forms asked new registrants, "Will you give aid and comfort to the enemies of the United States government or the government of the state of Alabama?" Kathleen Harris, a black woman with a bachelor of science degree who taught in the Selma school system, wrote in response: "Duties and obligations of citizenship are to obey the law, be loyal to our country and the state of Alabama, defend the country." Responding to the same question, Clissil McKay, a white registrant, wrote, "If Hurt would give comfort only if wonded [sic]." McKay was successfully registered as a voter while Harris, the black registrant, was rejected on the grounds that she had not specified the year she had become a resident of Dallas County. Such inconsistencies, Hart argued, pointed to the ways in which "registrars used immaterial errors to disqualify Negroes and then, accepted quasi-literate whites" (Kenworthy 1964m, 1).

Marveling at "the patience and self-control of the Negro who has been excluded from the American Dream for so long," these voices etched images of the "American Negro [who] has kept himself clean from the forces of subversion" (*Congressional Record* 1964, 6552). Echoing his poignant cry of "How long, O Lord, how long?" the Northern coalition narrated the Negro's plight in terms of exclusion from the voting booth and full citizenship (Kenworthy 1964m, 1).

Using emotionally potent anecdotes, these voices narrated particular tales of harassment and discrimination as they burdened black individuals. Each story justified the urgency of civil rights reform through dramatic accounts of individuated racial oppressions. Thus, the black family turned away from the park, Catholic nuns excluded from roadside restaurants, the competent but disenfranchised voter, and that most American of archetypes, the weary interstate driver who is refused a room to rest after a day's journey, each is a specific story of injustice, and the injury at the core of each tale focuses on individual harm and humiliation. As Humphrey put it: "When we deny a person employment because of his race, color, sex, or national origin, in a sense we steal his soul, his sense of identity . . . [his] spirit" (*Congressional Record* 1964, 6550).

The solution, Humphrey argued, involved putting "yourself in the other man's shoes, or as the old Indian said, 'Let me walk a mile in the other man's moccasins.' Do unto others as you would have them do unto you" (6542). Along the same lines, Kuchel argued that white Americans could choose no other course but to "judge [blacks] as you would be judged." Measuring fairness, justice, and decency in individual terms, each of these exhortations constructed the follies of segregation with narratives that provided a "flash of recognition," a sense of what it must feel like to be black and unwanted (Abrams 1991, 1022–23). Issuing an empathetic directive, the problem as defined demanded a personal and individual response.

Moreover, as Kuchel implored, the problem of racial segregation could only be solved if whites treated blacks in race-blind terms. "Judge me for my ability, for my qualifications, for my talent," he urged. "Do not judge me for the color of my skin" (*Congressional Record* 1964, 6554). Likewise, Senator Paul H. Douglas (D-Ill.), adding his voice in support of the civil rights bill, argued there could be "no differentiation between citizens. There are no first-class citizens and no second-class citizens; all, white or black, rich or poor, are citizens on equal terms" (6553). And in the same vein, President Lyndon B. Johnson, a strong advocate of the bill, speaking to a group of businessmen in Washington in April 1964, reminded his audience that "until education is blind to color, until employment is blind to color, you can free the slave of his chains but you can't free society of its bigotry" (Wicker 1964a, 1).

Thus, giving force to the individualist dictum of color blindness— if we could only look beyond a person's race, if we could only make ourselves blind to skin color—Northern voices of the sixties celebrated the incontrovertible sovereignty of the individual and articulated standards of color-blind liberalism as the principal means to racial reform. Echoing emotional appeals by Southern blacks, precisely the category of individual on whose behalf the Northern agenda made its claims, these grammars of liberalism served simultaneously to authenticate the liberal call to color blindness and, as well, to preclude sustained deliberation on alternate solutions to the problem of racial discrimination.

Reinforcing these themes, circulating vernaculars of news reports and other petit récits likewise emphasized the monstrous consequences of racial discrimination at the level of the individual. Caricatures in Northern newspapers of Eugene "Bull" Conner, the infamous police chief of Birmingham, Alabama, as the national symbol of Southern intransigence (Bennett 1993, 390), and news footage of the sheriff's deputies unleashing police dogs, fire hoses, and cattle prods on nonviolent civil rights demonstrators in Charlotte, Little Rock, and Selma, pitted violent whites against blameless blacks. These narratives gestured graphically to the unfairness of the Southern stand on civil rights, identifying racism against black Americans as the work of racist individuals—members of white citizens' councils and the Ku Klux Klan who detonated bombs to terrorize and kill. The problem, as defined, isolated the Southern bigot as "a moral evil" (Sitton 1964b, 17), urging the rehabilitation of these individuals.

The Southern position on civil rights arrived on the national scene, in a sense, prefabricated by these circulating accounts. Dixiecrats on the Senate floor played into these portrayals, corroborating national perceptions of Southerners as pathological and out of touch. Thus, Senator Allen J. Ellender (D-La.) engaged in a showy exchange with Humphrey, offering arguments for black biological inferiority that were based in discourses of heredity-perversion and eugenics. Justifying the actions of voter registrars who had "kept Negroes off the voting rolls by the discriminatory use of literacy tests and application forms" (Kenworthy 1964d, 1), Ellender argued: "If only the Northern Senator knew the capability of these people [blacks], he would be scared to death to have Negroes in charge of public office without qualification" (1).

Similarly, discourses of degeneracy and biological inferiority marked Senator Richard B. Russell's (D-Ga.) appeals to segregation as he led the Southern attack against the civil rights bill. Russell explained, "Southerners are concerned about amalgamation and mongrelization of the races. I know of no anthropologist who has been able to demonstrate that a mongrelized race has been able to bring forth a civilization or keep one going" (Kenworthy 1964c, 1). He continued that the civil rights bill was "a force bill designed to break up the 'separate but equal system' that the South has devised in the hope of solving the problem of two races living side by side without eventual amalgamation and mongrelization of birth" (Kenworthy 1964e, 1).

Revealing sharp differences between authorized knowledges circulating in the South and those in the North, such statements drew attention to bizarre Southern mentalities. Their claims about black inferiority, that "Negroes as a race were not equal to whites" and that "Negroes had made no contributions to Western civilization" (Handler 1964, 51) were amplified in press reports and on the Senate floor to "psychologize" civil rights opponents as prisoners of draconian customs. Condemned to the margins, these arguments remained laughable, odd, and impossible within the discourses of liberalism that reigned on the Senate floor.

As debate over the civil rights bill continued, a number of Dixiecrats turned to argue against civil rights reform using formulations that drew from discourses of liberalism themselves. Southern segregationists deployed counternarratives that portrayed the struggle over civil rights not as an attempt by blacks to achieve equality but rather as a grave threat to the American way in that it would "remake the social patterns of this country" (Kenworthy 1964k, 1). Senator Russell argued for the defeat of the civil rights measure because, as he put it, "this bill deals with every aspect of man's relations to man . . . It would destroy the free enterprise system, turn our social order upside down, and open up every private club in the country to Negroes" (Kenworthy 1964c, 1). Similarly, Senator George A. Smathers (D-Fla.) suggested: "Liberty is the right to select one course of action as opposed to another . . . Discrimination is thus the very heart and lifeblood of liberty . . . I do not advocate discrimination against any man . . . but this nation cannot afford to lose its very breath of life—individual liberty" (Kenworthy 1964i, 24).

In the same vein, Senator John J. Sparkman (D-Ala.) argued, "it is a characteristic, an inherent desire on the part of the individual to live among his own . . . [Such a choice is] a valuable civil right for the individual" (M. Hunter 1964, 45), and George C. Wallace, the segregationist governor of Alabama, suggested with characteristic flamboyance, "You may want to sell your house to someone with blue eyes and green teeth, but you should not be forced to do it. A man's house is his castle" (Franklin 1964c, 23).

Emphasizing fears that civil right reforms would "deprive the white majority of their private, inalienable, and constitutional rights to manage their own property" (Kenworthy 1964i, 25), Senator John Stennis (D-Miss.) argued that prohibitions on discrimination in employment and union membership would "constitute a drastic intrusion into private businesses . . . it would interfere with an employer's judgment of how best to build and maintain the most competent, efficient, and harmonious working force possible" (Kenworthy 1964h, 14).

The logical appeal of these arguments was not entirely ineffective, and Southern claims of the dangers that civil rights posed for the individual registered a growing public alarm. To wit, in a letter to the editor of the *New York Times*, one concerned citizen wrote:

> One hears much these days about civil rights, but very little about man's natural rights. Ever since the dawn of history [man] has had the right to control his property and select his associates. These rights are just as immutable as Jefferson's inalienable rights and are absolutely necessary for their fulfillment. They are the very warp and woof of the fabric of free man's priceless heritage. How can Congress, even under the noblest of motives, legislate them away? (Ponton 1964, 22)

Warring stories both—the oppressions endured by blacks and the injustice of forcing whites to integrate with them—these narratives appealed passionately to essentialized traits of the individual, to "man's natural rights," as Ponton put it in his letter to the *Times* in March 1964. Appointing sympathetic protagonists, the Southern strategy, much like the liberal consensus on civil rights, formulated its stock of narratives within a pervasive grammar of liberalism. Articulated in much the same terms, the incontrovertible logic of the "individual" offered urgent rationales for race reform and reappeared in Southern appeals to passionately urge its converse—the rejection of such reforms.

While the discursive context of the sixties—the televised parade of Southern brutalities, the folkloric record of racist violence in the Deep South, daily reminders on the Senate floor that despite their attempts to dress their arguments in liberal-speak, the Dixiecrats were an outmoded and illiberal lot—each of these factors worked to ensure that Southern claims failed to gain widespread credibility. Nevertheless, these comparisons point to the epistemic force of a pervasive grammar of liberalism in public debates over civil rights—opposing tales dressed in identical discursive garb. Whether for the humanity of blacks denied their constitutional rights or for the autonomy of whites facing constraints on their "natural" rights, the sixties were witness to Janus-faced narratives of individualism in both appeals for and against civil rights.

Liberalism thus emerges not simply as a facilitative discourse for one or another political agenda but instead as a grammar or syntax of knowing endemic to the emergence of specific truths, a mode of conceptual organizing. Whereas frames suggest strategic maneuvers in policy debates that willfully organize issues toward specific ends,[1] grammars reveal ossified usages as well as their vulnerabilities. Illuminating patterns of attention and inattention, the grammar of liberalism operates at the level of lexical distinctions, the syntax through which appeals and justifications are rendered intelligible. It directs our attention to organic distillations of truth, to the relations between vocabularies and their standing within reigning cultural discourses.

Paradoxical vestments of partisan appeals, each within the grammar of liberalism, thus dominated congressional debates over the civil rights bill in the mid-sixties and offer us crucial insights into reigning American ideologies about race. As critical race theorists have argued, the cultural transformations of the sixties and the seventies enabled consolidations of truths about racism from what Alan Freeman terms the "perpetrator perspective" (Crenshaw et al. 1995, xiv). That is, they allowed the broad cultural mainstream to explicitly acknowledge the fact of racism, while simultaneously being able to insist that the exercise of racial power was rare and aberrant rather than systemic and ingrained.

Such accepted knowledges embraced racial justice in terms that excluded radical or fundamental challenges to the status quo of institutional practices in American society. They limited dominant legal and cultural conceptions of racism to individual and identifiable acts of prejudice, and thus they perpetuated the invisibility of privilege that allows white Americans neither to be perceived as beneficiaries of systemic color preferences nor be held accountable for inequities harbored therein. As Thomas Ross argues, "practiced by no one in particular against no one in particular" (1995, 555), by the terms of reigning liberal grammars, systemic exclusions, oppressions, and privileges remained abstract and unfamiliar.

Thirty years later, discursive inheritances of these grammars were echoed in wide coverage of such incidents as the discovery of the Mark Fuhrman audiotapes in the media events of the O. J. Simpson criminal trial, the Texaco "black jelly beans" scandal, and the dragging death of James Byrd Jr. by three white males in Jasper, Texas. Dramatic and newsworthy, each of these integrative petit récits focused national attention on the pathologies of racist whites and the experiences of black individuals suffering at their hands. Whatever perspective the story is told from, the issues center on the individual and his/her pathologies and burdens. Instances of racism may thus be despised and subsequently punished. But portrayed as ugly confrontations between individuals, they erase the systemic or institutional operation of such oppressions.

Accompanied by their perspectival blindnesses—silencing accounts of group oppressions and exclusions and privileging knowledge of the individual costs of racial discrimination—narratives of individualism were reproduced in anti–affirmative action campaigns of the nineties. Thus, ballot pamphlets in California in 1996 observed that, beginning in the late sixties, affirmative action programs shifted "emphasis from individual rights to group entitlements" (Wilson, Connerly, and Lewis 1996). Ward Connerly proclaimed, "Our nation is desperately trying to embrace policies which place greater emphasis on the rights and responsibilities of individuals. The debate about affirmative action must be seen in that context" (Connerly 1996c, 14A). He continued:

> We are guaranteed the right to vote, the right to due process, the right to be free, not to be enslaved, as long as we conduct ourselves in accordance with the laws of the nation, and the right to equal treatment under the law,

regardless of our race, color, sex, religion, or national origin. These are rights [that] attach to us as individuals, not as members of a group.

As proponents of Initiative 200 in Washington recounted how the mythic American meritocracy had deteriorated into a "system of racial spoils . . . where some people are given an incentive to play up their race to get ahead" (Carlson 1998, B5), official voter pamphlets in California proclaimed likewise, "We are individuals! Not every white person is advantaged. And not every 'minority' is disadvantaged" (Wilson, Connerly, and Lewis 1996).

By the nineties, then, policy assaults on programs like affirmative action settled around the logics of circulating fears that while "a citizen should be judged by individual merit and not by special preference," social justice programs facilitated "a system that confers benefits on whole groups" (Wilson as quoted in Eljera 1996, 8). Liberal grammars of the sixties reappeared in these appeals to set merit against systemic preference, color blindness against racial exclusion. As congressional accounts of black families turned away from public parks and of weary travelers refused lodging in roadside motels had etched the ravages of racial segregation in terms of personal injuries and humiliations in the sixties, comparable tales of individuated wrongs served Connerly and his cohort in the nineties to vilify redistributive programs that benefited African Americans and to deny systemic advantages that accrued to whites.

Where these stories had compelled racial reform in the sixties, they reappeared thirty years later in the service of contrary ends. This polyvocality of authorized narratives, speaking stereophonically to opposite ends, cannot be explained by linguistic maneuver alone. This is not simply a matter of how well participants "do things with words." Rather, rearticulations of metanarratives of individualism as they enabled civil rights reforms in the sixties and, ironically, the elimination of those reforms by the nineties point to consonant shifts within discourses of contemporary liberalism.

In other words, the mobility of specific signifiers from one camp to the other, the reinvention of narratives so that they speak equivocally to multiple ends, reveal subtle yet remarkable transformations in larger discourses of liberalism. They foreground subtle discrepancies between liberalism and neoliberalism, suggesting that the particularities of liberal grammars are durable but malleable, and that shifts in these grammars echo the terms of larger transformations in the discourses of liberalism themselves.

At a glance, the liberalism that President Lyndon B. Johnson appealed to during the sixties to make the case for "the American Negro who for years, has been hobbled by chains" registers as keenly different from neoliberalisms that guided President Bill Clinton's "mend it, don't end it" mantra for overhauling race- and gender-based affirmative action during the nineties. Metonyms for shifts within the political discourses of liberalism, Johnson and Clinton mark the metamorphosis of New Deal Democrats into New Democrats, from traditional liberals to what John Brenkman refers to as "civic liberals" (1995, 19–22).

The terms of early liberalism set out a schema of the relationship between government and the governed in which individuals were identified on the one hand as "the *object* and target of governmental action" and, on the other hand, as "the necessary (voluntary) *partner* or accomplice of government" (Burchell 1996, 23, emphasis in original). Insisting upon clear limits on political authority, early liberalism championed the "sanctity of the opposition between public and private, politics and market, state and civil society" (Rose 1996, 39). And governance, as it was imagined, involved "pegging the principle for rationalizing governmental activity to *the rationality of the free conduct of governed individuals themselves*" (Burchell 1996, 23, emphasis in original).

Here the rational conduct of government was linked to "the *natural,* private-interest-motivated conduct of free market exchanging individuals," and individual freedom emerged as "a technical condition of rational government" (Burchell 1996, 23–24). Liberal government by these standards was preeminently "economic government" in the dual sense of cheap government as well as government geared to securing the conditions for optimum economic performance (26).

By contrast, discourses of neoliberalism that gained a foothold after the seventies enabled arguments about the arrogance of government over-reach and the dangers of imminent government overload. Taking hold apace in Thatcher's Britain and Reagan's America, these shifting discourses circulated claims that measures intended to decrease poverty had actually increased inequality, that attempts to assist the disadvantaged had actually worsened their disadvantage, that controls on minimum wages hurt the worse paid because they destroyed jobs (Rose 1996, 51). Echoing shades of traditional liberalism's deep distrust of government, neoliberalism emerged as "anti-statist" in its ideological representation. But reworked by the nineties, these truths embodied a highly contradictory strategy: they urged the dismantling of the welfare state and its programs of social and redistributive justice, while simultaneously remaining highly state-centralist in many of its strategic operations, championing repressive state apparatuses—the police, prison-industrial complex, military, and so on (Hall 1988, 152).

A politically salient assault on the rationalities, programs, and technologies of welfare and social justice was accordingly formulated over the course of the seventies and eighties from the left in terms of the "fiscal crisis of the state" and from the right in terms of the growth of an unproductive welfare and racial entitlements sector that created no wealth at the expense of the "productive" private sector in which all national wealth was actually produced (Rose 1996, 51). Positing the truth that the increasing levels of taxation and public expenditure required to sustain social, health, and welfare services, education, and the like were damaging to the health of capitalism as they required penal rates of tax on private profit (Rose 1996, 51), discourses of neoliberalism reproduced liberal imperatives for "a retreat from the state" but for keenly different reasons.

The rational principle for regulating and limiting governmental activity now entailed the promotion of an "enterprise culture" in all forms of conduct—the conduct of organizations hitherto seen as noneconomic, the conduct of government, and the conduct of individuals themselves. Here, the governed were encouraged to adopt "certain entrepreneurial forms of practical relationship to themselves as a condition of their effectiveness" such that a new form of "responsibilization" took form, which asked individuals to be responsible for the ways in which they assumed the status of being subjects of their lives, for the ways in which they fashioned themselves as certain kinds of subjects, and for the ways in which they practiced their freedom (Burchell 1996, 29–30).

Within the terms of neoliberalism, the meritorious self emerged as champion of self-help and self-fulfillment but with a vicious distrust of state mandates that made claims to private resources for public ends. Narratives about "active responsible individuals" reiterated narrowly defined rules of living to discipline individuals to proper standards of individualism. Celebrating a very specific kind of individual, these narratives championed a particular set of standards for professed ideals of "qualifications," "merit," and "equal protection" that took their cues from racialized and gendered narratives of "others" and "outsiders." These were individuals who "enterprised themselves," who maximized their quality of life through acts of choice, and who accorded their life meanings and values rationalized as the outcome of choices they made autonomously (Rose 1996, 57–58). Furthermore, they established standards for the nonracial self that were neither neutral nor objective, and that operated within rather than outside the bounds of social power and systems of racial privilege (Crenshaw et al. 1995, xv).

Within such a regime, individuals were to fulfill their national obligations not through their relations of dependency and obligation to one another but by seeking to fulfill themselves within a variety of "micromoral domains or 'communities'—families, workplaces, schools, leisure associations, neighborhoods" (Rose 1996, 57). As stock stories of individualism articulated with social hierarchies of race, class, and gender, they shaped the boundaries for what is "thinkable, doable, possible, and valued" to demand the elimination of protections geared to the civil and economic rights of individuals using the language of individualism itself.

As debates over social justice circled endlessly around metanarratives of individualism, the distance between neoliberal and neoconservative narrowed. Within the context of these discursive transformations, assaults on social justice could not but succeed, for they were the rightist consonants of neoliberalism itself. Serving to shore up a powerful new bloc, policy assaults against social justice programs as they played out over the course of the nineties steadied the field for an unprecedented, albeit unstated, meeting of minds between neoconservatives and neoliberals. Here, evocations of past wrongs, group rights, and racial reparations emerged as laughable, odd, and impossible. And as they winnowed out "discursive counteractions" that had been invented by the progressive resistance of the moment of the sixties (Goldberg 1993, 9), stock stories about individual responsibility and self-fulfillment, having cunningly erased the semiotic labor that produced them, emerged as the truths of our time.

This narrative mélange of attention and inattention, valorizing individual rights and neglecting group concerns bears the mark of the larger rightward shift from liberalism to neoliberalism. Documented by a number of scholars in recent years, such combinations of muting and amplification, of selection among partial details is found repeatedly in contemporary debates over social justice, including battles over social welfare, immigration, and redistributive justice (Cahn 1997, 965–1005; Fan 1997, 1202–40; Fraser and Gordon 1994, 309–36; Lubiano 1992; Santa Ana 1998, 137–76; Schram 1993, 249–70; Shulman 2000).

Every such narrativization reiterates grammars of liberalism refashioned within the discursive milieu of neoliberalism and enabling, as Terry Eagleton has suggested, "effects of closure whereby certain forms of signification are excluded, and certain signifiers 'fixed' in a commanding position" (1991, 194). Every such narrativization underscores a fixity to indeterminate concepts and cultural values and, as a consequence, sustains the dominant truth that social justice programs run afoul of them.

A key paradox of these formulations is that the policy changes they usher in have exacted the greatest price from individuals themselves— public aid recipients, working-class single parents, nonwhite immigrants, black and Latino college applicants, and so on. In an ironic and costly argumentative turn, contemporary knowledges of affirmative action, and social justice more generally, have thus been fixed in ways that place responsibility for an individual's economic and political viability entirely on his or her shoulders, while the excision of social justice from public discourse and its demise within public policy are justified precisely on the individual's behalf. As neoliberal policy mandates eviscerate civic safety nets for health care, public education, and public benefits, dominant ethics of individualism have been reworked toward a greater emphasis on responsibilization, demanding that, in order to be truly free, individuals must eschew the state and its redistributive programs and instead fulfill themselves through work, commodity consumption, and economic independence from public programs.

Flowing from their Janus-faced deployments during the sixties, narratives of individualism and color blindness returned thirty years later to attack civil rights reforms relying precisely on pervasive grammars of liberalism. Where Southern segregationist efforts to dress their arguments in liberal-speak had failed to gather legitimacy in the sixties, by the nineties, the discursive imperatives of neoliberalism ensured that Connerly and his cohort were able to reiterate tales of "natural" individual rights with potent credibility, tales that sustained the "truth" that social justice programs ran afoul of them.

What the present analysis clarifies in this context is that from the sixties to the nineties, attention to the work of policy narratives reveals an epistemic order of things constitutive of a common cultural sense about racism, racial exclusion, and its injustices. This stock of familiar tales—using identical grammars to opposing ends—reveals the constitutive work of race, or more precisely, a racial order of things, in deployments of the individual as s/he justified civil rights reform in the sixties and assaults on social justice by the nineties. We see how narrative encodations of "the individual" emerged in these episodes to give weight to appeals for natural rights to full citizenship as well as for individual responsibilization and self-reliance. We note, moreover, how these reigning grammars, whether for or against racialized reform, established unimpeachable standards of a raceless individualized self, standards that are neither neutral nor objective but work to sustain entrenched arrangements of social power and systems of racial privilege.

Narratives of Reversal, Reversals of Narrative

Where the sixties marked the Southern way of life as unethical and draconian, neoliberal appeals to individualism produced trenchant critiques of the "system of racial spoils" that affirmative action programs had wrought by the nineties. Profoundly shaped by grammars of individualism, the parade of white racial victimization that was orchestrated in the nineties drew from the terms of liberal indictments of the sixties. Thus, newfound gospels of reverse discrimination and white victimization were articulated using the persuasive reserves of the victors of the sixties, even though, thirty years earlier, those voices had argued for radically opposing policy ends.

Across decades, we are thus witness to remarkable and pointed reversals—warring stories reusing identical grammars. Enabling and repressing contrary knowledges about civil rights and discrimination, these maneuvers produced counterstories, each demanding legitimacy for specific interests that were disqualified in opposing stories using the same vocabulary. Every such narrativization reveals and anticipates counterstories and thus operates as a "discursive opening" to contrary ends. Constituting "reverse discourses," thus, each side is seen shifting and reutilizing "identical formulas for contrary objectives" (Foucault 1978/1990, 100–101).

Like the canvases of master painters, reused and painted over, civil rights reforms of the sixties themselves held the blueprints for assaults on social justice in the nineties. In other words, the decidedly progressive moment of civil rights reform in the sixties itself provided "discursive openings" for rightist assaults that would come thirty years later. The influence of such narrative reversals does not belittle vital social gains that the black civil rights movement made possible. Instead, narrative reversals offer key insights into the vulnerabilities of official discourses. They reveal the ways in which authorized tales carry within themselves the terms for their own undoing, which in the context of larger discursive shifts from liberalism toward neoliberalism facilitated a peculiar unraveling.

Using vocabularies inherited from the sixties, stories of "reverse discrimination" in the Proposition 209 and Initiative 200 campaigns of the nineties reutilized the formulae of individual race-based victimization toward critical reversals in public policy. At its most effective, the Proposition 209 campaign recounted plaintive stories of such reverse discrimination, integrative petit récits that poignantly testified to the individual costs of affirmative action. The experiences of James Cook, a white applicant for state university admissions, were frequently narrated in Connerly's speeches as a case in point:

> Ask the parents of James Cook, only one of two California students admitted to Johns Hopkins University in 1994, only to be denied admission to UC San Diego medical school because he is white . . . Ask . . . thousands of other middle class families who are forced to take out $80,000 to $100,000 second mortgages on their homes to send their kids out of state to college because racial preferences prevent them from being able to attend UC. (1996c, 14A)

Reiterating what Thomas Ross refers to as the "rhetoric of innocence," the white applicant to the medical school, the white contractor seeking city construction contracts, and so on, each is presumed innocent in an unexamined sense (1995, 551–52). Cook, likewise, enjoys a presumption of innocence as Connerly's tale serves subtly to impugn racial and gendered Others lurking within an ostensibly neutral meritocracy (Russell 1995, 56). Directed decisively at its target audience, the "thousands of middle class families" whom Connerly invokes are specifically *white* middle-class families whose racist frustrations are condoned and fanned in Cook's story.

Moreover, every such tale proffers an "insider narrative" hinting at other stories that exist but have not been told yet. Thus, James Cook's experiences are narrativized as a quotidian tale of the human costs of affirmative action. Circulating within a rich repertoire of anecdotes and hearsay, compiled second- and thirdhand, these stories take on the stature of the proverbial, needing no evidence for their substantiation. They work authoritatively to justify anxieties about the nightmare of affirmative action on grounds that it disadvantages some individuals as a matter of course. Social justice programs as a signifying category are thus fixed as

antithetical to liberal individualism and at odds with cultural values teth-
ered to those grammars.

Such narratives of reverse discrimination were not invented for the
first time during the nineties. Rather, the words "compensation," "reparations," and "preferences" had made their way into political discourse
by the mid-sixties, keeping pace with race reforms that were being promulgated in legislation and public policy (Steinberg 1995, 110). Thus,
the combination of jeers and applause that greeted Harold Franklin, the
first black student to attend Auburn University in Alabama, on his first
day on campus in early 1964 anticipated the rallying cry of "reverse discrimination" that would gain widespread appeal among voters thirty years
later. As hostile white students screamed at Franklin as he walked to the
library to register for classes, one voice was heard shouting, "I bet the nigger won't have to stand in line to register like we do" (Herbers 1964a, 1).

Reacting to a city ordinance that sought to prohibit racial discrimination in public accommodations in Kansas City, Missouri, in March
1964, members of the ultraconservative Association for the Freedom of
Choice distributed brochures that rejected the ordinance as "unadulter-
ated discrimination against the white race" (Janson 1964, 50). And similarly, supremacist organizations like the National States' Rights Party
took heart in Alabama governor George C. Wallace's vituperative jabs at
the civil rights bill, announcing in party bulletins: "Governor George C.
Wallace—Last Chance for the White Voter." The bulletins used overtly
racist scare tactics: "First, they demand a lunch counter. Now they want
to transport white children to Negro schools—next they will take your
paycheck and job. There is no end to the demands of a Communistic mob"
(Franklin 1964d, 27).

Dixiecrats on the Senate floor repeatedly referred to the "so-called
civil rights bill" as "giving preferential treatment to Negroes," and it was
not uncommon to hear Southern leaders voice concerns that "blacks would
be given preferential consideration just because of the injustices of the
past" (Lelyveld 1964, 67). When, on June 19, 1964, the civil rights bill
finally passed the Senate by a 73–27 margin, Southern leaders who had
attempted a variety of tactics to stall or derail the measure noted with

regret that "the measure goes beyond equal justice and provides special treatment for some people" (Kenworthy 1964p, 1).

These equivalences—the notion that civil rights for blacks as a group necessarily meant racial discrimination against white individuals—gained visibility over the course of the congressional hearings so that Northern voices in the House of Representatives found themselves deflecting Southern accusations, arguing pointedly that civil rights reforms as proposed in the bill would not result in "reverse discrimination" or "preferential treatment." As Representative Emanuel Celler (D-N.Y.), chairman of the Judiciary Committee and vocal proponent of the civil rights bill, put it:

> The grievances are real, the proof is in, and the gathering of evidence has gone on for over a century. The bill is not preferential. What it does do is place into balance the scales of justice so that the living force of the Constitution shall apply to all people, not only those who by accident of birth were born with white skins. (Kenworthy 1964a, 1)

Indeed, accounts of reverse discrimination that positioned individuals like Harold Franklin and whole groups of people as beneficiaries of racial favoritism were circulating with some regularity in public discourse as early as 1964. While news accounts reported that these efforts were "having little effect" because they were "too extreme to attract a large following" (Franklin 1964d, 27), racial reform in the sixties did facilitate an epistemic bricolage that combined, on the one hand, a firm commitment to racial equality, and on the other, a "constant wavering" over how much race ought to matter in deciding public policy (Wald 2000, 374).

Moreover, this constant wavering emerged just as race reforms were being promulgated in legislation and public policy, so that by the close of the civil rights era, hesitant divisions had emerged among liberals themselves. Thus, along with Northern appeals for black civil rights, the sixties also saw anxious liberal commentaries about the potential for racial reforms to degenerate into demands not just for legal equality but rather for "something more," including compensation, reparations, and preferences.

For many, including President Johnson, the problem of racial discrimination demanded more than just the opening of "the gates of opportunity . . . We seek not just freedom, but opportunity. We seek not just legal equity but human ability, not just equality as a right and a theory, but equality as a fact and equality as a result" (Johnson 1965). And in the same vein, the journalist Joseph Lelyveld quoted "leaders of civil rights groups" to explain that African Americans deserved preferential treatment because "the injustices of the past have not ended" (Lelyveld 1964, 67). Doing nothing to combat racial bias, Lelyveld explained, was, practically speaking, indistinguishable from condoning such bias. Thus, he concluded, preferences, while flawed, were better than nothing at all.

Recounting the events of a 1964 roundtable discussion sponsored by *Commentary* magazine entitled "Liberalism and the Negro," Stephen Steinberg explains that the discussants were sharply divided on the question of preferences and the extent to which they ran afoul of traditional liberalism. Foretelling the breakup of the liberal coalition that had functioned as the bulwark of the civil rights movement, Nathan Glazer warned that "blacks were now demanding not just equality of opportunity, but equality of results or outcomes" (Steinberg 1995, 104). And in contrast, Norman Podhoretz argued that the effort to "integrate deserving Negroes one by one into white society" could only result in tokenism. Thus, he proposed that "radical measures were now needed" that addressed the "Negro community *as a whole,*" measures that would help "overcome the Negro's inherited disabilities" (Steinberg 1995, 110–11, emphasis in original).

These divisions forced white liberals into a "political realism" by the close of the civil rights era that acknowledged the difficulty of moving the majority of the American electorate to support programs targeted specifically for blacks. They made room moreover for liberal acknowledgments of the "encroaching reach" of the welfare state, urging caution against its "caretaker" ethos. Consequently, in addition to the racial backlash taking shape on the right, Steinberg suggests that the end of the sixties was also witness to a liberal backlash. Based neither on racial animus nor on retrograde politics, the consolidating liberal backlash now argued that "the best or only way to help blacks was to help 'everybody.'" Reiterating tenets of traditional liberalism, liberal voices now abandoned their efforts toward race-based public policies, and as Steinberg puts it, joined the ongoing "retreat from race."

The grammar of liberalism thus cut an ever-widening division between what John Skrentny refers to as the "fair shakers," those who espoused a classically liberal "colorblind approach," and the "social engineers" who advocated an "affirmative action approach" that insisted upon "result-oriented and color-coded group rights" (1996, 21). As alarm over group rights and preferences mounted during the sixties, the social engineers were increasingly positioned as "radicals" and "racists" for urging race consciousness in politics and public policy (Skrentny 1996, 20). As these positions ossified, liberal capitulation on racial policies and programs enabled newfound, if uneasy, alliances, consolidating a neoliberal base that would ultimately empower organized assaults on racialized social justice by the nineties.

Over the course of decades, new poster children for the ignominies of racial discrimination emerged as the purveyor of tales of reverse discrimination morphed from the morally repugnant segregationist to the white college student. As James Cook's experiences were rendered authentic and proverbial, these narratives justified racialized anxieties about affirmative action and confirmed suspicions about its nonwhite, non-middle-class beneficiaries. Fueling an arrogant paranoia that relentlessly interpellates a demonic Other, the experiences of excluded whites drew attention to incompetent others who, it was assumed, were granted entry on account of their race, who invaded the comfort zone of the white workplace and called for discomforting transformations in workplace cultures by their very presence. These tales equated race-based remedies with racial discrimination and consequently valorized color and gender blindness as the only legitimate responses to lingering racism and sexism.

Traced back to discursive maneuvers of the sixties, the Proposition 209 and Initiative 200 campaigns are seen here strategically shifting and reutilizing existing vocabularies to their own ends. Consequently, the anxieties of white students at Auburn University in 1964 are reconstructed in James Cook's story. Suspicions about how black civil rights jeopardize the rights of white citizens—lifted, as it were, from Southern speeches on the Senate floor in 1964—saturated debates over affirmative action. Within the discursive context of neoliberalism, what had remained laughable, odd, and impossible in the sixties reappeared transformed from marginal to mainstream. As narratives of black nuns and weary travelers had captured the public imagination in the mid-sixties, now narratives about white males like James Cook reversed the story of civil rights. Although laments about reverse discrimination had begun to coalesce during the sixties, they failed to derail civil rights reform within the discursive context of sixties liberalism. By the neoliberal nineties, however, they gained nearly unimpeachable authority in public discourse as African American tales of continuing discrimination and oppression withered in terms of credibility.

Renewals of hegemonic individualism gave voice to suspicions about favoritism and entitlements, and about how special breaks for "whole groups" forced meritorious individuals out of the running. They added weight to assumptions about reverse discrimination and universalized the logic that "a true meritocracy [was] possible only by vigorously enforcing laws that [brought] an end to the existing system of group entitlements" (Wilson, Connerly, and Lewis 1996). In a milieu that relegated black grievances against whites to the past and situated white complaints about blacks in the present (Lipsitz 1998, 222), now women and black Americans were expected to show the occurrence of discrimination on an individual, case-by-case basis before they could demand relief, while it became possible to eliminate whole programs facilitating their inclusion on grounds that they were patently unfair for the individual.

Within reigning discourses of neoliberalism, narratives that highlighted group identities and urged rights and restitutions for entire groups emerged as laughable, odd, and impossible. The pro–affirmative action campaigns that came together to combat Proposition 209 in California and Initiative 200 in Washington offer examples of the ways in which the logics of group restitutions remained incoherent and inaccessible within the logics of individualism.

The narrative strategies of these campaigns orchestrated a parade of affirmative action beneficiaries, each as a justification for maintaining group-based affirmative action programs. In a series of radio and television advertisements, the Stop Prop 209 campaign in California, for example, narrated stories about programmatic benefits that accrued to women as a group. Math and sports programs for girls, public contracts for women-owned businesses in nontraditional fields like highway construction and masonry, targeted outreach used by police academies and medical schools—each was presented as an ethical and necessary means to equal opportunity for members of protected groups.

But with each example, the campaign inadvertently confirmed, precisely as the opposition had argued, that affirmative action was synonymous with a "system of group entitlements," a "program of special breaks that forced meritorious individuals out of the running" (Wilson, Connerly, and Lewis 1996). Interrupting pervasive grammars of individualism, these campaigns told stories about single mothers, lesbians, and businesswomen, each showcasing the benefits of group preferences. Untranslatable into the language of liberalism, these appeals registered the ways in which affirmative action programs privileged membership in groups over other attributes. Distinguishing individuals from historically disadvantaged groups on the one hand, and those who count as meritorious on the other, these accounts corroborated the "truth" that individual merit is inevitably trounced within systems of race- and gender-based social justice.

These campaigns reveal the liabilities of "narrative dissonance," as appeals for group restitutions emerged as incoherent and absurd within the reigning grammar of individualism. Within the terms of the responsibilized neoliberal self, group restitutions were untenable, for they asked the system to reward those who had failed to fulfill their "entrepreneurial obligations," those who had not "enterprised" themselves maximally, and those who remained dependent upon and obliged to others. In contrast with the work of narrative reversal, the dissonance of pro–affirmative action campaigns registered the case for affirmative action as a tedious vestige of the sixties, an unjust overcorrection that needed to be rectified.

Narrative Containment and the Therapeutic Motif

These genuflections before neoliberal narratives of responsibilization were offered in quotidian ways to justify assaults on social justice and made room for stock stories about America and its foundational commitments to inalienable individual freedoms. Articulating seamlessly with mythical notions of the American nation, the Northern defense of civil rights reforms during the sixties built on circulating nationalist mythologies of "the American promise" that remained unfulfilled as long as racial segregation reigned in the South. Thus, congressional debates over the civil rights bill set off a volley of nationalist clichés that included a ready repertoire of coming-of-age tales of the American nation itself.

In a speech celebrating Abraham Lincoln's birth, President Johnson invoked "the promise of our nation's birth" to justify the urgency of legislative reform for black civil rights. The president explained:

> The promise of our nation's birth—the promise that in due time the weights should be lifted from the shoulders of all men, and that all should have an equal chance—this is the unfinished work to which we the living must dedicate ourselves . . . The American promise will be unfulfilled while children lack schools and teachers, men lack jobs and houses, and Americans go without adequate medical care or are denied their full human rights . . . We stand with Lincoln for union and for the freedom of all men. ("Remarks by the President" 1964, 14)

Likewise, appealing to the common immigrant heritage that many white Americans shared, Senator Kuchel invoked cherished national icons like the Statue of Liberty to urge action on the civil rights bill.

> America—the beacon-hand of the Statue of Liberty which glows its worldwide welcome so symbolically—offers hope and the possibility to fulfill a dream: Give me your tired, your poor, your huddled masses yearning to breathe free, the wretched refuse of your teeming shore. Send these, the homeless, tempest-tossed to me: I lift my lamp beside the golden door. There is no sign on that golden door, America, which says: "Whites only are allowed here." (*Congressional Record* 1964, 6557)

The Southern Christian Leadership Conference and in particular its most famous spokesperson, Martin Luther King Jr., spoke in tune with such mythologies. Addressing thousands of civil rights supporters gathered at the historic March on Washington for Civil Rights in August 1963, King asserted:

> When the architects of our republic wrote the magnificent words of the Constitution and the Declaration of Independence, they were signing a promissory note to which every American was to fall heir. This note was the promise that all men, yes, black men as well as white men, would be guaranteed the inalienable rights of life, liberty, and the pursuit of happiness . . . America has defaulted on this promissory note insofar as her citizens of color are concerned. Instead of honoring this sacred obligation, America has given the Negro people a bad check; a check which came back marked "insufficient funds." We refuse to believe that there are insufficient funds in the great vaults of opportunity of this nation. And so we have come to cash this check, a check that will give us upon demand the riches of freedom and the security of justice.

Racial discrimination, by these measures, was unfair not only because of the price it exacted from black Americans but also because it burdened a mythically brave and beautiful America. The quintessentially un-American pestilence of racial injustice was morally wrong, according to these appeals, but it was especially wrong in America. Constructing the black civil rights movement of the sixties as a movement to "change America forever," as a profound social revolution to "save America's soul" and "repay colossal debts owed to the children of former slaves by the children of former slave owners," Northern leaders laid ethical claim to "the therapeutic motif" that cast their crusade for civil rights reform in terms of national healing and recovery (Ehrenhaus 1993, 77–96).

Thus, 1964 emerged as a historic moment in American history, a time when the nation faced up to its past and made amends for having turned its back on its black citizens. President Johnson proclaimed: "We intend to seek justice because that is what the nation needs. We intend to create hope because that is what the nation needs. We intend to build opportunity because that is what the nation deserves. We intend to pursue peace relentlessly because that is what the world demands" (Smith 1964, 64). And similarly, Senator Humphrey summoned white Americans to support black Americans in their struggle for civil rights because "we [whites] would be foolish to deny ourselves the opportunity of enlisting in the common cause of freedom for the millions of people who cry out to be a part of the great American Dream" (*Congressional Record* 1964, 6552). Inviting whites to enlist in the cause of freedom, the civil rights struggle was described as a momentous opportunity for catharsis, a chance to redeem white guilt and heal psychic scars.

Such appeals glossed over enduring patterns of violence, brutality, and colonization descriptive of the history of the American nation and instead drew attention to Southern segregation as uniquely troublesome. Stories of a lawless South circulated images of a place "seething with hatred," where civil rights warriors were shot in the back by "deviant and dangerous individuals," where police commissioners, judges, and mayors joined white citizens' councils to protect their "way of life," and where "freedom fighters" from the North disappeared in bloody acts of racist retribution. These representations served to denaturalize Southern customs and demonize Southern whiteness, highlighting key differences between outmoded habits of the South and progressive race politics associated with the North.

Contrasted with Southern villains, Northern leaders emerged as national heroes for demanding a thorough overhaul of deviant Southern customs. As John W. Reynolds, governor of Wisconsin who ran against Governor Wallace in the Wisconsin presidential primary in 1964, stated:

If what he [Wallace] stands for should prevail here it would give encouragement to hate mongers and racists through all America . . . Mr. Wallace personifies and symbolizes a state where dogs are set upon people, where churches are bombed, a state seething with hatred. Next to South Africa, their handling of the race problem is the worst in the world. ("Wallace Faces Wisconsin" 1964, 76)

Turning the focus to the discipline of Southern individuals, President Johnson urged the "Old Confederacy to bury forever its 'dead issues' and move fully into 'rewarding and fruitful union' with the rest of the nation" (Wicker 1964b, 1). A Southerner himself with "family roots in the red earth of Georgia," Johnson spoke to a crowd of supporters in Atlanta, Georgia, urging:

> I speak to you not as Georgians . . . or as Southerners, but as Americans. Your hopes are the nation's hopes. Your problems are the nation's problems. You bear the mark of a Southern heritage proudly, but that which is Southern is far less important than that which is American. (Wicker 1964b, 1)

Thick descriptions of a conflict-ravaged South marked by the brutalizing conditions of white supremacy and racial segregation thus marked out the distance that separated Americans from the fulfillment of the American promise. A reassuring saga of absolution is told here as resurrections of the mythic signifier "America" direct national attention to cultural absurdities of the American South. As the discipline of wayward Southerners took shape as the means to national redemption, the vast majority of Americans were exonerated by pointed vilifications of Southern customs as exceptional and un-American. Together with popular mythologies of the South as a site of intransigence and moral culpability during the sixties,[2] the civil rights movement was hailed as the social reformation that mended the social fabric once and for all. The sixties emerged, then, as a moment of therapeutic reform that successfully reined in the excesses of the South to heal the nation's racial wounds. This is a familiar story to most Americans, "poignant and reassuring in the closure it provides" (Ehrenhaus 1993, 78).

Thirty years later, recounting a dismal narrative of opportunities lost, of good intentions tragically thwarted, anti–affirmative action spokespersons returned to these themes. Promising voters a second chance at fixing the problems they had set out to address, the campaign urged: "A generation ago, we did it right. We passed civil rights laws to prohibit discrimination. But special interests hijacked the civil rights movement.

Instead of equality, governments imposed quotas, preferences, and set-asides" (Wilson, Connerly, and Lewis 1996). Now Proposition 209 granted these voters the chance to reclaim their "hijacked" efforts and redeem the civil rights movement by voting to end affirmative action.

Middle-class and wealthy black beneficiaries of affirmative action programs were portrayed in these assaults as "addicted" to state allotments of rights, and the elimination of affirmative action, the campaigns assured their audience, would rehabilitate these "quota addicts" out of their toxic reliance on race-based inclusion mechanisms. This rehabilitation promised black Americans liberation from the humiliations of tokenism, from the tyranny of racial classification itself. Likewise, working-class and poorer persons of color were constructed as belligerent and paranoid, as ascribing to a "slavish reliance" upon dependency and domination myths (Connerly and Brown 1995, 156–57); within the terms of neoliberalism, they had only themselves to blame for their woes.

And so, promising relief from a range of malefactions that race-based regimes had ostensibly wrought, appropriations of the therapeutic motif of the sixties recounted a partial history of blacks and whites who, thirty years earlier, were seen speaking with one voice for a hegemonic agenda of civil rights reform. Such appropriations renewed the work of healing and recovery, as sympathy-fatigued whites cast affirmative action for black Americans as an anachronous absurdity of the racial past, poisonous for America itself.

Like the Northern civil rights agenda of thirty years earlier, appropriations of the therapeutic motif in the nineties served prominently to contain and control. Adopted in suitably deradicalized form, the rallying cries and protest anthems of the black civil rights movement produced "a certain 'ghettoization' within state institutions that transformed militancy into constituency" (Omi and Winant 1994, 106). The democratizing challenge that the civil rights movement had posed was blunted as the Civil Rights Act—ultimately, a timid mandate of reform—delivered an overhaul of some areas while insulating other whole areas of potential conflict by defining them as "nonracial."

Disguising the racial terms of the mythic meritocracy, neoliberal conceptions of race and racism placed the entire range of everyday social practices—social practices developed and maintained throughout the period of formal American apartheid—beyond the scope of critical examination or legal remediation (Crenshaw et al. 1995, xv). As neoliberal visions of "freedom" for both black and white Americans were corralled into an internalized discipline of work and enterprise, of choice and self-fulfillment, discursive openings that had been briefly enabled by racial liberation movements of the sixties were sealed off. The destabilizing potential of racialized critique against the structural injustices of the racial order was consequently de-fanged, and a raceless universe discursively delineated to call out the deviance of race-based social justice.

The anti–affirmative action assault of the nineties emerged, by its own admissions, as a renewal of such containment, as a means to rein in the "absolutely stupid race regime and race mentality that we have in America" ("Interview with Ward Connerly" 1999). Both moments of reform—the sixties and the nineties—served critically to "absorb and insulate" radical interrogations of the racial order (Omi and Winant 1994, 106). Rumbling apparatuses of moderate reform, the racial reforms of the sixties and those of the nineties are in fact remarkably similar, even though they served radically opposing ends. Both moments were witness to narrative deployments of the therapeutic motif working to re-assure black and white Americans that shifts in racial regimes leveled the playing field, that they delivered recompense and atonement and thus solved the nation's race problems. Both moments reconfigured foundational cultural scripts that were resurrected with vigor to mold new champions, black and white, of the color-blind meritocracy.

The civil rights agenda of the sixties, not unlike the anti–affirmative action assault of the nineties, then, centrally reinforced mythic ideals of the meritorious self and the American Dream together with their bourgeois democratic accoutrements. Even as the passage of the civil rights bill ensured black citizens dignity, equality, and rights to the American political process, it effectively delivered large numbers of hitherto inaccessible black workers and consumers. Ushering black Americans into bourgeois economic life, racial reform in the sixties was not an aberration of bourgeois democracy; it was its fulfillment in much the same way that the rebellious tactics of the civil rights movement had not rejected the American Dream but instead were the necessary although ambiguous steps taken toward its culmination (Marable 1984, 71).

Thirty years later, the narrative containments of the anti–affirmative action assaults of the nineties centrally reinforced bourgeois democratic accoutrements into which black Americans had been invited during the sixties. Promoting an "enterprise culture" among these constituencies, the terms of neoliberalism now guided them toward investment rather than opposition. African Americans and others positioned in historically disadvantaged groups could no longer blame a racist America for their woes, not only because dominant narratives inherited from the sixties offered assurances that the nation had healed its racial troubles but also because within the discursive universe of neoliberalism, those who failed the standards of bourgeois economic life had only themselves to blame for deviating from the proper standards of individualism, for failing hegemonic standards of responsibilization.

The State as Storied Site

As an iconic "America" struggled through the sixties to emerge as a nation healed of its racial traumas, experiencing its growing pains with morality and integrity, public debates over race reiterated dilemmas over the proper place of American government in the lives of its citizens. Beyond circulating mythologies of the American nation, the civil rights debates of the sixties, as well as recent attacks on affirmative action programs, offer a rich repertoire of affirmations and denials about the state, its governmental apparatuses, and its relationship with the imagined category of an "American people." A range of concerns recurs in these debates about the proper relationship between human rights and fundamental liberties on the one hand and state powers and obligations to ensure justice and equality among citizens on the other.

Circling endlessly around how civil rights reforms would engorge the state and its power over the people, how racial reforms would usher in Communism and authoritarianism, how they would give free rein to an overzealous federal bureaucracy, narratives of power-hungry federal officials and a "judicial oligarchy" raised critical questions about the American state and its reach into the everyday lives of citizens.

Echoing Ku Klux Klan and white citizens' council rhetoric that "Communists were behind the integration movement in the South" (Herbers 1964d, 1), Southern voices identified the civil rights bill as part of a "damaging trend" that "threatened to eliminate trial by jury, union seniority rights, the right of businessmen to choose employers, local control of public education, freedom of thought, and club privacy" (Sitton 1964a, 28). Recalling "warnings" that Senator Joseph McCarthy (D-Wis.) had issued in the House Un-American Activities Committee hearings during the fifties, Governor Wallace now argued that "the left-wing influence in the American government and all this mobocracy around the world that's being led by either those who were in the Communist party or in . . . 'front' organizations" seemed to be coming to pass (Sitton 1964a, 28).

One of the hundreds of letters written to Northern Congressmen in mass letter-writing campaigns in early 1964 stated, "I have been under the impression that total equality under government regulation is called communism. Is that what we are so gently being led into?" ("Mail Protesting Rights Bill" 1964, 24). Another addressed to Senator Jacob K. Javits (R-N.Y.) asserted that "there are lots of commies in New York— don't help their cause," and in a more accusatory tone, "the civil (evil) rights bill is authored by the Communist red cell of New York of which you are the main spokesperson for Communism in Washington" (24).

If anti-communist rhetoric served Southern leaders to focus national attention on the un-American perils of racial reform, as Mary Dudziak argues, the perceived threat of Communism had also been a significant factor in the Northern push for civil rights reforms. Thus, Dudziak finds critical state incentives in pro–civil rights arguments that sought to "prove to the people of the world, of every nationality, race and color, that a free democracy is the most civilized and most secure form of government yet devised by man" (1995, 111, quoting U.S. Justice Department amicus brief in *Brown v. Board of Education*).

Similarly, in a letter to the editor of the *New York Times*, Sidney

Hook, a professor of philosophy at New York University, argued that "the greatest single handicap in the struggle against Communist totalitarianism abroad is the shameful humiliation of Negro citizens which the civil rights bill in some small measure attempts to counteract" (1964, 42). Much like Southern leaders who used circulating nightmares of the Communist threat to argue against civil rights reforms, Northern voices similarly denounced Communism and emphasized its opposition to American democratic principles as they championed contrary ends. Another instance of narrative reversal, the specter of Communism and narratives of its perils for Americans and "the American way" worked paradoxically to argue both for civil rights reform and against it.

Southern Senators pointed to the ways in which civil rights reforms warped the ethical obligations and responsibilities of American government. They argued that the proposed civil rights bill "gave unconstitutional powers to the federal government and deprived the states of powers reserved to the states and to individuals," thus disturbing the long-established balance of power in American government (Kenworthy 1964c, 1). Stock phrases such as "mushrooming bureaucracy," "unbridled administration," and "thought control," repeated frequently, served effectively to position individual rights and freedoms in opposition to governmental control and power.

Senator John G. Tower (R-Tex.), the only Republican to have enlisted in the anti–civil rights campaign, asserted that the civil rights bill would create a "police state with authority to dictate hiring and firing policy for 70 million Americans" (Kenworthy 1964g, 1). Senator Lister C. Hill (D-Ala.) argued in the same vein that "in the name of so-called civil rights" the proposed bill "would trample on the established rights of the overwhelming majority of Americans" and would "cripple and in many instances destroy the constitutional liberties, freedoms and safeguards fundamental to our form of government" (Kenworthy 1964i, 24).

In a concerted effort, the Coordinating Committee for Fundamental Freedoms (CCFF), an organization funded in large part by the Mississippi State Sovereignty Commission, sponsored an advertisement entitled "100 Billion Blackjack" as part of an anti–civil rights campaign. The ad appeared in more than two hundred newspapers nationwide and argued that "the American people are being set up for a blow that would destroy their right to determine for themselves how they will live" (Kenworthy 1964f, 1; "Mississippi Agency Channels" 1964, 21).[3] Pamphlets and other advertisements sponsored by the CCFF accused the civil rights bill of being "10 percent civil rights and 90 percent a federal power grab" ("Mail Protesting Rights Bill" 1964, 24), predicting that it would "abolish the rule of law and make the Attorney General a dictator" (Kenworthy 1964f, 1).[4]

Senator Russell suggested, "the bill is a bureaucrat's dream, and in the hands of an unscrupulous Attorney General it could be used as an instrument of unsurpassed tyranny" (Kenworthy 1964c, 1). Thus, Title VII provisions for inspection and record keeping were characterized by opponents as "the power to snoop," which would empower the proposed federal commission on equal opportunity to "make labor unions and employers keep records and send out inspectors to enter plants and union offices to gather data" on discriminatory practices (Kenworthy 1964a, 1).

Likewise, fears over restrictions on state autonomy found expression in concerns over Title VI of the proposed bill, which empowered federal agencies to enforce nondiscrimination by cutting off assistance to state programs. Opponents likened the measure to "a gun at the head of every state and community receiving any federal aid" and predicted liberal programs and allocations such as "roads, agriculture, unemployment relief, distribution of food to the indigent, school lunch programs, and so on" would pay the heaviest price for such penalties (Kenworthy 1964a, 1). Senator Sam J. Ervin (D-N.C.) similarly referred to the civil rights bill as a "monstrous blueprint for governmental tyranny," arguing that Title III, which barred racial discrimination in parks, playgrounds, and other publicly owned facilities, would give the attorney general "an autocratic power to be exercised at his uncontrollable discretion to browbeat all persons acting on behalf of state or local governments into submission to his will in virtually all of their dealings with virtually all of the people within their borders" (Morris 1964, 41).

Positioning themselves as concerned voices for innocent citizens who would pay an unfair price for civil rights reforms, Representative

William M. Colmer (D-Miss.) argued that the civil rights bill "under threat of blackmail would give every two-bit bureaucrat the power to cut the water off in your community" (Kenworthy 1964a, 1). Representative Basil L. Whitener (D-N.C.) called attention to the "suffering that would be visited upon blameless and helpless persons if federal contributions to unemployment relief were cut off from a community simply because officials, following local custom, required the recipients to stand in two lines—one for whites, the other for Negroes" (Kenworthy 1964a, 1).[5]

Outside Congress, conversations proliferated about the proper place of American government in the lives of its citizens. Governor John Love of Colorado, addressing the closing session of the annual Republican Women's Conference, directed his ire against "too much government services and too little reliance on the individual's hard work." He continued, "unless there arises a solid, responsible air of discontent in this nation, unless it sweeps through every region and state and hamlet in America, we are in for a grave future" (Loftus 1964, 55). While government programs were important and had served well in retraining and education, Love argued, "success will come largely through hard work, education, ambition, and the dedication of the individual. . . . We can't be for economy in government without being against continual expansion of government services" (Loftus 1964a, 55).

Senator Barry Goldwater (R-Ariz.), campaigning for the Republican presidential nomination in the 1964 primaries, announced his "philosophy of government" by demanding that "government mind its own business where business is concerned" (Loftus 1964b, 26). Arguing against the civil rights bill on the Senate floor, Goldwater suggested:

> To give genuine effect to the prohibitions of this bill will require the creation of a federal police force of mammoth proportions. It also bids fair to result in an "informer" psychology in great areas of our national life— neighbors spying on neighbors, workers spying on workers, businessmen spying on businessmen, where those who would harass their fellow citizens for selfish and narrow purposes will have ample inducement to do so. These, the federal police force and an "informer" psychology, are the

hallmarks of the police state and landmarks in the destruction of a free society. (1964, 18)

Likewise, Governor Wallace of Alabama announced his decision to run for president, as he put it, "to tell the truth about the so-called civil rights bill and how it would destroy the private enterprise system in this country" ("Alabama Governor Files" 1964, 8). Identifying a dangerous "left-wing influence in the American government" (Sitton 1964a, 28), he predicted that the civil rights bill would "destroy the right of free ownership of private property" (Franklin 1964a, 29).

Specifically, the governor characterized federal courts as "the judicial oligarchy," equating court decrees mandating racial desegregation with the "dictatorial tactics of Hitler's Germany and Mussolini's Italy" (Franklin 1964e, 18). From this perspective, the civil rights bill was a dangerous "imposition on working men and women of intrusive 'social' policies by an insulated, elitist, liberal cabal of lawyers, judges . . . and government bureaucrats" (Edsall and Edsall 1991, 77), and its chief defect was that it reversed the relationship between "a government subservient to the people to that of a sovereign state and a subservient people" (Franklin 1964e, 18).

In response, Northern voices like Senator John O. Pastore (D-R.I.) demanded on the Senate floor if "it was fair to use the money which belongs to all the taxpayers of the United States in a discriminatory manner" (Kenworthy 1964j, 20). Pastore explained that it was "wrong for a local agency to give $20 to a white widow with four children and $2 to a Negro widow with four children." The civil rights bill was not intended to enable the federal government to "tell a hospital in South Carolina receiving federal funding how the hospital is to be operated," as Southern leaders had suggested, but instead, Pastore explained, "if a man is struck by an automobile and is brought to the hospital, [this bill would make it impermissible] for the hospital to deny him admission because he is colored."

As each side spoke on behalf of an imagined "silenced majority" and against an incursive and domineering state, they served to firm up the state's legitimacy and its political affectivity. In other words, stories about the state and its apparatuses that circulated within public debates over civil rights during the sixties did not just sanction the state. They also lent their legitimizing power to narratives about various phenomena that fell within the purview of the state. Whether they depicted feckless bureaucrats or protectors of the people, venal politicians or passionate leaders, these debates keenly reflected the "special potency associated with the ability of the state to act even when its legitimacy is subject to cynical suspensions of disbelief" (Schram and Neisser 1997, 14).

Beyond its politico-economic apparatuses of power, its legislative, regulatory, and military institutions and agencies, then, the state emerges through these articulations as a profoundly contested and mythic entity. As Slavoj Žižek argues, the state itself is a "storied site" (1989) constructed through a range of accounts as oppressor and benefactor, as vulnerable and valiant, as heroic and villainous.

Revealing the perpetual mix of authority and vulnerability that discourses of the modern state navigate, such arguments reappeared within recent assaults on affirmative action. Thus, young, white, college-going males were positioned as victims of "government preferences and set-asides" who now emerged as new "warriors for democracy" (Connerly 1997d) poised to rehabilitate a wayward state out of its dysfunctional habits and mentalities. As Connerly and his cohort argued in California, what affirmative action had done was to "empower government to make decisions about people's lives on the basis of a government melanometer" (Connerly 1996a). By the logic of these appeals, the ultimate indignity of affirmative action was that its follies were state-sponsored. Commanding intense emotional legitimacy, popular mythologies of the state and its agents highlighted both the ways in which state regimes constructed race as well as how contests over race legitimized state controls (Crenshaw et al. 1995, xxv).

Distinguishing themselves from more radical tales of armed militias poised for self-defense against the federal government and media events like the Branch Davidian standoff with the FBI in Waco, Texas, narrative portrayals of state abuses of public funds, threats to individual choices, and unfair anti-white quotas were carefully scripted. They did not suggest that regulatory, legislative, and creative governmental activities should be rejected altogether. Instead, they defined positive tasks for government, resecuring the state's legitimacy as the arbiter of judicious reform.

Consequently, while these narratives held the state responsible for reneging on the neoliberal meritocratic self, they nevertheless directed attention to the image of a state in distress, "hijacked by special interests." As a liberal cabal in Washington was portrayed as callously acquiescing to un-American quota systems to serve its petty political ambitions, these appeals privileged a highly contradictory strategy of redress: they urged a "retreat from the state" and simultaneously a recentering of the state with stipulations for an enterprise culture and its attendant ethics of individual responsibilization.

Among those thousands of voices from the sixties who defended racial segregation based on the principle that federal mandates for integration offered proof of an increasingly incursive, domineering, power-grabbing state, many also found justifications for segregation on grounds that it worked as an effective technology of state control, that is, it enabled a more effective and efficient state. Thus, for example, as Don Brooks, a white taxi driver from Indianapolis, Indiana, explained to a news reporter at the height of public speculation preceding Alabama governor George C. Wallace's run in the Indiana presidential primary in May 1964: "We've got a problem here of white women and colored men. And of course the white male population resents that. We're very conservative." Acknowledging his segregationist sympathies, Brooks continued, "I definitely think they [blacks] should be segregated. For one thing, we have a terrific crime problem here and if you segregate them, it's easier to police them" (Sitton 1964e, 83). Defining racial segregation precisely as a technology of state control, Brooks incisively articulated the imbrications of racial discipline and state incentives for carceral control and police.

But if segregation facilitated physical and spatial control over black Americans, training and retraining them to "know their place" in the social order, desegregation similarly invented key rationales for state interventions into social and cultural life. For instance, upon their inception in the sixties, civil rights reforms sanctioned a profusion of techniques for monitoring race and gender. Bureaucratic agencies were set up to mark, count, categorize, and order the population by race and gender. Public employers were asked to devise targeted outreach to include members of "historically disadvantaged groups." State and federal commissions were established to ensure compliance with assigned goals and timetables, and "experts" scientifically forecast integration needs and evaluated the effectiveness of integration schemes. Thus, while civil rights reforms of the sixties broke open ossified local customs of racial exclusion and color supremacies, they also instituted new state technologies that would serve bourgeois economic interests and liberal state incentives. Indeed, viewed as technologies of state control, segregation and desegregation are of a piece, each delineating a range of activities as properly under the purview of the state.

As the workings of admissions and hiring committees were opened up to scrutiny, cultural categories such as "black" and "white," and the differences between these categories, took particular shape. And the modalities of racism and sexism developed not as aberrations within the mythic meritocracy that liberal discourses championed but instead as descriptive of the order of things—of accepted wisdom about the proper place of race in public life, as a productive technology of individuation, and an effective technology of state control.

It must be noted here that early liberalism, even in its emphasis on individual realization and self-improvement, did not suggest that regulatory, legislative, and creative governmental activity should be abandoned wholesale. Likewise, modern forms of neoliberalism, even as they call for the extrication of the state from the lives of individual citizens, define positive tasks for governmental activity. Thus, despite critiques of the deadening consequences of intrusions of the state into the life of the individual, these appeals nonetheless provoked the invention and deployment of a "wide array of organizational forms and technical methods in order to extend the field within which a certain kind of economic freedom might be practiced in the form of personal autonomy, enterprise, and choice" (Barry, Osborne, and Rose 1996, 10).

Along the same lines, over the nineties, the demonization of black beneficiaries and unfair state-sponsored programs that harbored them reflected the growing legitimacy of images of a state plagued by crises in its abilities to manage the meritocracy. Widespread portrayals of the state as fumbling, wasteful bungler or as a force of villainous corruption suggested that abandoning affirmative action at that moment in time would restore public confidence in state authorities as gatekeepers of the meritocracy. Forcefully implicating specific racial histories and zealously celebrating individuals who enterprise themselves within neoliberal norms of productivity and morality, the contemporary retreat from affirmative action points to entrenched incentives of the modern governmentalized state.

This retreat suggests that while the state must continually offer rational justifications for its tactics, those justifications reinforce the rationality of the state and thus contour the possibilities and limitations of political struggle and contestation. While governmentality works to force accountability from the state for its tactics and devices, in so doing, it also insulates the governmentalized state from devastating assaults. And as grand transformations in racial regimes serve to reassert the legitimacy and affectivity of the state, we begin to see, in the historical detail of these specific moments, how race and its regulatory regimes remain a key technology of the modern, neoliberal state.

Conclusion

I began this book with a series of questions that were, for me, an entry point into what I witnessed over the course of the nineties as an enduring impasse in America: the problem of the color line. Growing up in India, I knew people who had suffered broken bones that healed without a cast into knobby, crooked reminders of accidents long past. Race in America, it seemed to me, was like those bent bits, healed into knotty, scarred deformities. These were old wounds that throbbed with every change of season, injuries that lasted a lifetime.

It had been barely thirty years since the formal end of Jim Crow segregation, but every news night streamed televisual images of African American dysfunction—drugs, crime, gangs, baby factories. As middle-class African Americans moved to the suburbs, rising up the ranks as middle-management tokens in the meritocracy, a staggering number of black men sat "warehoused" in prisons and other institutions of carceral control. Each election season served up fresh reminders of failing inner-city schools and "unteachable" black youth, and as political candidates played mercilessly on white guilt and fear, poor blacks remained an effective foil for the eviscerated white American Dream. Demonizing immigrants for "stealing American jobs" and African Americans for cashing in on "melanin merit," neoconservative "experts" dominated network news programs to blame the most disenfranchised segments of the population for the worsening plight of American workers.

Two disparate cultural sound tracks emerged over the course of this post-soul era: one revealing the "hidden transcripts" of black working-class rage that exploded on MTV in the form of hip-hop and gangsta rap, and the other, sounding the eerie silence of retreat from racial justice, white "sympathy fatigue" metastasizing to racial resentment and wrath. The scarred anatomy of the color line throbbed with every change in political season and, true to W. E. B. Du Bois's famous line, survived as the greatest problem of the twentieth century.

My entry into these complex sociological shifts was spurred by a series of assaults against social justice that took shape in the closing decades of the twentieth century. As grassroots efforts to organize these populist attacks on welfare, affirmative action, and immigrant rights gained in political strength and visibility, a number of baffling questions surfaced. How was it possible that programmatic reforms that had emerged thirty years ago as the only mechanism that could, ethically and effectively, rectify deep-seated biases in public life had turned around by the nineties to epitomize the "worst excesses of the sixties"? By what circumstances had affirmative action, the poster child of the civil rights era, transformed into a "toxic system of quotas, preferences, and set-asides"? What did these assaults reveal about race and racism in the contemporary United States? What could they tell us about public consciousness, and the power and vulnerability of cultural imaginaries?

As the chapters of the book specify, my responses to these questions substantiate two conceptual insights: the epistemic power of race in American public discourse, and the paradoxical schema of the contemporary neoliberal state. Here at the end of the book, I want to pursue a few final observations—points of caution and emphasis—that allow me to look over these insights, and draw out a little further what these analyses have enabled me to say about the racial order of things at the beginning of the twenty-first century.

I begin with feminist scholars who in recent years have issued eulogies for feminism (Brown 2002), their voices noting, with some despair, the "death of Western feminism" and the rise of a self-indulgent, commodified "post-feminism" in its place. This sense of loss is substantiated by what Susan Douglas (1994) has noted as the "I'm not a feminist, but . . ." stance that is increasingly normalized among younger generations of American women. Growing up in a culture dominated by backlash politics, this new generation constitutes a powerful electoral demographic, well-schooled in the villainies of bad girls like feminazis and welfare queens.

For feminist scholars seeking clues into the demise of white feminism, recent assaults on social justice offer important insights. For one, they reveal that race remains an effective strategic wedge between women, a critical means by which white women are recruited to vote in racial solidarity with white men. The position of women within these attacks merits close attention because it illuminates not only how reigning discourses of post-soul culture have disarmed the radical impulses of feminism but also that co-optation from within has proved an effective strategy to contain the structural threat that feminism had posed.

Within the cultural imaginaries of the post-soul era, white women are positioned as tireless lookouts guarding the margins of white male-dominated workplaces. These female protagonists, variously vilified and valorized in the affirmative action genre of the nineties, rail against color and gender consciousness. Thus, normalizing neoliberal claims about objectivity and individual merit, they illuminate the ways in which women, and particularly white women, have come to serve as highly credible witnesses against racialized and gendered social justice.

But as white women from the "model majority" of political campaigns morph into "workplace martyrs" of the affirmative action genre, they reveal that mainstream anxieties about black squatters in the workplace are of a piece with concerns over the threat posed by white female upstarts. It follows, then, that one of the ways that white feminism can revitalize itself in the post-soul era is by taking on, through analytic and political critique, the ways in which women have been co-opted into complicity within the hegemonic discourses of neoliberalism.

If contemporary modalities of neoliberalism inscribe a key role for white women within racist assaults of the moment, the feminist answer to such cooptation must be to enlist white women as strategic allies within anti-racist battles. As the neoliberal project ascends to dominance by cleaving race and class divisions among women—and this, as the present analysis reveals, is a key element of post-soul culture—the unfinished project of feminism must be to find the racist labors of neoliberalism at cause in the withering away of contemporary feminism.

Cultural imaginaries of the post-soul era are characterized likewise by narrow and regimented portrayals of docile, well-behaved African Americans. Here, archetypes of black helpers in the affirmative action genre work in consonance with African Americans endowed with political "superstanding," exceptional black voices rewarded with a bounty of privileges for their willingness to be recruited as racially correct voice-overs in racist assaults of the decade. As black conservatives like Ward Connerly collect their dues by cozying up to neoliberal challenges to social justice, African Americans who appeared in films of the nineties are cast similarly in heroic servitude, calling out troublesome Others and shoring up white male authority in the mythic meritocracy.

Striking a discordant chord within this milieu, cultural interventions of the hip-hop generation produced artists, poets, and filmmakers who emerged in the nineties as explorers at the frontiers of a new black politics. To the poorest and most disenfranchised of these voices, the civil rights movement was marred by dismal failures. As Manning Marable has noted, "lower class blacks [were] virtually unaffected by civil rights legislation, affirmative action, and federal government initiatives to diminish unemployment" (1984, 176–77). And the victories of the sixties—the end of legal segregation, the growth and suburbanization of the black middle class, and the hegemonic ascent of discourses of multiculturalism—had moved apace with sharp declines in the socioeconomic circumstances of the majority of black Americans. By the nineties, black college enrollments were dropping, and real incomes for black workers showed precipitous declines (Aronowitz 2000; Lyne 2000).

In this context, Martin Luther King Jr. and Rosa Parks lingered as distant icons disappearing into an irrelevant past. Here, the mandates of commercial viability limited recording and studio contracts to those of this generation who would champion black commodity fetishism and "gettin' mine" as the only plausible responses to entrenched black disempowerment. Collapsing the dynamic heterogeneity of the hip-hop generation, the public face of post-soul culture grew synonymous with performers who would syncopate the fighting anthems of Black Power to the drumbeats of the marketplace. These voices celebrated black super-stardom in music and sports as markers of the African American Dream, championing a new paradigm of racial protest that focused much of its wrath on the politics of "playa hatin'."

Engaging in mutual and gregarious backslapping, these "new H.N.I.C. Head Niggas In Charge" (Boyd 2003) appear unperturbed by vanishing modes of grassroots struggle and the displacement of black anti-racist politics by the shiny new accoutrements of the "bling bling" aesthetic (Mukherjee, in press). Bearing a striking resemblance to neolib-eral mantras of the nineties, these voices, inadvertently perhaps, take sides with the likes of Connerly, urging African Americans to take individual responsibility for their self-fulfillment. A key characteristic of post-soul culture, the hegemonic dominance of neoliberalism, ensures, and perhaps necessitates, the gutting of African American transformation politics as blacks themselves rap and rhyme in celebration of these "truths."

The dubious distinction of the post-soul era, then, is a double-edged meter of progress that traces a sobering narrative arc from resistance to co-optation. As discourses of feminism and civil rights are de-fanged into empty spectacles of commodity culture, they reveal a critical ontological paradox within accepted truths—discursive dominance is always already contested. That is, knowable and sayable truths hold the blueprints for their own undoing, and the discursive history of civil rights, as this book has shown, is no exception.

At the end of this tale, the racial order of things offers a final point of caution that emerges from the specious logics of the gathering global "war on terror." For one, the affective dimensions of the "governmen-talized" state at the helm of this war have enjoyed a remarkable reprieve since September 11, 2001. Shaking off critiques leveled at "Washington excess" and "big government" that had circulated with relative ubiquity in previous decades, the neoliberal state is reinvested with legitimacy as vast bureaucracies of the racial state proliferate anew under the auspices of "national security."

The terms of the racial order that this book has explored are ever more ensconced within the "audit cultures" of this burgeoning national security state. Census protocols, immigration and unemployment applications, incarceration reports, birth and death certifications, medical and educational statistics, travel and purchasing patterns—each facilitates racial discipline in quotidian terms, and each is incorporated wholesale into state tactics of the "war on terror." Here, as Marable reminds us, the slow evolution of the liberal welfare state of the sixties toward the neoliberal state of the nineties is consolidated rather than muddled by the events of September 11.

Like racialized assaults on affirmative action that were inscribed in keenly race-neutral terms, current campaigns issued by law enforcement agencies urging ordinary citizens to "Say Something If You See Something" erase their reference to race even as they reinscribe it. As state tactics of racial surveillance and discipline proliferate within the microdomains of everyday life—in airports, on subway trains, and at freeway rest stops—they render palatable a host of carceral techniques—detention, torture, murder alike—not as racist retribution against a foreign enemy but rather as necessary and rational protocols for the security and safety of all (Marable 2001).

As the neoliberal state thus flexes its carceral muscle, it corrals homeland orthodoxies with sanguine efficiency. Here, militaristic "superpatriotism" plays around the clock on television stations nationwide emerging as the new standard of political correctness (Parenti 1994), which, while it denies them, nevertheless hinges on racist presumptions about wily Arabs and their barbarous fundamentalisms. African Americans and Latinos join in these vicious plays of belonging and Othering, partaking in racist repression and violence as a means to make their way, however temporarily and partially, into the elusive fraternity of "colorblind" citizenship (Mukherjee 2003, 29–46). As new archetypes of "conservative macho" assert their dominance within the cultural imaginary of the American empire (Goldstein 2004, 175–77; Roy 2004), unveiled Afghani women like sodomized Iraqi prisoners serve crucially to secure the racial dominance of white masculinity.

As the "war on terror" capitalizes on tactics of discipline already in place within the racial order of the post-soul era, popular initiatives that had sounded the death knell for social justice programs over the course of the nineties offer us clues to understanding how racialized hegemonies of the "age of terror" are being assembled. They remind us that we should not be fooled by the deracialized rhetoric of this "new race war" (Monbiot 2002). Rather, we must recognize "terror," "patriotism," "security," and so on as retooled taxonomies of the abiding racial order. These are the fresh new faces of an old familiar episteme, beguiling in their simplicity and horrific in intent.

Notes

Introduction

1. White women have by far reaped the greatest rewards from federally mandated affirmative action programs. The percentage of women in executive, administrative, and managerial positions rose from 17.6 percent in 1972 to 43.8 percent in 1996 (Equal Rights Advocates 1999).

2. The text of the initiative contains three exceptions. It does not impact the practices of private corporations and nongovernmental groups. It does not apply to state affirmative action programs that are needed to maintain eligibility for federal aid. Also excluded are positions where "bona fide qualifications based on sex are reasonably necessary for normal operation." This last exception would allow, for instance, the hiring of female prison guards in women's correctional facilities.

3. For example, the Citizens' Initiative on Race and Ethnicity, an organization that sought to bring "a number of Americans together to focus on how to protect the civil rights of all Americans" (www.cire.org), issued a list of "commission members," each with an impeccable right-wing pedigree, including Clint Bolick of the Institute for Justice, Elaine L. Chao, previously with the Heritage Foundation, Linda Chavez of the Center for Equal Opportunity, Ward Connerly of the American Civil Rights Institute, Tamar Jacoby and Abigail Thernstrom of the Manhattan Institute, Barbara J. Ledeen, a U.S. senator who was previously one of the co-founders of the Independent Women's Forum, and Shelby Steele of the Hoover Institution.

4. The measure was defeated by a vote of 62 to 38 (Branscomb 2003, A11).

1. Race, Gender, and the Constitution of Subjects

1. See for instance, Frankenberg 1997; Haney Lopez 1996; Hill 1997; Ignatiev 1995; Ignatiev and Garvey 1996; Lipsitz 1998; Lott 1993; Nakayama and Martin 1999; Pfeil 1995; Roediger 1991; Wray and Newitz 1996.

2. The No on 209 campaign that split away from the Stop Prop 209 organizers in August 1996 as a consequence of internal fractiousness produced a second television commercial with financial support from the Democratic National Committee in October 1996. This commercial featured the ex-Klansman David Duke in an effort to indict Proposition 209 supporters of racisms comparable to those preached historically by members of the Ku Klux Klan. I turn to a full discussion of the No on 209 campaign in a later section of this chapter.

3. Reiterating the myth that women and nonwhites are typically unqualified for their jobs, such suspicions find themselves reproduced in everyday, casual conversations. The commonplace of anecdotes that recount the experiences of white males who do not survive short lists for job interviews because "the department was looking for a black woman to *colorize* its offices" is a case in point.

4. Here the campaign unwittingly corroborates James Baldwin's wry observation that "it is true that two wrongs don't make a right, as we love to point out to the people we have wronged" (1969, 8).

5. Ultimately, Goldwater did not deliver this portion of his speech, but it is instructive that such an argument was included in his campaign's stock speeches.

6. The emphasis on Chicano farm workers battling unscrupulous grape growers in fifties California and black civil rights workers confronting the racist excesses of Southern segregation during the Jim Crow era, moreover, inevitably returned public attention to the nation's racial rather than gendered history. Thus, the Stop Prop 209 campaign's target—the gender gap—was unwittingly subordinated in these appeals as the fight over affirmative action was once again aligned along race but not gender lines.

2. The Affirmative Action Film of the Nineties

1. There are several subsequent racialized exchanges between McClane and Carver, but these are scripted as playful banter.

2. The gentleness of this new sensitive white hero deserves a careful and critical regard, however, for the image of the sensitive man calls up the male person who, while enjoying the position of unbelievable privilege, also has the privilege of gentleness.

3. The rise of a new generation of independent black filmmakers over the course of the eighties and nineties may offer another explanation for the generic silence on racial themes. Young black filmmakers, fresh out of the film schools of New York and Southern California, opened up room for cathartic narrations of continuing black struggles in ghetto-centric "gangsta" films and other didactic race dramas including Spike Lee's *Do the Right Thing* (1989), *Jungle Fever* (1991), *Clockers* (1995), and *Bamboozled* (2000); John Singleton's *Boyz N the Hood* (1991), *Higher Learning* (1995), and *Rosewood* (1997); and Allen and Albert Hughes's *Menace to Society* (1993). Reflecting strategic calculations of the mainstream audience's "sympathy fatigue" over tales of black struggle along with box office demands for large mainstream audiences, the absence of racial scenarios in the affirmative action genre suggests strategic moves by Hollywood studios to pull out of the business of race films over the course of the nineties.

4. The third chapter of this book turns to a discussion of such nostalgia films addressing the conservative revisionism of narrations of civil rights history that position white Southerners as "men before their time," and the enduring therapeutic motif of the American South that emphasizes Southern anachronism and distance from the rest of America to enable the fantasy of a nation freed from its hideous past and healed of its racial troubles. Likewise, films like James Foley's *The Chamber* (1996) and Tony Kaye's *American History X* (1998) showcase traumatic run-ins between contemporary white youth and anachronistic white supremacist ideologies to similarly therapeutic ends.

5. Celebrating the cultural syncretism that accompanies the appropriation of that which is alternate, oppositional, and rebellious into the mainstream, the mining of marginal cultures in the service of mainstream visual pleasure thus remained a staple of Hollywood fare into the nineties.

6. While younger generations of working men might shy away from wishing out loud that women in the workforce return to traditional "pink-collar" positions, they are nevertheless seen harboring a childlike petulance toward women co-workers. As Don Cherry (Nicholas Sadler), the twenty-three-year-old, nerdy, technical whiz-kid who works on Sanders's team, puts it in a later scene: "They [women] are stronger, they're smarter, and they don't fight fair. It's the next step in human evolution. It's like the Amazons—keep a few of us around for sperm and kill off the rest." The generational distance that may have been visible at the start of the narrative is progressively muddled as the film conflates the obsolescent patriarch who has been ousted from the workforce with the

neophyte who claims a helpless paranoia about the formidable adversary he finds in women.

7. Such an analogy is reiterated in the film's dramatization of Sanders's nightmare later that night in which he finds himself being sexually accosted in the office elevator by his boss, Bob Garvin. Here again, the film appears to draw connections between the ways in which the new American workplace has "sodomized" the older ousted male and a similar fate awaiting Sanders when he returns to work the next day.

8. The phrase "going postal" refers to a series of post office shootings beginning with the Oklahoma postman Patrick Sherrill who walked into work in 1986 and shot and killed fifteen fellow employees in less than ten minutes (Gumbel and Carrell 2002, 5).

9. In an outburst typically reserved for the white patriarch, the scene continues with Sanders screaming, "Why don't I be that evil white guy you're all complaining about?" Calling out to the Vietnamese nanny who cares for his children, he continues, "Hey Chau-Minh! Why don't you come down here and let me exercise my dominance?" The film uses this moment to absolve Sanders of his color and gender privileges despite the ironic fact that Sanders does in fact enjoy the services of a Vietnamese nanny to care for his children.

10. As Runyon explains to the White House chief of staff: "I'm not confirming a woman just because she's a woman. Laine Hanson has an extra burden. She has to come on the world scene with perfect credentials . . . A woman better be pretty damn qualified to have nobody to answer to and Laine Hanson is not that."

11. See chapter 1 for full details.

12. The closing dedication of the film reads ingratiatingly, "For our daughters," which reasserts the film's ultimately hollow commitments to gender equity in the workplace.

13. Kaplan's contrasting sterile competence also fortifies the narrative's woefully sexist assumption that a woman may be beautiful or competent but not both.

14. Kaplan guides Sanders to Katharine Alvarez, the lawyer who represents him in the sexual harassment mediation, and alerts him to enemies and problems he has not yet apprehended in a series of mysterious e-mail messages that simply state: "Solve the problem. A friend."

15. The racial implications of this allusion are neither probed nor critiqued in the narrative.

16. Hayes and the "defense boys," we learn in the following scene, have no intentions of making any serious effort to smooth the progress of a gender-integrated military. In an effort to thwart these ambitions, they decide upon the Combined Reconnaisance Team within the elite SEALS force as the first test program for DeHaven's female candidates, confident that "no woman would last a week" in a program that boasts a 60 percent dropout rate for men.

17. The term "feminazi" emerged in the context of the ultraconservative radio personality Rush Limbaugh's vitriolic radio addresses over the course of the eighties and nineties and is defined in Limbaugh's words as "a woman to whom the most important thing in life is seeing to it that as many abortions as possible are performed" (1992, 192–93).

18. Armed as they are with representations of themselves as lacking, as always subordinated to white males whose approval they need to survive, black men and white women "are uniquely positioned to compete with one another for the favors white 'daddies' can extend to them" (hooks 1996, 84). Bell hooks explains that patriarchy invites them to "learn how to 'do it for daddy,'" and to find ultimate pleasure, satisfaction, and fulfillment in that act of performance and submission" (83). G.I. Jane offers us ground to consider the ways in which black men and white women may not always compete with one another in this context. Rather, the film suggests that white women may form fleeting coalitions of convenience with black men while they learn how best to "do it for daddy."

19. O'Neil is also notably refeminized in these concluding scenes—a nurse to Urgayle on the helicopter ride back to base and tearful at her locker as she receives Urgayle's sentimental tokens. McCool is the only other soldier on the team who assists O'Neil in her ministrations on the wounded Urgayle. Thus, by film's end, the African American and the woman on the team return to familiar roles, tending for and nursing white men back to health.

20. A long-time friend, Tom Boylar (Tim Ransom), was an armored tank commander serving under Serling's command at Al Bathra, and one of the men killed in the incident.

21. Gartner is repeatedly positioned as a benevolent father figure in his interactions with Serling. Unable to bring himself to confide in his wife, Meredith (Regina Taylor), Serling finds a patient listener in Gartner at the height of his crisis over Al Bathra. He arrives sloppy drunk at the lobby of his hotel one evening and makes a full confession "way, way off the record" to the attentive Gartner. Later, when Serling approaches Gartner for help on the Walden report,

Gartner agrees and, showing an affectionate regard for the younger man, urges, "Serling, eat something. You look awful."

3. Civil Rights, Affirmative Action, and the American South

1. Martyrdom has traditionally been one of the main paths to sainthood in the Roman Catholic faith (Paulson 2000, A1).

2. As the controversy grew, the widow, Coretta Scott King, was accused of "greed," of "misrepresent[ing] what her husband stood for," and of "attach-[ing] a price tag to every piece of her late husband's legacy" (Tucker 1999, 7Q).

3. Earlier in the nineties, the black-owned toy manufacturer Olmec Corporation introduced a "Powerful Past" collection of action figures to celebrate famous black heroes including King and Malcolm X (McGhee 1992, 30; Poole 1992, 2). For Yla Eason, founder and president of Olmec, the figures were geared to foster "a positive self-image among black children."

4. Lipsitz acknowledges that Mississippi in the sixties and California in the nineties are dissimilar in key respects. For one, as he explains, the battle-ground has shifted from a largely binary struggle between blacks and whites to the intercultural conflicts and collusions of the present. Nevertheless, given their long and consonant histories of racial oppression and interracial conflict, discourses of neoliberal color blindness authorized in 1996 California and supremacist discourses of Southern segregation from the sixties are comparable, he argues, in that they have both enabled deliberate and vengeful deployments of a "possessive investment in whiteness" (1998, 229).

5. Included here are such texts as Alan Parker's *Mississippi Burning* (1988), Richard Pearce's *A Long Walk Home* (1990), the highly acclaimed television series *I'll Fly Away* (Joshua Brand, 1991–93), Jonathan Kaplan's *Love Field* (1992), Jessie Nelson's *Corrina, Corrina* (1994), Carl Franklin's *Devil in a Blue Dress* (1995), Kasi Lemons's *Eve's Bayou* (1997), and Boaz Yakin's *Remember the Titans* (2000).

6. Golub includes *Dances with Wolves, Schindler's List, Amistad, Glory, Mississippi Burning, Ghosts of Mississippi, Long Walk Home*, and *City of Joy* among films that epitomize the Hollywood redemption history genre.

7. Canton Academy is one among many examples of private schools that opened strategically in Southern towns soon after Congress approved the Civil Rights Act in 1964 requiring integration of public schools in the South.

8. On May 6, 1997, the people of Canton, Mississippi, re-elected Alice Scott to a second term as mayor. In October 2002, Scott lost to another African

American, Fred Esco Jr., who has since won re-election to a second term (Burns 2005, A1). In the three mayoral elections since Alice Scott first defeated Sidney Runnels in 1994, every candidate for mayor has been black except for one white hopeful, Elizabeth Parsons, who received a mere ninety votes in the 2002 race (Burns 2002, 1).

9. *48 Hours* produced a second feature story in 1996 that offered a follow-up on the first story, which aired a few weeks after *A Time to Kill* was released in theaters. The follow-up show recycles material from *Lights, Camera, Canton* with the addition of post-production scenes and footage of a special movie premiere held in Jackson, Mississippi, that was attended in large numbers by residents of Canton who had participated in the production.

10. Some local residents who appear in *Waking in Mississippi* do articulate a guarded optimism about shifts in race relations in the South. Asked if she thought Schumacher's Hollywood production had been "good for Canton," Linda Johnson, the local children's librarian, an African American, replies, "It gave everybody a good feeling to be a part of it. It was something to be very proud of. It was a great accomplishment." In the same vein, a journalist, Doris Luckett, another African American, explains: "I heard a lot of people say it really brought them together and they learned to have conversations. And not just passing of words. So that's good. And that's positive. And I hope we continue. I heard some folks say, 'We don't want to stop here.' Because when the movie people leave, we want to keep this up."

11. Although the Canton Country Club had no nonwhite members before it admitted Samuel Jackson, club officials claimed the facility had an "open policy" on memberships.

12. In an effort to prove that she does finally understand his reasons for taking Carl Lee's case, Carla, Jake's wife, articulates his motivations near the end of the film: "The truth is that I've been blaming you for all that's happened. But it's not your fault. You didn't kill those boys. You were trying to make things right. I know that now. I thought you took this case because you wanted to prove to everybody what a big time lawyer you were. But I was wrong. You took this case because if those boys had hurt Hannah the way that they hurt Tonya, you would have killed them yourself."

13. Ellen is gradually "softened" as the narrative progresses. The lingering sexual attraction between her and Jake, her "kittenish" performance with the male administrator at the Whitfield psychiatric facility, which allows her access

to key rebuttal evidence, the near rape she suffers at the hands of Klansmen, her subsequent confinement in the hospital, and her tears in response to Jake's presence at her bedside—all work to feminize Ellen, containing the feminist threat she posed earlier in the narrative.

14. Deputy Dwayne Looney is the police officer caught in the line of fire as Carl Lee shoots down Billy Ray and James Louis on the courthouse stairs. Looney suffers bullet wounds to his right knee and as a consequence is forced to have his leg amputated. When a remorseful Carl Lee insists on visiting Looney in the hospital, Sheriff Walls arranges for the prisoner to be smuggled out of his cell and driven to the local hospital under the cover of dark. Alone in the hospital room, the injured officer receives Carl Lee's apology with tears. A few weeks later, Looney is invited by the prosecution to testify against Carl Lee, given that the accident has forced Looney "out of the police business" and into a "desk job" at the precinct offices. But on the witness stand, Looney has a surprise in store, demanding of the jury: "You set this man free! He's a hero!"

15. These portrayals return to a revival of the "white man's burden," where once again civilized cultures stand "duty-bound to uplift the so-called savage ones" (Rosaldo 1989, 108). Such tales patronizingly recount how whites, in the footprints of the Great Emancipator, "deliver[ed] full freedom for the American Negro" and assert that, absent the generous and sympathetic labors of whites, black Americans would have remained enslaved, segregated, and victimized by neglect.

4. Of Heroism and Healing, Racism and Redemption

1. Following the work of the sociologist Erving Goffman, a frame is "a conceptual means of organizing and delimiting the scope of what one pays attention to" (1974). For Todd Gitlin, frames are "cognitive schema or packages with a central core that help in interpretation and processing" (1980). Frames delimit descriptions of the critical issues of the day, giving shape to what gets focused on in a policy dispute and what gets eclipsed (Entman 1993; Gamson 1992; Gitlin 1980; Schön and Rein 1994). Framing is an interpretive process that constructs situations in particular ways so as to illuminate some aspects and obscure others. Any frame through which an issue is described is neither free of ideology nor impartial. "All organization, conceptual or otherwise, is bias. Each frame, privileging as it does a particular unit, relation, and level of analysis, conditions the questions that are asked, and thereby the answers obtained" (Samarajiva and Shields 1992, 398).

2. Listing statistics on school integration in Southern and border states in April 1964, the *New York Times* reported that Mississippi remained the only state where no black students were enrolled in schools with whites. Alabama (.0004 percent), Arkansas (.968 percent), Florida (.53 percent), Georgia (.052 percent), Louisiana (.602 percent), North Carolina (.538 percent), South Carolina (.0004 percent), Texas (4.29 percent), and Virginia (1.57 percent) reported that under 5 percent of their black students were enrolled in integrated schools by this time. Delaware, Kentucky, Missouri, Oklahoma, and West Virginia reported higher than 20 percent integration (A. Lewis 1964, D5).

3. As part of its strategy to animate concerns over the costs of the civil rights bill for working-class whites, the CCFF advertised heavily in non–English language dailies geared to new immigrant and working-class audiences. For instance, *Zgoda*, a Chicago Polish-language daily newspaper that reached southern Milwaukee and northern Indiana, ran anti–civil rights advertisements funded by the CCFF for several weeks before the presidential primaries in Indiana in May 1964 (Kenworthy 1964o, 6).

4. Similar letter-writing campaigns were organized by the archconservative John Birch Society in March and April 1964. Robert H. W. Welch, society president, boasted in one of the organization's newsletters, "Our members are responsible for pouring more than half a million messages into Washington during the last month." In a well-coordinated effort, members ran "anonymous" advertisements with the headline "Every vote for the Civil Rights Act of 1964 is a Nail for the Coffin of the American Republic" (Franklin 1964, 1).

5. While Southern leaders repeatedly raised concerns that the civil rights measure would "turn the clock back on human freedoms" and violate the equal protection clause of the Constitution, evidence collected by the Civil Rights Commission suggested that several Southern states and counties were themselves guilty of cutting off federal funds from African Americans in reprisals against attempts to register to vote (Kenworthy 1964n, 19).

Bibliography

Abrams, Kathy. 1991. "Hearing the Call of Stories." *California Law Review* 79: 971–1052.

Ackerman, Todd. 2004. "UT Wants to Put Cap on Top 10 Admissions." *Houston Chronicle*, May 12, A20.

Adarand Constructors v. Peña, 115 S. Ct. 2097 (1995).

Addelston, Judi. 1999. "Doing the Full Monty with Dirk and Jane: Using the Phallus to Validate Marginalized Masculinities." *Journal of Men's Studies* 7, no. 3: 337–52.

Ainslie, Ricardo, and Kalina Brabeck. 2003. "Race, Murder, and Community Trauma: Psychoanalysis and Ethnography in Exploring the Impact of the Killing of James Byrd in Jasper, Texas." *Journal for the Psychoanalysis of Culture and Society* 8, no. 1: 42–50.

"Alabama Governor Files in Wisconsin." 1964. *New York Times*, March 7, 1964, 8.

American Civil Liberties Union. 1996. *Affirmative Action: Myths and Facts*. http://www.aclu.org.

———. 1997. *Briefing Paper on Affirmative Action*. http://www.aclu.org.

"An Interview with Ward Connerly." 1999. *Interracial Voice*, April 24, 1999. http://www.acri.org/spchbkrvw/index.html.

"And the Walls Came Tumbling Down." 1964. *Time*, July 17, 25–26.

Anson, Sam Gideon 1996. "Ward Connerly's Female Trouble." *LA Weekly*, October 11, 15.

"Anti-Affirmative Action Campaign Will Target '06." 2004. *Associated Press State and Local Wire*, June 15.

Aronowitz, Stanley. 2000. "Misidentity Politics." *Nation*, November 6, 28–31.

Asadullah, Samad A. 1996. "Between the Lines: The California White Civil Rights Initiative: Don't Be Confused." *Los Angeles Sentinel*, June 3, A7.

Autman, Samuel. 2002. "Beyond the Numbers: UC Schools Expand Criteria for Who Gets Admitted." *San Diego Union-Tribune*, March 17, A1.

Ayres, B. Drummond, Jr. 1996. "A Reign of Confusion in Affirmative Action." *New York Times*, December 1, 1.

Azreal, Deb. 1997. "Waking in Mississippi." *Video Eyeball:* 48.

Baldwin, James. 1969. *Black Anti-Semitism and Jewish Racism*. New York: R. W. Baron.

Balibar, Etienne, and Immanuel Wallerstein. 1991. *Race, Nation, Class: Ambiguous Identities*. London: Verso.

Bancroft, Ann. 1994. "Assembly Panel Quickly Kills Reverse-Bias Plan." *San Francisco Chronicle*, August 11, A19.

Barry, Andrew, Tony Osborne, and Nikolas Rose. 1996. "Introduction." In *Foucault and Political Reason: Liberalism, Neo-Liberalism, and Rationalities of Government*, ed. A. Barry, T. Osborne, and N. Rose, 1–17. Chicago: University of Chicago Press.

Barry, Dan, David Barstow, Jonathan D. Glater, Adam Liptak, and Jacques Steinberg. 2003. "Correcting the Record: *Times* Reporter Who Resigned Leaves Long Trail of Deception." *New York Times*, May 11, 1.

Bearak, Barry. 1997. "Questions of Race Run Deep for Foe of Preferences." *New York Times*, July 27, 1.

Beason, Tyrone, and Tom Brune. 1998. "High-Profile Backers, Opponents Tiptoe Around I-200 Debate." *Seattle Times*, September 1, A1.

Bell, Derrick. 1992. *Faces at the Bottom of the Well: The Permanence of Racism*. New York: Basic Books.

Bennett, Lerone, Jr. 1993. *Before the Mayflower: A History of Black America*. 6th ed. New York: Penguin.

Bermanzohn, Sally Avery. 2003. *Through Survivors' Eyes: From the Sixties to the Greensboro Massacre*. Nashville, Tenn: Vanderbilt University Press.

"Bishops Want Vatican to Name King a Martyr." 2000. *St. Petersburg Times*, January 15, 7.

Biskupic, Joan. 1997. "High Court Is Asked to Block Proposition 209." *Washington Post*, August 30, A10.

Blau, Francine D., and Marianne A. Ferber. 1992. *The Economics of Women, Men, and Work*. Englewood Cliffs, N.J.: Prentice Hall.

Bogle, Donald. 1997. *Toms, Coons, Mulattoes, Mammies, and Bucks: An Interpretive History of Blacks in American Films*. New York: Continuum.

Bolick, Clint. 1993. "Clinton's Quota Queens." *Wall Street Journal*, April 30, A12.

Bonilla-Silva, Eduardo. 2001. *White Supremacy and Racism in the Post Civil Rights Era*. Boulder, Colo.: Lynne Rienner.

Bordo, Susan. 1997. "Can a Woman Harass a Man?" *Philosophy Today* 411: 51–66.

Boudreau, John. 1994. "Effort to Outlaw Affirmative Action Promoted in California." *Washington Post*, December 27, A3.

Bowen, William G., and Derek Bok. 1998. *The Shape of the River: Long-Term Consequences of Considering Race in College and University Admissions*. Princeton, N.J.: Princeton University Press.

Boxall, Bettina. 1996. "Opponents of Prop. 209 Target Women Voters." *Los Angeles Times*, August 20, A1.

Boyd, Todd. 2003. *The New H.N.I.C. Head Niggas in Charge: The Death of Civil Rights and the Reign of Hip Hop*. New York: New York University Press.

Branscomb, Leslie Wolf. 2003. "Defeat of Prop. 54 is Called Win for Grassroots Politics." *San Diego Union-Tribune*, October 8, A11.

Brenkman, John. 1995. "Race Publics: Civic Deliberation, or Race after Reagan." *Transitions* 66: 4–36.

Broder, David S. 1999. "For 2000, an Issue of Race." *Washington Post*, January 23, A1.

Bronner, Ethan. 1997. "Group Suing U. of Michigan over Diversity." *New York Times*, October 14, A24.

Brown v. Board of Education, 347 U.S. 483 (1954).

Brown, Wendy. 2002. "Women's Studies Unbound: Revolution, Mourning, Politics." UK Women's Studies Network Conference, Belfast.

Brune, Tom. 1998a. "I-200 Supporters Diversify Leadership: African American Woman Joins Campaign." *Seattle Times*, June 16, B1.

———. 1998b. "Poll: I-200 Passage Was Call for Reform." *Seattle Times*, November 4, A1.

———. 1998c. "Locke Keeps Diversity as Goal." *Seattle Times*, December 1, B1.

———, and Joe Heim. 1998. "Initiative 200: New Battle Begins." *Seattle Times*, November 4, B1.

———, and Lynne Varner. 1999. "Affirmative Action Not Dead Here, It Just Morphed, Most Agree." *Seattle Times*, July 7, A1.

Burchell, Graham. 1996. "Liberal Government and Techniques of the Self." In *Foucault and Political Reason: Liberalism, Neo-Liberalism, and Rationalities of Government*, ed. A. Barry, T. Osborne, and N. Rose, 19–36. Chicago: University of Chicago Press.

Burdman, Pamela. 1999. "UC Regents to Approve 4% Admissions Policy." *San Francisco Chronicle*, March 19, A1.

———. 2002. "Connerly Initiative Would Ban Collection of Racial Data." *Black Issues in Higher Education* 19, no. 9: 18–20.

———. 2003. "Exposing the Truth and Fiction of Racial Data." *California Journal* 52, no. 8: 40.

Burka, Paul. 1998. "Jewel of the Forest." *Texas Monthly*, August, 9.

Burns, Nikki. 2002. "Former Alderman Beats Canton's First Black Mayor." *Mississippi Link*, October 30, 1.

———. 2005. "Blacks Flex Political Muscle in Mississippi Mayoral Races," *Mississippi Link*, June 9–15, A1.

Butler, Judith. 1996. "An Affirmative View." *Representations* 55: 74–83.

Cahn, Naomi R. 1997. "Representing Race Outside of Explicitly Racialized Contexts." *Michigan Law Review* 944: 965–1005.

Caldwell, Christopher. 2003. "California's Other Race: The Dishonest Assault on the Racial Privacy Initiative." *Weekly Standard*, September 15.

California Civil Rights Initiative Web page. http://www.ccri/Yeson209.

California Constitution, Article 1, §31a.

California Department of Finance/Demographic Research Unit. 2000. *Race/Ethnic Report*. Sacramento.

Canton Convention and Visitors Bureau. 2003. Press Release. May 5.

Carlson, John. 1998. "Initiative 200: Should Washington Put an End to Race-Preference Programs?" *Seattle Times*, February 1, B5.

Chakravorty-Spivak, Gayatri. 1990. "Questions of Multiculturalism." In *The Post-Colonial Critic: Interviews, Strategies, Dialogues*, ed. S. Harasym, 59–66. New York: Routledge.

Chávez, Lydia. 1998. *The Color Bind: California's Battle to End Affirmative Action*. Berkeley: University of California Press.

Chen, Howard Henry. 1997. "Black and White Documentary." *The News and Observer* [Durham, N.C.], May 8, 1E.

Chiang, Harriet. 1996a. "Judge Wants 'Affirmative Action' in Prop. 209 Summary." *San Francisco Chronicle*, August 2, A19.

———. 1996b. "Top State Court Lets CCRI Blurb Remain As Is." *San Francisco Chronicle*, August 13, A16.

———. 1999. "State Appeals Court Invalidates Minority Outreach Program." *San Francisco Chronicle*, May 28, A22.

Christian, Barbara. 1996. "Camouflaging Race and Gender." *Representations* 55: 120–28.

Chua-Eoan, Henry. 1998. "Beneath the Surface." *Time*, June 22, 34–35.

"Citizens for a United Michigan Asks Michigan Supreme Court to Take Up Connerly Petition Challenge." 2004. *PR Newswire State and Regional News*, June 30.

City of Canton, Mississippi. Official Web site. http://www.cityofcanton.net/about.htm.

City of Richmond v. J.A. Croson Co. 488 U.S. 469 (1989).

Claiborne, William. 1995. "Gov. Wilson Deftly Plays Up to Middle-Class Angst." *Washington Post*, August 27, A1.

Clayton, Mark. 2001. "The Woman behind the Law School Admissions Suit." *Christian Science Monitor*, April 3, 14.

"Closing Up." 1964. *New York Times*, July 4, 4.

Coalition for Economic Equity v. Wilson. 1996. Case No. C96-4024 TEH, December 23.

Coalition for Economic Equity v. Wilson. 1997a. Case Nos. 97-15030 & 97-15031, April 8.

Coalition for Economic Equity v. Wilson. 1997b. Case Nos. 97-15030 & 97-15031, August 26.

Cohn, Bob. 1993. "Crowning a 'Quota Queen'?" *Newsweek*, May 24, 67.

Congressional Record. 1964. Washington D.C.: GPO: 6538–74.

Connerly, Ward. 1996a. "With Liberty and Justice for All." Speech delivered March 8, 1996, to the Heritage Foundation, Washington, D.C. Reprinted in *Vital Speeches* 6214: 434–37.

———. 1996b. "An Ugly Campaign to Preserve Quotas." *Wall Street Journal*, September 25, A22.

———. 1996c. "End Government Bias." *USA Today*, October 22, 14A.

———. 1997. "Remarks to the Lincoln Leadership Award for Civic Virtue," February 12. Washington, D.C. http://www.acri.org/spchbkrvw/feb12.html.

———. 2003. "We Are Multi-Racial—But We Should Be Colorblind." *Daily Telegraph* [U.K.], October 2, 26.

————, and Thomas L. Rhodes. 1997. "Prop 209 Won't Gut Affirmative Action." *Wall Street Journal*, February 11, A20.

————, and Willie Brown. 1995. "Choosing Sides." *Black Enterprise* 264: 156–57.

Conrad, Cecilia. 1997. "California Torpedoes Affirmative Action." *Black Enterprise* 27, no. 7: 32.

Cordova, Jeanne. 1997. "'Suck My Dick!' The Latest Feminist Message?" *Lesbian News* 23, no. 4 (November): 34.

Cose, Ellis. 1997. *Color-Blind: Seeing beyond Race in a Race-Obsessed World*. New York: HarperCollins.

Cover, Robert M. 1983. "Foreword: Nomos and Narrative." *Harvard Law Review* 97: 4–68.

Crenshaw, Kimberle W. 1997. "Color Blindness, History, and the Law." In *The House That Race Built*, ed. W. Lubiano, 280–88. New York: Vintage.

————, Neil Gotanda, Gary Peller, and Kendall Thomas. 1995. "Introduction." In *Critical Race Theory: The Key Writings that Formed the Movement*, ed. K. Crenshaw, N. Gotanda, G. Peller, and K. Thomas, xiii–xxxii. New York: New Press.

Currivan, Gene. 1964. "Kepple Acclaims School Agitation." *New York Times*, February 16, 61.

Custred, Glynn. 1997. "Individual Rights and Equality before the Law." *Academic Questions* 102: 15–18.

Davies, Jude. 1995. "Gender, Ethnicity, and Cultural Crisis in *Falling Down* and *Groundhog Day*." *Screen* 363: 214–32.

Davis, Angela Y. 1977/1998. "Reflections on Race, Class, and Gender in the USA." In *The Angela Y. Davis Reader*, ed. J. James, 307–25. Malden, Mass.: Blackwell.

————. 1997. "Race and Criminalization: Black Americans and the Punishment Industry." In *The House That Race Built*, ed. W. Lubiano, 264–79. New York: Vintage.

Delgado, Richard. 1989. "Storytelling for Oppositionists and Others: A Plea for Narrative." *Michigan Law Review* 87: 2411–41.

Dillard, Angela D. 2001. *Guess Who's Coming to Dinner Now? Multicultural Conservatism in America*. New York: New York University Press.

Dolny, Mark. 2003. *Spectrum Narrows Further in 2002: Progressive, Domestic Think Tanks See Drop*. http://www.fair.org/extra/0307/thinktanks2002.html.

Douglas, Susan J. 1994. *Where the Girls Are: Growing Up Female with the Mass Media*. New York: Three Rivers Press.

Dudziak, Mary L. 1995. "Desegregation as a Cold War Imperative." In *Critical Race Theory: The Cutting Edge*, ed. R. Delgado, 110–21. Philadelphia: Temple University Press.

Duke, Lynne, and Darryl Fears. 2003. "Putting Diversity in the Line of Firing: Minority Staffers at the *Times* Feel the Loss and Fear the Fallout." *Washington Post*, June 7, 2003, C1.

Duster, Troy. 1998. "Individual Fairness, Group Preferences, and the California Strategy." In *Race and Representation: Affirmative Action*, ed. R. Post and M. Rogin, 111–34. New York: Zone Books.

Dyer, Richard. 1988. "White." *Screen* 294: 44–65.

Dyson, Michael Eric. 2000. *I May Not Get There with You: The True Martin Luther King, Jr.* New York: Free Press.

Eagleton, Terry. 1991. *Ideology: An Introduction*. London: Verso.

Edsall, Thomas B., and Mary D. Edsall. 1991. *Chain Reaction: The Impact of Race, Rights, and Taxes on American Politics*. New York: W. W. Norton.

Ehrenhaus, Peter. 1993. "Cultural Narratives and the Therapeutic Motif: The Political Containment of Vietnam Veterans." In *Narrative and Social Control: Critical Perspectives*, ed. D.K. Mumby, 77–96. Newbury Park, Calif.: Sage.

Eichenwald, Kurt. 1996. "The Two Faces of Texaco." *New York Times*, November 10, 1.

Eljera, Bert. 1996. "Californians to Vote on Affirmative Action: It's Official— California Civil Rights Initiative Qualifies for November Ballot." *Asianweek*, April 19, 8.

Entman, Robert M. 1993. "Framing: Toward Clarification of a Fractured Paradigm." *Journal of Communication* 434: 51–58.

———. 1997. "Manufacturing Discord: Media in the Affirmative Action Debate." *Harvard International Journal of Press and Politics* 24: 32–52.

Equal Employment Opportunity Commission. 1995. *The Status of Equal Opportunity in the American Workforce*. Washington D.C.: GPO.

Equal Rights Advocates. 1999. *Why Women Still Need Affirmative Action*. http://www.equalrights.org/AFFIRM/stats.html.

Everett-Haynes, La Monica, and Todd Ackerman. 2004. "A&M Programs to Consider Race." *Houston Chronicle*, May 29, 37.

"Excerpts from Justices' Opinions on Michigan Affirmative Action Cases." 2003. *New York Times*, June 24, 2003, 24–25.

"Extremism Loses in the Schools." 1964. *New York Times*, March 17, 35.

Fair Employment Council of Greater Washington. 1994. "Measuring Employment: Discrimination through Controlled Experiments." *Review of Black Political Economy*.

Fan, Stephen Shie-Wei. 1997. "Immigration Law and the Promise of Critical Race Theory: Opening the Academy to the Voices of Aliens and Immigrants." *Columbia Law Review* 97: 1202–40.

Fanon, Frantz. 1967. *Black Skin, White Masks*. New York: Grove Press.

Fergerson, Gerard. 1997. "Tales of Black Criminality: Racial Determinism and Fatal Narratives." In *Tales of the State: Narrative in Contemporary U.S. Politics and Public Policy*, ed. S. F. Schram and P. T. Neisser, 125–35. New York: Rowman Littlefield.

Firestone, David. 2001. "U. of Georgia Cannot Use Race in Admission Policy, Court Rules." *New York Times*, August 28, A1.

Fiske, John. 1994. *Media Matters: Everyday Culture and Political Change*. Minneapolis: University of Minnesota Press.

Fix, Michael E., and Margery Austin Turner. 1998. *A National Report Card on Discrimination in America*. Washington, D.C: Urban Institute.

Fletcher, Michael A. 2000. "Use of Race in Admissions Upheld." *Washington Post*, December 14, A2.

Folbre, Nancy, and Heidi Hartmann. 1989. "The Persistence of Patriarchal Capitalism." *Rethinking Marxism* 24: 90–96.

Foucault, Michel. 1970. *The Order of Things: An Archaeology of the Human Sciences*. New York: Vintage.

———. 1978. "About the Concept of the 'Dangerous Individual' in Nineteenth Century Legal Psychiatry." *International Journal of Law and Psychiatry* 1: 1–18.

———. 1978/1990. *The History of Sexuality: Volume I*. Trans. R. Hurley. New York: Vintage.

———. 1978/1991. "Governmentality." Trans. C. Gordon. In *The Foucault Effect: Studies in Governmentality*, ed. G. Burchell, C. Gordon, and P. Miller, 87–104. Chicago: University of Chicago Press.

———. 1979. *Discipline and Punish: The Birth of the Prison*. New York: Vintage.

———. 1980. *Power/Knowledge: Selected Interviews and Other Writings, 1972/1977*. New York: Pantheon.

Fowler, Bree. 2004. "Michigan Attorney General Plans Appeal of Court Ruling on Affirmative Action Petition." *Associated Press State and Local Wire*, March 30.

Fraiman, Susan. 1994. "Geometries of Race and Gender: Eve Sedgwick, Spike Lee, Charlayne Hunter-Gault." *Feminist Studies* 201: 67–84.

Frankenberg, Ruth, ed. 1997. *Displacing Whiteness: Essays in Social and Cultural Criticism*. Durham, N.C.: Duke University Press.

Franklin, Ben A. 1964a. "Wallace Enters Maryland Race with Attack on Civil Rights Bill." *New York Times*, March 10, 29.

———. 1964b. "Birch Drive Seeks Rights Bill Death." *New York Times*, April 21, 1.

———. 1964c. "Wallace Keying Maryland Campaign to Prayer and Anecdotes." *New York Times*, May 11, 23.

———. 1964d. "Hate Groups Back Wallace Bid." *New York Times*, May 14, 27.

———. 1964e. "Wallace Scores U.S. Judiciary as Dictatorial in Racial Cases." *New York Times*, June 5, 18.

Fraser, Nancy, and Linda Gordon. 1994. "A Genealogy of Dependency: Tracing a Keyword of the U.S. Welfare State." *Signs* 19: 309–36.

Freedberg, Louis. 1997. "GOP Trying to Ban Affirmative Action." *San Francisco Chronicle*, June 18, A1.

Gamson, William A. 1992. *Talking Politics*. Cambridge: Cambridge University Press.

———, and Andre Modigliani. 1987. "The Changing Culture of Affirmative Action." *Research in Political Sociology* 3: 137–77.

George, Maryanne. 1998. "Affirmative Action Challenge Has Put U-M on Racial Edge." *Detroit Free Press*, April 15, 1A.

George, Nelson. 1992. *Buppies, B-Boys, Baps, and Bohos: Notes on Post-Soul Black Culture*. New York: HarperCollins.

———. 2004. *Post-Soul Nation: The Explosive, Contradictory, Triumphant, and Tragic 1980s as Experienced by African Americans*. New York: Viking.

Gibson, James W. 2000. "Warrior Dreams." In *Signs of Life in the U.S.A.*, ed. S. Maasik and J. Solomon, 496–505. Boston: Bedford/St. Martin's.

Gilhool, Thomas K., Eleanor K. Holmes, Gillian Russell, J. Douglas Shrader, and Allen Thomas. 1964. "Letters to the Editor: Rights Protest Upheld." *New York Times*, March 15, 8.

Gingrich, Newt, and Ward Connerly. 1997. "Face the Failure of Racial Preferences." *New York Times*, June 15, 15.

Gitlin, Todd. 1980. *The Whole World Is Watching: Mass Media in the Making and Unmaking of the New Left*. Berkeley: University of California Press.

Glaeser, Edward L., Jacob L. Vigdor, and Terry Sanford. 2001. *Racial Segregation in the 2000 Census*. Washington, D.C.: Brookings Institution Survey Series/ Center on Urban and Metropolitan Policy.

Glass Ceiling Commission. 1995. *Good for Business: Making Full Use of the Nation's Human Capital: A Fact Finding Report of the Federal Glass Ceiling Commission*. Washington, D.C.: GPO.

Glater, Jonathan D. 2004. "Diversity Plan Shaped in Texas Is under Attack." *New York Times*, June 13, A1.

Goffman, Erving. 1974. *Frame Analysis: An Essay on the Organization of Experience*. New York: Harper and Row.

Goldberg, David Theo. 1993. *Racist Culture: Philosophy and the Politics of Meaning*. Cambridge, Mass.: Blackwell.

———. 1997. *Racial Subjects: Writing on Race in America*. New York: Routledge.

———. 2002. *The Racial State*. Malden, Mass.: Blackwell.

Goldstein, Richard. 2004. "Bush's Basket: Why the President Had to Show His Balls." In *The W Effect: Bush's War on Women*, ed. L. Flanders, 175–77. New York: Feminist Press.

Goldwater, Barry. 1964. "Text of Goldwater Speech on Rights." *New York Times*, June 19, 18.

Golub, Mark. 1998. "History Died for Our Sins: Guilt and Responsibility in Hollywood Redemption Histories." *Journal of American Culture* 213: 23–46.

Gone South Productions. 1995. Promotional materials for the film *Waking in Mississippi*.

Gooding-Williams, Robert. 1993. "Look, a Negro!" In *Reading Rodney King, Reading Urban Uprising*, ed. R. Gooding-Williams, 157–77. London: Routledge.

"GOP Backs Off King Speech Ad; Spot Used 'I Have a Dream' to Promote Anti-Affirmative Action Measures." 1996. *St. Louis Post-Dispatch*, October 24, 5B.

Graham, Allison. 2001. *Framing the South: Hollywood, Television, and Race during the Civil Rights Struggle*. Baltimore, Md.: Johns Hopkins University Press.

Gray, Herman. 1995. *Watching Race: Television and the Struggle for Blackness*. Minneapolis: University of Minnesota Press.

Greenhouse, Linda. 1997. "Justices Allow Anti-Bias Law to Go into Effect." *New York Times*, September 5, A16.

———. 2002. "Court Revisits Colleges Efforts to Gain Diversity." *New York Times*, December 3, A1.

————. 2003. "U. of Michigan Ruling Endorses Value of Campus Diversity." *New York Times*, June 24, A1.

Griffith, Pat. 1997. "U. of Michigan to Fight Lawsuits that Challenge Its Push for Minorities." *Pittsburg Post-Gazette*, December 4, A12.

Gubar, Susan. 1997. *Race Changes: White Skin, Black Face in American Culture*. New York: Oxford University Press.

Guerrero, Ed. 1993. "The Black Image in Protective Custody: Hollywood's Biracial Buddy Films of the Eighties." In *Black American Cinema*, ed. M. Diawara, 237–46. New York: Routledge.

Guillermo, Emil. 1995. "Emil Amok: The Color of Conservatism." *Filipino Express* 950 (December 17): 11.

Gumbel, Andrew, and Severin Carrell. 2002. "Once Again, a Killing Rage Breaks through the Surface of Everyday Life." *Independent*, April 28, 2002, 5.

Hall, Stuart. 1988. *The Hard Road to Renewal*. London: Verso.

————. 1992. "What Is This 'Black' in Black Popular Culture?" In *Black Popular Culture*, ed. G. Dent, 21–33. Seattle: Bay Press.

Handler, M. S. 1964. "White and Negro Clash at Parley." *New York Times*, February 9, 51.

Haney Lopez, Ian F. 1996. *White by Law: The Legal Construction of Race*. New York: New York University Press.

Hanke, Robert. 1992. "Redesigning Men: Hegemonic Masculinity in Transition." In *Men, Masculinity, and the Media*, ed. S. Craig, 185–98. Newbury Park, Calif.: Sage.

Hardt, Michael, and Antonio Negri. 2000. *Empire*. Cambridge, Mass.: Harvard University Press.

Harris v. Forklift Systems, Inc. 1993. 510 U.S. 17.

Harris, Louis. 1995. *Women's Equality Poll: A Survey of the Attitudes of a Cross-Section of American Women and Men and a Cross-Section of Voters in California on Affirmative Action, Abortion, and Other Key Issues Affecting Women and Minorities*. Prepared for the Feminist Majority Foundation.

————. 1996. "The Future of Affirmative Action." In *The Affirmative Action Debate*, ed. G. E. Curry, 326–35. Reading, Mass.: Addison-Wesley.

Hartmann, Heidi. 1996. "Who Has Benefited from Affirmative Action in Employment?" In *The Affirmative Action Debate*, ed. G. E. Curry, 77–96. Reading, Mass.: Addison-Wesley.

Hasian, Marouf A., Jr., and Fernando Delgado. 1998. "The Trials and Tribulations of Racialized Critical Rhetorical Theory: Understanding the Rhetorical Ambiguities of Proposition 187." *Communication Theory* 83: 245–70.

Haskins, Jim. 2002. *Black Stars of the Civil Rights Movement*. Hoboken, N.J.: John Wiley and Sons.

Hayden, Tom, and Connie Rice. 1995. "California Cracks Its Mortarboards." *Nation*, September 18, 264.

Hechinger, Fred M. 1964. "Class or Race? Economic Status Held Key Issue in Urban School Integration." *New York Times*, March 15, 7.

Herbers, John. 1964a. "Auburn U. Calm as Negro Enters." *New York Times*, January 5, 1.

———. 1964b. "10,000 March for Rights in Kentucky's Capital." *New York Times*, March 6, 27.

———. 1964c. "School Is Center of Race Protests." *New York Times*, March 15, 48.

———. 1964d. "Klan to Organize Its Own Towns as Havens from Desegregation." *New York Times*, March 23, 1.

Herring, Caroline. 1997. "Documentary Film *Waking in Mississippi* Shown at Center." *Southern Register*, Fall 24.

Hill, Lance. 2004. *The Deacons for Defense: Armed Resistance and the Civil Rights Movement*. Chapel Hill: University of North Carolina Press.

Hill, Mike. 1997. *Whiteness: A Critical Reader*. New York: New York University Press.

———. 2003. *After Whiteness: Unmaking an American Majority*. New York: New York University Press.

Holbrook, Damian J. 2003. "Forget the Madonna Song." *TV Guide Online*. January. http://www.tvguide.com.

Holmes Norton, Eleanor. 1996. "Affirmative Action in the Workplace." In *The Affirmative Action Debate*, ed. G. E. Curry, 39–48. Reading, Mass.: Addison-Wesley.

Holmes, Steve A. 1998. "Victorious Preferences Foes Look for New Battlefields." *New York Times*, November 10, A25.

Honan, William H. 1996. "Efforts to Bar Selection Based on Race: Moves Are Made across the Nation." *New York Times*, March 31, 14.

Hook, Sidney. 1964. "Fulbright's Rights Stand." *New York Times*, April 8, 42.

hooks, bell. 1984. *Feminist Theory: From Margin to Center*. Boston: South End Press.

———. 1992. *Black Looks: Race and Representation*. Boston: South End Press.

———. 1994. *Outlaw Culture: Resisting Representations*. New York: Routledge.

———. 1996. *Reel to Real: Race, Sex, and Class at the Movies*. New York: Routledge.

Hopwood v. Texas. 1996. 78 F.3d 932.

Hornbeck, Mark. 1998. "Engler Quiet on Racial Quotas." *Detroit News*, May 18, D1.

HoSang, Daniel. 2001. "Hiding Race." *Colorlines*, December 1.

"Houston Thinks Globally in OK of Preferences." 1997. *Los Angeles Times*, November 6, A1.

Howard, John. 1996. "Supreme Court Upholds Lundgren on Prop. 209: Ruling Bars Language Describing It as Repeal of Affirmative Action." *Fresno Bee*, August 13, A3.

Hunter, Ian. 1988. *Culture and Government: The Emergence of Literary Education*. Houndmills, Basingstoke: Macmillan.

Hunter, Marjorie. 1964. "Debate on Rights Often Tangential." *New York Times*, March 15, 45.

Hunter, Stephen. 1997. "G.I. Jane: Demi Grunts, You Bear It." *Washington Post*, August 22, D1.

Ignatiev, Noel. 1995. *How the Irish Became White*. New York: Routledge.

———, and John Garvey, eds. 1996. *Race Traitor*. New York: Routledge.

Impoco, Jim. 1995. "The Mother of All Wedge Issues." *U.S. News and World Report*, June 5, 30.

"Initiative 200: Another Blow to Affirmative Action." 1998. *Star Tribune*, November 7, 18A.

Inness, Sherrie A. 1999. *Tough Girls: Women Warriors and Wonder Women in Popular Culture*. Philadelphia: University of Pennsylvania Press.

Jackson, Derrick Z. 1998. "When Women Spurn Equality." *Boston Globe*, November 13, A27.

James, Caryn. 1994. "Tales from the Corner Office." *New York Times*, December 11, B1.

Janson, Donald. 1964. "Kansas City Bill on Rights Fought." *New York Times*, March 22, 50.

Jeffords, Susan. 1993. "The Big Switch: Hollywood Masculinity in the Nineties." In *Film Theory Goes to the Movies*, ed. J. Collins, H. Radner, and E. Preacher Collins, 196–208. New York: Routledge.

Johnson, Lyndon B. 1965. "Commencement Address at Howard University: To Fulfill These Rights." June. Reprinted in *Affirmative Action and the Constitution: vol. 1*, 1998. ed. Gabriel J. Chin, 21–26. New York: Garland.

Johnson, Roberta A. 1990. "Affirmative Action Policy in the United States: Its Impact on Women." *Policy and Politics* 182: 77–90.

Jones, Jackie. 1992. "The Accusatory Space." In *Black Popular Culture*, ed. G. Dent, 95–98. Seattle: Bay Press.

Katz, Nancy L. 1997. "How Prop. 209 Affects Claudia Ramsey's Shop." *Christian Science Monitor*, November 18, 2.

Kelley, Robin D. G. 1994. *Race Rebels: Culture, Politics, and the Black Working Class.* New York: Free Press.

———. 1997. *Yo' Mama's Disfunktional! Fighting the Culture Wars in Urban America.* Boston: Beacon Press.

Kenworthy, E. W. 1964a. "House Rights Bloc Beats Attacks on Heart of Bill." *New York Times*, February 6, 1.

———. 1964b. "Jobs Issue Blocks Attempt in House to Vote on Rights." *New York Times*, February 9, 1.

———. 1964c. "Senate Starts Rights Fight; Russell Bars Compromise." *New York Times*, March 10, 1.

———. 1964d. "Ellender Agrees Some Registrars Bar Negro Votes." *New York Times*, March 12, 1.

———. 1964e. "Relocate Negroes Evenly in States, Russell Proposes." *New York Times*, March 17, 1.

———. 1964f. "To Get Rights Bill before Senators." *New York Times*, March 18, 1.

———. 1964g. "Senate Rights Test Expected in Weeks." *New York Times*, March 20, 1.

———. 1964h. "Churches Termed Key to Rights Bill." *New York Times*, March 21, 14.

———. 1964i. "G.O.P. Senator Declares Liberals Are Contributing to Rights Bill Delay." *New York Times*, March 24, 24.

———. 1964j. "Fund Raises Rights-Bill Clash." *New York Times*, March 25, 20.

———. 1964k. "Rights Bill Wins 2 Tests in Senate by Wide Margins." *New York Times*, March 27, 1.

———. 1964l. "The South's Strategy." *New York Times*, March 28, 25.

———. 1964m. "Civil Rights Forces Assail Denial of Vote to Negroes." *New York Times*, April 2, 1.

———. 1964n. "Keating Attacks Mississippi Bills." *New York Times*, April 7, 19.

———. 1964o. "Civil Rights: Politics." *New York Times*, April 26, 6.

———. 1964p. "Revised Measure Now Goes Back to House for Concurrence." *New York Times*, June 20, 1.

King, Coretta Scott. 1996. "Man of His Word." *New York Times*, November 3, D15.

King, Deborah. 1995. "Multiple Jeopardy, Multiple Consciousness: The Context of Black Feminist Ideology." In *Words of Fire: An Anthology of African-American Feminist Thought*, ed. B. Guy-Sheftall, 294–318. New York: New Press.

King, Joyce. 2002. *Hate Crime: The Story of a Dragging in Jasper, Texas*. New York: Pantheon.

King, Martin Luther, Jr. 1963/1986. "I Have a Dream." In *A Testament of Hope: The Essential Writings and Speeches of Martin Luther King, Jr.*, ed. J. M. Washington, 217–20. New York: HarperCollins.

Knickerbocker, Brad. 1998. "Affirmative Action's Future on Line in Washington State." *Christian Science Monitor*, October 16, 3.

Kotkin, Joel. 1995. "The Hot Zone: Why Did the New Affirmative Action Debate Erupt in California?" *The New Democrat*, May/June.

Krock, Arthur. 1964. "In the Nation: Significance of Wisconsin Primaries." *New York Times*, April 9, 30.

Leff, Laurel. 1993. "From Legal Scholar to Quota Queen." *Columbia Journalism Review* (September/October): 36.

Lelyveld, Joseph. 1964. "Negroes Intensify Their Demands for Jobs." *New York Times*, January 6, 67.

Lesher, Dave. 1996. "State GOP Plans TV Ad Blitz for Prop 209." *Los Angeles Mirror*, October 22, A20.

———. 1997. "Connerly Leads New Assault on Preferences." *Los Angeles Times*, January 16, A3.

———, and Bettina Boxall. 1996. "Clashes within GOP Delay Ad Campaign for Prop 209." *Los Angeles Mirror*, October 23, A3.

Levering Lewis, David. 2001. "Harlem's Visible Man." *New York Times*, August 2, A21.

Lewis, Anthony. 1964. "Token Integration Now Faces Sharp Court Test." *New York Times*, April 12, D4.

Lewis, Neil A. 2003. "Some on the Right See a Challenge." *New York Times*, June 24, A1.

Limbaugh, Rush H. 1992. *The Way Things Ought to Be*. New York: Pocket Star Books.

Linville, Susan E. 2000. "The Mother of All *Courage Under Fire* Battles and the Gender-Integrated Military." *Cinema Journal* 39, no. 2: 100–120.

Lipsitz, George. 1990. *Time Passages: Collective Memory and American Popular Culture*. Minneapolis: University of Minnesota Press.

———. 1998. *The Possessive Investment in Whiteness: How White People Profit from Identity Politics*. Philadephia: Temple University Press.

Loftus, Joseph A. 1964a. "Gov. Love Calls for Discontent." *New York Times*, April 12, 55.

———. 1964b. "Goldwater Gives Stand on Issues." *New York Times*, May 14, 26.

"Longing for the Days When There Were No Blacks Competing for Admission to College." 1995. *Journal of Blacks in Higher Education*, December 31, 40.

Lorde, Audre. 1984. *Sister Outsider*. Freedom, Calif.: Crossing Press.

Los Angeles Times Exit Poll. 1996. http://www.acri.org/209.

Lott, Eric. 1993. *Love and Theft: Blackface Minstrelsy and the American Working Class*. New York: Oxford University Press.

Lubiano, Wahneema. 1992. "Black Ladies, Welfare Queens, and State Minstrels: Ideological War by Narrative Means." In *Race-ing Justice, En-gendering Power: Essays on Anita Hill, Clarence Thomas, and the Construction of Social Reality*, ed. T. Morrison, 323–61. New York: Pantheon.

Lucas, Greg. 1996. "Anti-Affirmative Action Bill Defeated." *San Francisco Chronicle*, May 29, A11.

Lyne, William. 2000. "No Accident: From Black Power to Black Box Office." *African American Review* 34, no. 1 (Spring): 39–60.

"Mail Protesting Rights Bill Rises." 1964. *New York Times*, March 18, 24.

Malcolm X. 1963. *Message to the Grassroots*. November 12, Detroit, Mich. Reprinted in *Malcolm X Speaks: Selected Speeches and Statements*, ed. G. Breitman. New York: Pathfinder Press, 1965.

———. 1964/1991. "The Harvard Law School Forum of December 16, 1964." In *Malcolm X: Speeches at Harvard*, ed. A. Epps, 161–82. New York: Paragon House.

Manegold, Catherine S. 2000. *In Glory's Shadow: Shannon Faulkner, the Citadel, and a Changing America*. New York: Knopf.

Marable, Manning. 1984. *Race, Reform, and Rebellion: The Second Reconstruction in Black America, 1945–1982*. London: Macmillan.

———. 1992. "Clarence Thomas and the Crisis of Black Political Culture." In *Race-ing Justice, En-gendering Power: Essays on Anita Hill, Clarence Thomas, and the Construction of Social Reality*, ed. T. Morrison, 61–85. New York: Pantheon.

———. 1996. "Staying on the Path to Racial Equality." In *The Affirmative Action Debate*, ed. G. E. Curry, 3–15. Reading, Mass.: Addison-Wesley.

———. 2001. "Terrorism and the Struggle for Peace." *Along the Color Line*. October. http://www.manningmarable.net.

Marks, Milton. 1996. "Is the California Civil Rights Initiative Civil? Is It Right?" *Sun Reporter*, August 8, S5.

Maslin, Janet. 1994. "Sex and Terror: The Male View of the She-Boss." *New York Times*, January 14, C1.

McBride, Kelly. 1998. "I-200 Campaign Embitters Advocate: African American Says She Was Vilified for Her Views." *Seattle Times*, November 30, B4.

McGhee, Minette. 1992. "Blacks Press Toymakers for Diversity Dolls." *Chicago Sun Times*, February 27, 30.

Millones, Peter. 1964. "Negroes in South Test Rights Act; Resistance Light." *New York Times*, July 4, 1.

"Minorities, Engineers Protest Depiction in *Falling Down*." 1993. *Atlanta Journal and Constitution*, March 3, B12.

"Mississippi Agency Channels $260,000 to Anti-Rights Drive." 1964. *New York Times*, March 19, 21.

Mohr, Charles. 1964. "Goldwater Urges Study of the Poor." *New York Times*, January 16, 1.

Moland, John, Jr. 1996. "Social Change, Social Inequality, and Intergroup Tensions." *Social Forces* 1.

Monbiot, George. 2002. "Race War." March 5. http://www.monbiot.com/dsp_article.cfm?article_id=493.

Morris, John. 1964. "Rights Bloc Sees New Johnson Aid." *New York Times*, April 12, 41.

Moynihan, Daniel Patrick. 1965. *The Negro Family: The Case for National Action*. Washington, D.C.: U.S. Department of Labor.

Mukherjee, Roopali. 2002. "Single Moms, Quota Queens, and the Model Majority: Putting 'Women' to Work in the California Civil Rights Initiative." In *Sex and Money: Feminism and Political Economy in the Media*, ed. E. Meehan and E. Riordan, 100–111. Minneapolis: University of Minnesota Press.

———. 2003. "Between Enemies and Traitors: Black Press Coverage of September 11 and the Predicaments of National 'Others.'" In *Media Representations of*

September 11, ed. S. Chermak, F. Bailey, and M. Brown, 29–46. New York: Praeger.

———. In press. "The Ghetto Fabulous Aesthetic in Contemporary Black Culture: Class and Consumption in the *Barbershop* Films." *Cultural Studies.*

Murphy, Caryle. 2000. "Vatican Honor for King Is Applauded; Catholic Church Plans to Designate Civil Rights Leader as Christian Martyr." *Washington Post*, January 17, B3.

Murphy, Dean. 2003. "Affirmative Action Foe's Latest Effort Complicate California Recall Vote." *New York Times*, August 3, 13.

Murray, Charles, and Richard Herrnstein. 1994. *The Bell Curve.* New York: Simon and Schuster.

Nakagawa, Gordon. 1993. "Deformed Subjects, Docile Bodies: Disciplinary Practices and Subject-Constitution in Stories of Japanese-American Internment." In *Narrative and Social Control: Critical Perspectives*, ed. D. K. Mumby, 143–63. Newbury Park, Calif.: Sage.

Nakao, Annie. 2003. "A Funny Way to Stop Thinking about Race." *San Francisco Chronicle*, September 11, E14.

Nakayama, Thomas K., and Judith N. Martin, eds. 1999. *Whiteness: The Communication of Social Identity.* Thousand Oaks, Calif.: Sage.

Neal, Mark Anthony. 2002. *Soul Babies: Black Popular Culture and the Post-Soul Aesthetic.* New York: Routledge.

Nieves, Evelyn. 2003. "California Battles over Racial Identification." *Washington Post*, September 13, A4.

Nissimov, Ron. 2000. "Admissions Issue May Go to High Court; Rulings Are Split on Allowing Race Factor in College Policies." *Houston Chronicle*, December 11, A19.

Nolan, Bruce. 2000. "Make King a Martyr, Bishops Say; Civil Rights Hero is on Pope's List." *Times-Picayune* [New Orleans], January 14, A1.

Oates, Stephen B. 1994. *Let the Trumpet Sound: The Life of Martin Luther King, Jr.* New York: Perennial Harper Collins.

Omi, Michael, and Howard Winant. 1994. *Racial Formation in the United States: From the 1960s to the 1990s.* New York: Routledge.

Parenti, Michael. 1994. *Land of Idols: Political Mythology in America.* New York: St. Martin's.

Parker, Beth. 1998. *The Impact of Proposition 209 on Education, Employment, and*

Contracting: Opportunities for Women in California. http://www.equalright.org/
AFFIRM/Full209.html.

Pashler, H. 1996. *Would Civil Rights Pioneers have Supported CCRI?* http://www.
ccri/Yeson209.

Paulson, Michael. 2000. "U.S. Bishops List King as Martyr Candidate." *Boston
Globe,* January 13, A1.

Perlmutter, Emanuel. 1964. "Murphy Says City Will Not Permit Rights Violence."
New York Times, March 16, 1.

Petition for Rehearing and Suggestion for Rehearing En Banc Filed by the Coalition for Economic Equity et al., April 23, 1997.

Pfeil, Fred. 1995. *White Guys: Studies in Postmodern Domination and Difference.* New
York: Verso.

Pierre, Robert E. 2004. "Affirmative Action Foes Seek Michigan Referendum."
Washington Post, March 5, A3.

Pipes, Sally, and Michael Lynch. 1996. *Women Don't Need Affirmative Action.* http://
www.heritage.org/commentary/op-sp1.html.

"Police Fear Crisis in Jackson, Miss." 1964. *New York Times,* March 8, 52.

Ponton, Cooper D. 1964. "For Man's Natural Rights." *New York Times,* March
7, 22.

Poole, Sheila. 1992. "Business Report: On Minorities." *Atlanta Journal and Constitution,* December 9, F2.

Pooley, Eric. 1997. "Fairness or Folly." *Time,* June 23, 32–36.

Postman, David. 1998a. "California Group Pays for I-200 Radio Ad." *Seattle Times,*
September 26, A7.

———. 1998b. "Debate Focuses on Fix for White Privilege." *Seattle Times,* October 10, A11.

Prashad, Vijay. 2000. *The Karma of Brown Folk.* Minneapolis: University of Minnesota Press.

Prichard, James. 2004. "Connerly Avows Michiganians Will Get Chance to Vote
on Racial Preferences." *Associated Press State and Local Wire,* May 6.

Projansky, Sara, and Kent A. Ono. 1999. "Strategic Whiteness as Cinematic Politics." In *Whiteness: The Communication of Social Identity,* ed. T. K. Nakayama and J. N. Martin, 149–74. Thousand Oaks, Calif.: Sage.

"Prop. 209 Chair Condemns Anti-209 Ad." 1996. California Civil Rights Initiative Press Release.

Purdum, Todd S. 1998. "Judge Nullifies Most of California's Immigration Law." *New York Times*, March 19, A12.

Rainwater, Lee, and William L. Yancey. 1967. *The Moynihan Report and the Politics of Controversy.* Cambridge, Mass.: MIT Press.

Ramirez Berg, Charles. 1992. "Bordertown, the Assimilation Narrative, and the Chicano Social Problem Film." In *Chicanos and Film: Representation and Resistance*, ed. C. Noriega, 29–46. Minneapolis: University of Minnesota Press.

Reed, Adolph, Jr. 1999. *Stirrings in the Jug: Black Politics in the Post-Segregation Era.* Minneapolis: University of Minnesota Press.

Regents of University of California v. Bakke. 1978. 438 U.S. 265.

Rein, Lisa. 2001. "An Opportunity to Be Officers and Alumnae." *Washington Post*, May 19, B1.

"Remarks by the President." 1964. *New York Times*, February 13, 14.

Robertson, Rob. 1997. "Confronting Mississippi: Duke Filmmakers Go behind the Scenes to Study Racial Perceptions in the South." *Southern Register* (Fall): 14.

Robinson, Amy. 1994. "It Takes One to Know One: Passing and Communities of Common Interest." *Critical Inquiry* 20: 715–36.

Rodriguez, Gregory. 2001. "The Nation: Who Are You." *New York Times* (Week in Review), June 3, 1.

Roediger, David R. 1991. *The Wages of Whiteness: Race and the Making of the American Working Class.* London: Verso.

———. 1997. "White Workers, New Democrats, and Affirmative Action." In *The House that Race Built*, ed. W. Lubiano, 48–65. New York: Vintage.

———. 2002. *Colored White: Transcending the Racial Past.* Berkeley: University of California Press.

Roffman, Peter, and Jim Purdy. 1981. *The Hollywood Social Problem Film: Madness, Despair, and Politics from the Depression to the Fifties.* Bloomington: Indiana University Press.

Rosaldo, Renato. 1989. "Imperialist Nostalgia." *Representations* 26 (Spring): 107–22.

Rose, Nikolas. 1996. "Governing Advanced Liberal Democracies." In *Foucault and Political Reason: Liberalism, Neo-Liberalism, and Rationalities of Government*, ed. A. Barry, T. Osborne, and N. Rose, 37–64. Chicago: University of Chicago Press.

Rosen, Jeffrey. 2003. "How I Learned to Love Quotas." *New York Times Magazine*, June 1, 52–55.

Ross, Thomas. 1995. "Innocence and Affirmative Action." In *Critical Race Theory: The Cutting Edge*, ed. R. Delgado, 551–63. Philadelphia: Temple University Press.

Rowan, Carl T. 1994. "The Protest behind Proposition 187." *Chicago Sun-Times*, October 30, 42.

Roy, Arundhati. 2004. "The New American Century." *Nation*, February 9.

Russell, Margaret M. 1995. "Race and the Dominant Gaze: Narratives of Law and Inequality in Popular Film." In *Critical Race Theory: The Cutting Edge*, ed. R. Delgado, 56–63. Philadelphia: Temple University Press.

"Sacramento Bee Editorial Smear by Association." 1996. California Civil Rights Initiative Press Release.

Salisbury, Mark. 1993. "He's an 'Ordinary Man at War with the Everyday World.'" *Empire* (July): 76–78.

Samarajiva, Rohan, and Peter Shields.1992. "Emergent Institutions of the 'Intelligent Network': Toward a Theoretical Understanding." *Media, Culture, and Society* 143: 397–419.

Sample, Herbert A. 1998. "Prop. 209's Backer Has New Goals." *San Diego Union-Tribune*, November 10, A10.

Sanchez, Rene. 1997. "Final Exam for Campus Affirmative Action? White Applicant's Test of Michigan Admissions Could Set National Policy." *Washington Post*, December 5, A1.

Santa Ana, Otto. 1998. "Awash under a Brown Tide: Immigration Metaphors in California Public and Print Media Discourse." *Aztlán* 232: 137–76.

———. 1999. "'Like an Animal I Was Treated': Anti-Immigration Metaphor in U.S. Public Discourse." *Discourse and Society* 10, no. 2: 191–224.

Savage, David G. 1993. "Paper Trail Could Block Nominee for Justice Post." *Los Angeles Times*, May 22, A1.

Schemo, Diana Jean. 2001. "U. of Georgia Won't Contest Ruling on Admissions Policy. *New York Times*, November 10, A10.

Scheppele, Kim Lane. 1989. "Foreword: Telling Stories." *Michigan Law Review* 87: 2072–98.

Schevitz, Tanya. 2001. "UC Regents Set to Alter Admissions." *San Francisco Chronicle*, November 15, A1.

———. 2002. "Racial Privacy Initiative Ignites Upset." *San Francisco Chronicle*, March 15, A1.

———. 2003. "State Initiative on Racial Privacy Raised Issues about Health, Education." *San Francisco Chronicle*, October 8, A12.

Schön, Donald A., and Martin Rein. 1994. *Frame Reflection: Toward the Resolution of Intractable Policy Controversies*. New York: Basic Books.

Schram, Sanford F. 1993. "Postmodern Policy Analysis: Discourse and Identity in Welfare Policy." *Policy Sciences* 263: 249–72.

———, and Paul T. Neisser. 1997. "Introduction." In *Tales of the State: Narrative in Contemporary U.S. Politics and Public Policy*, ed. S. F. Schram and P. T. Neisser, 1–14. Lanham, Md.: Rowman, Littlefield.

Scott, James C. 1990. *Domination and the Arts of Resistance*. New Haven, Conn.: Yale University Press.

Seger, Linda. 2000. "Creating the Myth." In *Signs of Life in the U.S.A.*, ed. S. Maasik and J. Solomon, 308–17. Boston: Bedford/St. Martin's.

Shah, Sonia, ed. 1997. *Dragon Ladies: Asian American Feminists Breathe Fire*. Boston: South End Press.

Shapiro, Michael J. 1990. "Strategic Discourse/Discursive Strategy: The Representation of 'Security Policy' in the Video Age." *International Studies Quarterly* 343: 327–40.

Shaw v. Reno. 1993. 113 S. Ct. 2816.

Shepard, Paul. 1999. "MLK Contemporaries Fear 'Marketing' of Civil Rights Leader." *Indiana Daily Student*, January 15, 7.

Shome, Raka. 2000. "Outing Whiteness." *Critical Studies in Media Communication* 173: 366–71.

Shulman, George. 2000. "Narrating Clinton's Impeachment: Race, the Right, and Allegories of the Sixties." *Theory and Event* 41.

Shultz, Vickie. 1992. "Women before the Law: Judicial Stories about Women, Work, and Sex Segregation on the Job." In *Feminists Theorize the Political*, ed. J. Butler and J. W. Scott, 297–338. New York: Routledge.

Simpson, Mark. 1994. *Male Impersonators: Men Performing Masculinity*. New York: Routledge.

Sitton, Claude. 1964a. "Wallace Asserts Popular Response Calls for a Serious Bid in Wisconsin." *New York Times*, March 18, 28.

———. 1964b. "Clerics Hostile to Gov. Wallace." *New York Times*, March 19, 17.

———. 1964c. "Wisconsin Vote Hailed in South by Rights Foes." *New York Times*, April 9, 1.

———. 1964d. "Wallace: South's Mood." *New York Times*, April 12, E5.

———. 1964e. "Johnson Prestige on Line in Indiana." *New York Times*, April 19, 83.

Skelton, George. 1996. "Capitol Journal: The Risks of Wooing Strange Bedfellows." *Los Angeles Times*, October 28, A3.

Skrentny, John D. 1996. *The Ironies of Affirmative Action: Politics, Culture, and Justice in America*. Chicago: University of Chicago Press.

Smith, Frederick. 1964. "Johnson Pleads for Civil Rights at a Reception for U.S. Editors." *New York Times*, April 18, 14.

"South's Leaders Hold Bill Illegal." 1964. *New York Times*, July 3, 9.

SP-1: Resolution of the University of California Board of Regents Adopting a Policy "Ensuring Equal Treatment" of Admissions. July 20, 1995.

Spencer, Jayne. 1999. "Life Is More Than a Moment." *Indiana University Home Pages*. October 22. http://www.iuinfo.indiana.edu/HomePages/102299/text/counts.htm.

Staples, Brent. 2001. "Putting a Price Tag on the Legacy of Martin Luther King." *New York Times*, November 28, A26.

"State GOP Pulls TV Ads with King's Famed Speech." 1996. *Fresno Bee*, October 25, A3.

Steinberg, Stephen. 1995. *Turning Back: The Retreat from Racial Justice in American Thought and Policy*. Boston: Beacon Press.

Stephens, Angela. 1998. "Court Upholds Three California Affirmative Action Policies." *Community College Week*, December 28, 12.

Stith, Andrew. 1996. *Breaking the Glass Ceiling: Racism and Sexism in Corporate America: The Myths, the Realities, and the Solutions*. Orange, N.J.: Bryant and Dillon.

Stoler, Ann Laura. 1995. *Race and the Education of Desire: Foucault's "History of Sexuality" and the Colonial Order of Things*. Durham, N.C.: Duke University Press.

Strathern, Marilyn, ed. 2000. *Audit Cultures: Anthropological Studies in Accountability, Ethics, and the Academy*. London: Routledge.

Tahmincioglu, Eve. 2001. "Vigilance in the Face of Layoff Rage." *New York Times*, August 1, C1.

Takaki, Ronald. 1980. *Iron Cages: Race and Culture in Nineteenth-Century America*. London: Oxford University Press.

———. 1993. *A Different Mirror: A History of Multicultural America*. Boston: Back Bay.

Temple-Raston, Dina. 2002. *A Death in Texas: A Story of Race, Murder, and a Small Town's Struggle for Redemption*. New York: Henry Holt.

Terte, Robert H. 1964. "5 Cities May Join Schools Boycott." *New York Times*, January 7, 22.

Themba, Makani N. 1999. *Making Policy Making Change: How Communities Are Taking the Law into Their Own Hands*. Berkeley, Calif.: Clarendon Press.

Tucker, Cynthia. 1999. "King Family Stops at Nothing in Pursuit of Profits." *Atlanta Journal and Constitution*, November 7, 7Q.

Tyson, Timothy B. 2004. *Blood Done Sign My Name: A True Story*. New York: Crown.

U.S. Census Bureau. 1998. *Profile of General Demographic Characteristics*. Washington, D.C.: GPO.

———. 2000. *Money Income in the United States*. Washington, D.C.: GPO.

"Uneasiness in South Deepening." 1999. *The Age* [Melbourne], February 20, 25.

U.S. Commission on Civil Rights. 1995. *Briefing Paper on the Legislative, Executive, and Judicial Development of Affirmative Action*. Washington, D.C.: GPO.

U.S. Office of Professional Management. 2002. *The Fact Book*. Washington, D.C.: GPO.

Varner, Lynne K. 1998. "Riddle Illustrates Division over I-200." *Seattle Times*, July 2, B1.

Verhovek, Sam H., and B. Drummond Ayres, Jr. 1998. "The 1998 Elections: Voters Back End to State Preferences." *New York Times*, November 4, B2.

Wald, Gayle. 2000. "The Vestments and Investments of Race." *American Quarterly* 522: 371–80.

Walker, Robert. 1998. "California's Collision of Race and Class." In *Race and Representation: Affirmative Action*, ed. R. Post and M. Rogin, 281–307. New York: Zone.

"Wallace Faces Wisconsin Fight." 1964. *New York Times*, March 8, 76.

Watkins, S. Craig. 1998. *Representing: Hip Hop Culture and the Production of Black Cinema*. Chicago: University of Chicago Press.

Watters, Ethan. 1997. "Ward Connerly Won the Battle, Now He's Facing the War." *Mother Jones* (November/December: 71–73).

Wehrwein, Austin C. 1964a. "Wallace Called Advocate of Evil." *New York Times*, March 25, 25.

———. 1964b. "Democratic Race Rouses Wisconsin." *New York Times*, March 29, 40.

Weiss, Kenneth R. 1999. "Regents May Reconsider UC Affirmative Action Ban." *Los Angeles Times*, January 14, A1.

West, Cornel. 1993. *Race Matters*. New York: Vintage.

Westbrook, Bruce. 2000. "Sleazy Politics: *The Contender* Gets Good and Dirty Playing Hardball." *Houston Chronicle*, October 13, 1.

White, Gayle. 2000. "U.S. Catholics Nominate King as Martyr." *Atlanta Journal and Constitution*, January 14, 10A.

White, Hayden. 1978. *Tropics of Discourse: Essays in Cultural Criticism*. Baltimore, Md.: Johns Hopkins University Press.

White, Mimi. 1998. "'Reliving the Past Over and Over Again': Race, Gender, and Popular Memory in *Homefront* and *I'll Fly Away*." In *Living Color: Race and Television in the United States*, ed. S. Torres, 118–39. Durham, N.C.: Duke University Press.

Wicker, Tom. 1964a. "Businessmen Hear Johnson Rights Plea." *New York Times*, April 10, 1.

———. 1964b. "Johnson Appeals in South for End to Race Barriers." *New York Times*, May 9, 1.

Wiegman, Robyn. 1995. *American Anatomies: Theorizing Race and Gender*. Durham, N.C.: Duke University Press.

———. 1999. "Whiteness Studies and the Paradox of Particularity." *Boundary 2* 63: 115–50.

Willis, Sharon. 2001. "Race as Spectacle, Feminism as Alibi: Representing the Civil Rights Era in the 1990s." In *Keyframes: Popular Cinema and Cultural Studies*, ed. M. Tinkcom and A. Villarejo, 98–114. London: Routledge.

Wilson, Pete, Ward Connerly, and Pamela A. Lewis. 1996. *Argument in Favor of Proposition 209: The Right Thing to Do*. Ballot pamphlet.

Wilson, Yumi. 1995. "Affirmative Action Fight Heats Up." *San Francisco Chronicle*, January 26, A1.

Wiltenberg, Mary. 2004. "Affirmative Action Battle Brews Anew in Michigan." *Christian Science Monitor*, January 20, 18.

Winant, Howard. 1994. "Racial Formation and Hegemony: Global and Local Developments." In *Racism, Modernity, and Identity: On the Western Front*, ed. A. Rattansi and S. Westwood, 266–89. Cambridge, Mass.: Polity Press.

"Women Helped Push Through 209." 1996. *Fresno Bee*, November 12, A3.

Woodson, Robert, and William J. Bennett. 1994. *The Conservative Virtues of Dr. Martin Luther King*. Heritage Lectures, no. 481. January 14.

Wray, Matt, and Annalee Newitz, eds. 1996. *White Trash: Race and Class in America*. New York: Routledge.

Zachary, G. Pascal. 1997. "Leader of California Proposition 209 Bringing Campaign to Other States." *Wall Street Journal*, January 14, A22.

Žižek, Slavoj. 1989. *The Sublime Object of Ideology*. London: Verso.

Index

affirmative action: and African Americans, 11–12, 71–72; and alibis, 48, 75–76; and Asian Americans, 48, 69, 76; assault on, 9, 18–20, 26–27, 39, 62–65, 232, 237; categories of, 1–2, 14, 34–35, 45, 78, 229; and civil rights movement, 5, 80–82, 148–49, 218–19; and economic shifts, 15–19; and feminism, 6, 13, 54–55; in Florida, 26, 31; in Georgia, 31, 33; history of, 2–10; and hyphenated Americans, 13, 75; and Latinos, 16, 18, 71, 205; legal basis for, 10–12; legal challenges to, 13, 28–29, 31; and media coverage, 75–76; and melanin merit, 9–10, 13, 231; and "mend it, don't end it," 22; in Michigan, 9, 28–29, 31–33; and model minority, 34, 48–49; and Northern civil rights agenda, 44, 219; and Philadelphia Plan, 11–12; and postfeminism, 6, 123; and preferences, 9, 21, 24–25, 61, 64, 81, 209; and quota addicts, 72, 75, 219; and quota queens, 14, 34, 60–63; race- and gender-conscious project of, 105, 110; and racially correct voice-overs, 6, 65–68, 180; and resegregation, 27, 78; and reverse discrimination, 13, 21, 30, 51, 60–62, 207, 212–14; and single mothers, 14, 60–63, 205; in Texas, 26, 31, 33; and token hires, 13, 21, 34, 105, 240n3, 242n10; and truly needy, 61–64, 72; and warriors for democracy, 41, 43, 227; in Washington, 26, 27–31, 33; and white men, 12–13, 15–16, 19, 240n3; and white women, 18, 46–52, 70, 93, 239n1. *See also* Connerly, Ward; Initiative 200 campaign; merit; meritocracy; Proposition 209; Proposition 209 campaign

affirmative action films. *See* film, Hollywood

G.I. Jane, 119–32, 140
glass ceiling. *See* workplace, American
Goldberg, David Theo, 37, 140
governmentality. *See* racial order of
 things; state, neoliberal
Gratz v. Bollinger, 9, 28–29, 31–33
Gray, Herman, 89
Grutter v. Bollinger, 9, 29, 31–33
Guerrero, Ed, 83–84
Guinier, Lani, 62–63

Hall, Stuart, 86
Harris v. Forklift Systems, Inc., 98
hidden transcripts, 59, 130, 232. *See
 also* No!200 campaign
Hill, Anita, 91, 98
hooks, bell, 243n18
Hopwood v. Texas, 31

immigrants: and assimilation
 narratives, 88; history of, 13; and
 immigrant rights, 19–20, 22, 71;
 and social problem film, 88. *See
 also* Proposition 187
Initiative 200 campaign: black
 spokesperson for, 65, 67–68; and
 Connerly, 30, 65; and Proposition
 209, 26–27, 58, 65; and race,
 68–71, 201, 207; and reverse
 discrimination, 51

Jackson, Jesse: in debates with
 Connerly, 66; on Martin Luther
 King Jr., 148; in Stop Prop 209
 campaign, 24, 55, 81
Jasper, Texas, 158

Jeffords, Susan, 85, 90
Jim Crow system. *See* segregation
Johnson, Lyndon B.: and black civil
 rights, 195, 211, 215, 218; and Bill
 Clinton, 202; executive orders by,
 11

Kelley, Robin D. G., 85
Kennedy, John F., 10
King, Coretta Scott, 148, 244n2
King, Martin Luther, Jr.: and amnesia,
 146; as appropriated by neoconservatives, 80–81, 148–49;
 commodification of, 146–47; at
 March on Washington, 216; and
 nomination as martyr, 145–46; and
 nostalgia, 146–47, 234; in public
 memory, 183
knowledges, public. *See* racial order
 of things

Lee, Spike, 169
Lewis, Pamela, 46–49, 61
liberalism: backlash against, 211–12;
 bourgeois Lockean, 3; and color-
 and gender-blindness, 113, 195,
 201, 206, 212; cultural imaginaries
 of, 147; and feminism, 104, 125;
 grammar of, 82, 197–203; and
 individualism, 3, 187, 192–95, 197–
 202, 206; and neoliberalism, 3, 34,
 202, 205, 213, 228–29; and responsibilization, 34, 44, 203–4, 206
Lights, Camera, Canton, 164–67, 184,
 186–87, 245n9
Lipsitz, George, 150–51, 165, 244n4

Roopali Mukherjee is assistant professor of media studies at Queens College of the City University of New York.